BEECHING

Britain's Railway Closures and Their Legacy

THE DEFINITIVE GUIDE

BEECHING

Britain's Railway Closures and Their Legacy

THE DEFINITIVE GUIDE

ROBIN JONES

First published as Beeching: 50 Years of the Axeman (2011) and Beeching: The Inside Track (2012)
by Mortons Media Group Ltd.

This edition published in 2020 by Gresley Books,
an imprint of Mortons Books Ltd.
Media Centre
Morton Way
Horncastle LN9 6JR
www.mortonsbooks.co.uk

ISBN 978-1-911658-14-6

The right of Robin Jones to be identified as the author of this work has been
asserted in accordance with the Copyright, Designs and Patents Act 1988.

Typeset by Kelvin Clements
Printed and bound by Grafo, Spain

To Jim and Kevin Edwards, who toured Britain's railways with their grandad Bert Glazebrook and saw the Changeover Years first hand

Contents

Introduction

DESPITE THE fact that Britain invented the steam railway and introduced it to the rest of the world, surprisingly few of the names associated with this globe-shaping transport technology have become commonplace household words well outside the domains of the enthusiast and historian.

Among the elite group that have clearly managed this feat are *Flying Scotsman*, Stephenson's *Rocket* (no — despite the widespread popular misconception, George Stephenson did not invent the steam railway locomotive, that was down to Richard Trevithick), maybe *Royal Scot*, if only because of the marketing of the biscuit brand, perhaps *Mallard*, officially the world's fastest locomotive, and, dare I say it, *Thomas* the little blue engine. Another name that can be added to this list is that of Dr Richard Beeching.

The much-reviled British Railways chairman has long been popularly portrayed as an axe-wielding ogre who closed as many railways as he could, rid us of the universally loved steam engines and left communities all over Britain with no access to trains.

Indeed, a mistake often made in print is referring to a particular branch line as a 'Beeching closure' when he had nothing at all to do with it, the particular withdrawal of services taking place before his appointment to the British Railways Board in 1961.

Many people still hold the view that if the dreaded doctor had not descended on the nation's railways in the Sixties, many of the closed lines would still be running today. Beeching has been described as the most hated civil servant of all time.

The criteria used by him and those who followed in his wake to justify the closure of individual routes, particularly those serving large centres of population, have repeatedly been questioned in depth. Mountains of hindsight regularly express the view that Beeching was wrong in this or that case, that route closures were premature, and if only the powers that be had foreseen the expansion of rural communities in commuter-belt country, and the nightmarish road congestion from the 1980s onwards, in which households on even very modest incomes support two or maybe three second-hand cars, the decisions regarding the wholesale pruning of the rail network in the Sixties may have been very different.

In several, though by no means all, of these 'lost line' scenarios, it is difficult not to sympathise or agree wholeheartedly, but it is so easy to pass judgment long after the event, without looking at the circumstances that prevailed at the time when many hard decisions were made.

Coming into the sector from a purely business point of view, Beeching in 1963 produced his landmark report, The Reshaping of British Railways, which immediately became one of the seminal documents of British railway history.

The recommendations contained within the report led to the closure of around a third of the nation's railway network, throwing tens of thousands of railwaymen on to the dole queue, disenfranchising some of the country's biggest towns from train services as well as country branch lines, in a vain bid to cut the soaring British Railways deficit in an age where passenger numbers dwindled as car ownership ran rampant.

On the other hand, the closures also streamlined the network in a way that helped ensure its survival into the 21st century, an era in which passenger numbers are now at their highest for many decades, and Beeching also set the wheels in motion to yank freight haulage by rail into the modern age, so that it could compete with roads.

So was Beeching a villain — or a hero? Here is the story of the man who probably had the biggest impact on the nation's railways since George and Robert Stephenson invented *Rocket*.

This book also takes a look behind the scenes at Beeching's planning team, which drew up the top-secret 'Blue Book of Maps' which predicted not only the closures of railway lines but also those of coal mines and steelworks as far ahead as two decades, the routes which had lucky escapes from the axe, in one case by the skin of its teeth, and those lines which have since been reopened, Scotland's Borders Railway being the standout case. The route which one of the British Rail planners since says never should have been axed — the East Lincolnshire line from Grimsby to Peterborough — is also looked at in depth.

Reversals of Beeching closures are also highlighted, arguably the most successful in recent years being that of Scotland's aforementioned Borders Railway, the northernmost third of the Waverley Route which ran between Carlisle and Edinburgh. And there is more on the way: in August 2019, the Scottish Government announced plans to restore passenger services to the Levenmouth area of Fife after an absence of half a century.

The rise of the heritage railway sector is also examined, with a plethora of closed lines being revived by enthusiasts and now forming a sizeable plank of many a local tourist economy.

CHAPTER ONE

The road back to roads

THE ESSENCE of the postwar controversy about rail closures has its roots long before Dr Richard Beeching, and might be considered to date back to the birth of the steam locomotive itself.

Cornish mining engineer Richard Trevithick, frustrated at his home county's isolation from the canal network which provided the trade arteries of the Industrial Revolution, and indeed the poor communications between Cornwall and the rest of Britain apart from by sea, followed up earlier rudimentary experiments by others involving horseless carriages by building his own steam locomotive — but one which would run on roads.

Trevithick and engineer Andrew Vivian built a steam road carriage which, on Christmas Eve 1801, climbed Camborne Hill under its own power. Startled onlookers jumped aboard for a ride — and so was born the world's first motor car!

The obvious advantage of road transport over rail is its great versatility. It does not rely on the provision of railway tracks and offers almost infinite personal choice and freedom for travel.

However, back in the early 19th century, the great Roman art of roadbuilding had largely been forgotten and in those days before the invention of tarmacadam, most of them were muddy potholed affairs which even horses and carts found difficult to negotiate.

In 1802, Trevithick demonstrated his pioneer London Steam Carriage in the capital, offering trips from the city centre to Paddington and back, with up to eight guests on board. Here was the world's first motor bus, and the first official public run of a self-powered passenger vehicle.

However, steering was the big problem and the steam carriage ended up crashing into railings. The fault lay not with the vehicle but the poorly maintained, bumpy roads of the day. Trevithick built a second such carriage for London in 1803. Standing 13ft high, it proved too big and could not compete economically with the horse-drawn versions.

He finally overcame the problem of inadequate roads by using rails on which to run his steam locomotives. The tramway or waggonway concept was by then well established: track made from wooden or cast iron rails would link collieries, foundries and factories to the nearest transshipment point, usually river ports or harbours, and horses would pull trucks loaded with the finished product and return, often with the raw materials to make them.

In 1802, Trevithick constructed a steam railway locomotive for private use at Coalbrookdale ironworks in Shropshire and, two years later, gave the world's first public demonstration of one on the Penydarren Tramroad near Merthyr Tydfil.

Had the roads of the day been capable of carrying his road steam locomotives, would there have been any point in him looking at rail? Nevertheless, the world at large was slow on the uptake of Trevithick's locomotives, and he eventually gave up on the idea, finding very few takers.

However, the acute shortage of horses caused by the army needing so many for the Napoleonic Wars led to mine owners in the north of England looking for alternative traction for their private tramways in the early part of the decade that followed, and they began looking afresh at Trevithick's futuristic but novelty ideas. But it was not until 1825 that the world's first public steam-operated railway, the Stockton & Darlington, opened for business, and even then locomotives were at first used for freight, with horses pulling passenger trains. It was George Stephenson's *Rocket*'s triumph in the Rainhill Trials of 1829 and the Liverpool & Manchester Railway's adoption of steam locomotive traction that finally steered the railway concept on the course to transport supremacy and opened the floodgates for the years of Railway Mania, in which a multitude of speculative schemes sought to connect city with city, town with town and, in carving up the British mainland, created the basis of the national network for the centuries that followed.

Steam railways linked industrial centres far more efficiently than their horse-drawn predecessors to ports, facilitated the development of dormitory towns and commuter belts, took farming produce to national markets and opened up the seaside to mass tourism, among many other benefits too numerous to mention here. They made it easier for country folk to migrate to the expanding cities in search of a better life. In Victorian times, the railway not only reshaped society but became a backbone of it.

EXPANDED TO ITS LIMITS

By and large, the railway network had expanded to its maximum size by the dawn of the 20th century. Towards the end of Victorian times, efforts were made to connect the remaining parts of the country not deemed profitable enough to warrant attention from the major railway operators to the national network.

The Light Railways Act 1896 was a response to the economic downturn of the previous decade that had hit agriculture and rural communities hard. It brought the railways into less populated areas of the country that had been ignored by the established railway companies who saw no profit to be made there. This leglislation made it far easier to build a rural railway 'on the cheap' without having to apply for a costly Act of Parliament.

The 1896 Act limited weights to a maximum of 12 tons on each axle and line speeds to a maximum of 25mph. Such limitations allowed the use of lightly laid track and relatively modest bridges in order to keep costs down. Also, level crossings did not have to have gates, and just cattle grids would suffice.

The Act led to nearly 30 local standard and narrow gauge railways being built under its powers, the best-known examples perhaps being the Kent and East Sussex Light Railway, which opened in 1900, the Basingstoke and Alton Light Railway of 1901, the Vale of Rheidol Railway in 1902, the Welshpool & Llanfair Light Railway in 1903, the Leek & Manifold Valley Light Railway and the Tanat Valley Light Railway of 1904.

By contrast, in 1899, under railway magnate Edward Watkin, the Manchester, Sheffield & Lincolnshire Railway opened its 'London Extension' from Annesley, north of Nottingham, to Marylebone, and changed its name to the Great Central Railway. It would be the last trunk railway to be built in Britain until the Channel Tunnel Rail Link from St Pancras International a century later: indeed, it was Watkin's intention for it to link up with a proposed Channel Tunnel, and accordingly was built to continental loading clearances to allow potential through running of trains to and from Europe.

Also in 1899, the Great Western Railway obtained an Act of Parliament permitting construction of a double-track railway between Honeybourne and Cheltenham and doubling of the single-track route from Stratford-upon-Avon to Honeybourne. This would link in with the North Warwickshire Line being built from Tyseley to Stratford via Bearley Junction to provide a through route from the Midlands to the South West to compete with the Midland Railway route via the Lickey Incline.

Work began on construction of the Honeybourne-Cheltenham line in November 1902, and it was opened throughout four years later. In 1910, the first through trains over the route between Wolverhampton, Birmingham and the West Country and Cardiff were introduced. It may be considered as the last great cross-country route to be completed.

Railway building did not end there, but new lines that were subsequently opened were very much local affairs, such as the North Devon & Cornwall Junction Light Railway, which made use of existing mineral lines to link Halwill Junction to Torrington from July 27, 1925.

However, history recorded that, in short, virtually everywhere that was going to be connected to the rail network had been reached by Edwardian times — often several times over.

THE BIGGEST CHALLENGE OF ALL ARRIVES

The improvements in roads made in Britain following the development of the 'Macadam' type of surface pioneered by Scotsman John Loudon McAdam around 1820 led to renewed interest from inventors looking at self-propelled forms of transport that could run over them.

The International Exposition of Electricity in Paris, held in November 1881, saw French inventor Gustave Trouvé demonstrate a working three-wheeled automobile powered by electricity. German engineer Karl Benz is generally hailed as the inventor of the modern car.

He constructed a three-wheeled carriage-like road vehicle powered by his own four-stroke cycle gasoline engine in Mannheim in 1885, and the following year his company, Benz & Cie, was granted a patent. The company began to sell automobiles off its production line in 1888, and sold around 25 of them between then and 1893, when his first four-wheeler appeared. In 1896, Benz designed and patented the first internal-combustion flat engine and by the end of the century was the world's largest automobile company. The first design for an American automobile with a gasoline internal combustion engine was produced by George Selden of New York in 1877. In Britain, Thomas Rickett tried a production run of steam cars in 1860. Charles Santler of Malvern is regarded as having built the first petrol-powered car in the country in 1894, but it was a one-off. The first production automobiles in Britain came from the Daimler Motor Company in 1897.

Industrial-scale car production began in the US in 1902, at the Oldsmobile plant in Lansing, Michigan. Henry Ford's Model T came on the scene in 1908, and soon his Detroit factory was turning out cars at 15-minute intervals. Not only that, but he had made the car affordable: by 1914, when 250,000 Model Ts had been sold, an assembly line worker could buy a Model T with four months' pay. Ford of Britain was founded in 1909 and in 1921, Citroen became the first European car manufacturer to adopt Ford's ground-breaking production line methods. By 1930, all manufacturers had followed suit, and while it was at first much regarded as a rich man's plaything, with railway travel the primary option for much of the population, car ownership was very much in the ascendancy.

RAILWAYS COMPETING AGAINST RAIL

The title 'railway company' does not necessarily imply that an organisation exists to promote the railway concept; the key word is 'company', a body that is created to generate profits, by the best means possible.

When the dawn of the 20th century saw that motor road vehicles would shape the future of transport later if not sooner, the Great Western

Railway looked at providing bus services not only as a feeder to its train services, but also as a cheaper alternative to building new branch lines in sparsely populated rural areas which would never pay. The GWR balked at the idea of spending £85,000 on extending the Helston branch with a light railway to Britain's southernmost village, Lizard Town, and decided to try motor buses instead.

Two vehicles that had been used temporarily by the Lynton & Barnstaple Railway were acquired; the service was launched on August 17, 1903, the summer before GWR City class 4-4-0 No. 3440 *City of Truro* unofficially became the first steam locomotive in the world to break the 100mph barrier, with a speed of 102.3mph recorded hauling the 'Ocean Mails Special' from Plymouth to Paddington on May 9, 1904.

The idea of a railway company running a motor bus dated back to 1890, when the Belfast & Northern Counties Railway fitted seats to a petrol-engined parcels delivery van and took fares for rides in it. The Lizard buses proved so popular and profitable that other routes were soon established, first locally to Mullion, Ruan Minor and Porthleven, and then further afield at Penzance.

A bus route from Slough station to Beaconsfield was launched on March 1, 1904, followed by routes to Windsor on July 18 that year. The first GWR double deckers appeared on the Slough-Windsor service in 1904 onwards. A route from Wolverhampton to Bridgnorth was briefly operated from November 7, 1904 using steam buses, motor buses replacing them the following year.

By the end of 1904, 36 buses were in GWR operation, and when the Great Western Railway (Road Transport) Act was passed in 1928, the company boasted the biggest railway bus fleet. This Act paved the way for the services to be transferred to bus companies, although the railway was to be a shareholder in these operations. On January 1, 1929, the GWR routes in Devon and Cornwall went over to the new Western National Omnibus Company, 50% owned by the railway and the other half by the National Omnibus and Transport Company. That year the GWR acquired 30% of the shares in the Devon General Omnibus and Touring Company.

The final bus services operated by the GWR began in the Weymouth area in 1935, jointly run with rival the London & South Western Railway, and they were transferred to Southern National on January 1, 1934. Never afraid to compete with the railway concept, on April 11, 1933, the GWR launched its first air service, flying from Cardiff to Exeter and Plymouth.

The GWR and the other major railway operators built up extensive fleets of lorries and vans to supplement rail freight services. Yet what would happen when the day came that road vehicles would no longer supplement goods trains, but carry freight from start to finish in their own right?

ROAD FREIGHT ON THE RISE AND CLOSURES BEFORE BEECHING

Britain would never be the same in the wake of the First World War. One of the marked changes after 1918 was the blurring of the distinction between social classes: public schoolboys and labourers alike had experienced the horrors of the Western Front together, and never again would it be a case of one doffing their cap to the other. Similarly, churchgoing rapidly declined after the conflict, with religion becoming less relevant to a population bemused at why it had not been able to prevent the carnage of the trenches. There was a fresh spirit of entrepreneurship among the soldiers returning from the front. Large quantities of road vehicles were sold off as military surplus, and many were eagerly bought up by those wishing to launch their own haulage businesses. In doing so, freight was switched slowly but surely from rail to the cheaper and more versatile road alternative. In turn, local authorities began building more roads to cater for the increase in traffic.

Because of the growth of road haulage, the railways' profit margins began to suffer. Road hauliers could offer significantly lower prices than the railways, while offering the benefit of door-to-door delivery, while railways were hampered by their original charters of the 1840s and 50s to act as common carriers, and legally were unable to refuse unprofitable cargoes and lower their transportation costs accordingly.

A series of Royal Commissions into the problem was held in the Thirties, but failed to find a solution. Chancellor of the Exchequer Neville Chamberlain, who as prime minister is best known for his later 'peace in our time' appeasement of Hitler, increased vehicle excise duty, leaving the hauliers paying all of the Annual Road Fund.

This move came as a big boost to the railways, who were now theoretically back in the driving seat, but before they could reap big dividends from of it, the Second World War broke out. However, the railways were still not released from their historic common carrier obligations until 1957. Dr Beeching did not invent main line railway closures: that was a process that may be deemed to have begun more than a century before he came on the transport scene. In 1851, the Newmarket & Chesterford Railway closed its Great Chesterford to Six Mile Bottom section after opening a more viable length linking Six Mile Bottom straight to Cambridge.

The First World War saw a comparatively small number of rural railways closed, with their tracks lifted for use on the Western Front military lines, never to reopen again. These included the Bideford, Westward Ho! & Appledore Railway, and the GWR line from Rowington to Henley-in-Arden, which had been superseded by the abovementioned North Warwickshire Line from Birmingham to Stratford-upon-Avon via Henley, but these country lines were still very much small beer in the overall scheme of railways.

The 1930s, however, saw a swathe of closures of many 'rural fringe' lines, the like of which had been empowered by the 1896 Light Railways Act. Some, like the GWR-run narrow gauge Welshpool & Llanfair and Corris railways, lost their passenger services but remained open for freight, while others, like the Lynton & Barnstaple — by then part of the Southern Railway — the Welsh Highland Railway and the Leek & Manifold Valley Railway, closed outright.

The standard gauge Charnwood Forest Railway in Leicestershire ceased running passenger trains in 1931, and Birmingham's Harborne branch closed to passengers in 1934 in the face of direct competition from city trams and motor buses.

The Weston, Clevedon & Portishead Railway, the only direct route of any description that ever existed between those three coastal towns, ran its last public train in 1940.

Few of these lines can be regarded as mainstays of the railway network; indeed, regardless of their historical or romantic appeal, it is debatable whether some of them should have been built at all: once the motor road vehicle provided a credible alternative, it is all but certain that they would not have been. In any event, so many of the lines built under 1896

Light Railways Act concern had a lifespan of only around three decades, and their demise gave a strong pointer to the future of rural routes in the age of the motor car, bus and lorry.

NATIONALISATION: THE 'BIG FOUR' BECOME ONE

The biggest watershed in the history of Britain's railways came in 1948 when the national network was taken into permanent public ownership for the first time.

The nation's railways had been placed under state control during the First World War, and it was clear that the network could be run more efficiently with fewer operators. Afterwards there were calls for complete nationalisation — a move first mooted as early as 1850. However, the Railways Act 1921 provided a compromise with the grouping of most of the country's 120 railway companies into four main ones. These were the 'Big Four' comprising the Great Western Railway, the London, Midland & Scottish Railway, the London & North Eastern Railway and the Southern Railway.

Yet the Second World War again saw the nation's railways acting as one company, a time when the network saw more use than at any other point in its history.

Luftwaffe air raids inflicted heavy damage, particularly around London and Coventry, while the diversion of resources from maintenance led to the network falling into disrepair. After the war, it was soon realised that the private sector could not afford to put right the damage and decay, and so Clement Attlee's Labour government decided to nationalise the railways under the Transport Act 1947. British Railways came into existence as the business name of the Railway Executive of the British Transport Commission.

It was clear from the start that there would be closures. The Railway Executive was fully aware that some lines on the very dense network were unprofitable and also difficult to justify on social grounds. Going back to the Victorian era of Railway Mania, it is easy to argue that many lines, particularly local branches, were built, only for history to show that they could never really be justified.

In terms of long-distance travel, there soon arose competition between different companies for the same passengers. One famous example was the 'Races to the North' whereby rivals competed to see who could take passengers from London to Scotland fastest, while the GWR and London & South Western Railway, later Southern Railway, competed strongly for the London-Exeter-Plymouth markets, as did the GWR and LMS for London-Birmingham, to quote another of many examples.

While such rival routes served different communities along the way, if inter-city travel was considered of paramount importance, then a logical step forward would be to pick the best route and divert all the resources to that, and maybe consider the other for closure.

The first official closure under British Railways was the goods-only line from Mantle Lane East to the foot of Swannington Incline in Leicestershire, by the new London Midland Region, in February 1948.

The first passenger services to be withdrawn were those from Woodford & Hinton station on the Great Central route, to Byfield on the Stratford & Midland Junction Railway, on May 31, 1948, also by the LMR.

Another of the very early closures was that of the 2ft 3in gauge Corris Railway, inherited from the GWR, which was axed following flood damage on August 21, 1948.

The following year, the British Transport Commission set up the Branch Lines Committee, with a remit to close the least-used branch lines.

The modest programme of closures continued in 1949 with passenger services withdrawn from Liverpool Lime Street to Alexandra Dock, Stratford-upon-Avon to Broom, and Fenchurch Street to Stratford (Bow Junction).

In 1950, a total of 150 route miles were closed, rising to 275 in 1951 and 300 in 1952.

STILL STEAMING

By the late Forties, Britain was lagging behind other major countries in terms of the phasing out of steam traction.

The LMS produced its first diesel shunter in 1931, and in December 1947, the month before nationalisation, unveiled Britain's first main line diesel locomotive to the press.

Derby-built Co-Co No. 10000 had made its first run the month before, and after proving trials entered service in February 1948, followed by sister No. 10001. They became British Railway's D16/1 class. In 1950-51, the Southern Region's Ashford Works turned out two prototype main line diesel locomotives, which became Class D16/2.

In 1934, the Great Western Railway introduced the first of a very successful series of diesel railcars, which were used on cross-country services and which survived in regular use into the 1960s. The GWR also ordered two gas turbine locomotives.

However, all of these developments were a drop in the ocean compared to the modernisation taking place in the United States and elsewhere.

While steam locomotives are labour intensive regarding maintenance and operation, diesels need much less time and labour to operate and maintain. A fire has to be built in a steam locomotive firebox several hours before it runs: a diesel is not unlike a car, which just needs the turning of an ignition key. Also, while electrification of railway lines by providing overhead masts has a high capital outlay, the operating costs are much lower.

Following legislation of 1923 banning the use of steam locomotives within New York City, railroads turned to diesels, the Central Railroad of New Jersey introducing its first in 1925. By the Thirties, dieselisation was well under way, and by the mid-Fifties, most trunk railroads had retired all of their steam locomotives, although some, albeit in ever-diminishing numbers, continued on short lines into the Sixties, with rare stragglers lasting in revenue-earning service until the Seventies. For the record, the Crab Orchard & Egyptian Railroad, a steam-using tourist line which added regular revenue freight service in 1977, is said to be the last US railroad of any kind to use steam locomotives in regular service, as opposed to operation for tourist or heritage purposes.

Canadian Pacific ordered its first diesel in 1937, turned out its last new steam locomotive in 1949 and completed dieselisation by 1960.

Much closer to home, the Irish Republic introduced main line diesel railcars in 1950, the same year that its railways were nationalised into Córas Iompair Éireann, a move which led to widespread closures of lossmaking lines. In 1955, it made large-scale diesel purchases and within five years, virtually all steam on scheduled main line passenger services was over. CIE eliminated steam altogether in 1962.

In the early years of nationalisation, Britain was still emerging from the effects of the war and years of austerity. British Railways had inherited a locomotive fleet which included numerous ancient types that had long since been overtaken by technology, and needed new motive power — and fast.

Dieselisation, a move which was clearly inevitable, was seen by the powers that be as taking a leap in the dark at that time, and so when Robert Riddles, the Ministry of Supply's director of transportation equipment during the Second World War and a former vice-president of the LMS, was appointed member of the Railway Executive for Mechanical and Electrical Engineering in 1948 — effectively the old post of chief mechanical engineer — he stuck with steam.

British Railways continued to build locomotives to old 'Big Four' designs, and turned out a total of 2537. Riddles, meanwhile, oversaw the development of new 'Standard' designs, of which 999 were built. The Standards drew largely from LMS designs, but incorporated some features from the other Big Four companies' locomotives.

The first Standard was Pacific No. 70000 *Britannia*, which emerged from Crewe Works in 1951, the year of the Festival of Britain.

Many believe that the BR Standard 9F 2-10-0s were the best of the Riddles designs. They were built to last 40 years. The final Standard design was a one-off, 8P Pacific No. 71000 *Duke of Gloucester*, built in 1954.

Despite the excellence of many Standard designs, history records that they were just a stop-gap, with their days numbered as the UK economy began to recover.

That is not to say that steam was not capable of holding its own. By the late Fifties, and maintenance had been slowly but surely brought back up to date, long-distance schedules were generally back on par with those of the 1930s. Measures were taken to enhance the performance of pre-war locomotives working in postwar conditions: for example, the Western Region equipped all the King 4-6-0s and many Castle 4-6-0s with double chimneys to improve their steaming; Bulleid's streamlined Pacifics were rebuilt without their distinctive air-smooth casings and all of the Gresley Pacifics had been fitted with Kylchap blastpipes and double chimneys, a move especially effective with the A3s.

However, in 1954, the Leeds/Bradford area of the West Riding of Yorkshire was chosen by British Railways as a pilot area in which to test the first of its diesel multiple units, a type of vehicle following on from the GWR diesel railcars, and previous LMS experimental vehicles. Also, in June that year, the electrified Woodhead Route between Manchester and Sheffield, a project first proposed by the LNER, was completed, with the electric services inaugurated that September.

Another big factor at this time which was carving into the railways' viability was the denationalisation of road transport. The road haulage industry had bitterly opposed nationalisation by the Attlee government, but the Conservatives were elected in 1951, and road haulage was soon denationalised and deregulated. Again, it could offer charges which greatly undercut those of rail, while the still-heavily regulated railways, which had to meet the extra burden of safety costs, remained under the control of the British Transport Commission.

THE BRITISH RAILWAYS MODERNISATION PLAN

As the postwar financial situation eased, the inevitable happened on December 1, 1954: British Railways unveiled its blueprint for the future. The report known as Modernisation and Re-Equipment of the British Railways, or the 1955 Modernisation Plan for short, despite the fact it was published at the end of the previous year, set out to combat the threat presented to the railways by road transport. The target was to increase speed, reliability, safety and line capacity, while making services more attractive to passengers and freight operators.

The most notable aim was the complete phasing-out of steam locomotives by diesel and electric alternatives. It also proposed the electrification of principal main lines, including the East Coast Main Line to Leeds and possibly York, the Great Northern suburban system, Euston to Birmingham/Manchester/Liverpool, Chelmsford to Clacton/Ipswich/Felixstowe; the Liverpool Street north-east suburban system; Fenchurch Street to Tilbury and Shoeburyness; and the Glasgow north suburban network. Initial proposals to employ the overhead 1500V of the Woodhead Route were discarded once the advantages of the 25kV AC were fully realised. South of the Thames, in long-established third-rail electric territory, it was intended to electrify all main lines east of Reading-Portsmouth. Elsewhere, diesels would replace steam.

The report also proposed a new fleet of passenger and freight rolling stock, the creation of large goods marshalling yards with automated shunting to streamline freight handling, mass resignalling and track renewal, and the closure of more unprofitable lines and routes which duplicated others. The report proposed to spend £1240 million over 15 years to achieve these goals.

In 1956, a government White Paper confidently stated that modernisation would help eliminate BR's financial deficit by 1962. However, at a time when British Railways was still turning out large numbers of steam locomotives, the observer might be forgiven for getting the impression that the left hand did not know what the right hand was doing. History records that this indeed turned out to be the case, and the nation's railways' deficit would certainly not disappear purely because of the measures contained in the Modernisation Plan — far from it.

The Railway Executive's initial plan to keep steam on busy routes until it was superseded by electric traction was abandoned, and instead, diesels would provide a stop-gap until electrification, while on secondary lines they would provide the long-term solution. Steam continued to be built for the national network until March 25, 1960, when Swindon Works ceremoniously outshopped the last Standard 9F, No. 92220 *Evening Star*, while at the same time, British Railways rushed headlong into ordering a motley assortment of main line diesel types which were to show that they might have been far more rigorously tested before being bought. Some of them would end up being withdrawn even before the last steam locomotives disappeared. What conformed to a changing policy and looked good on paper failed to live up to the mark.

Just as the Great Western Railway had tried to go it alone with Isambard Kingdom Brunel's 7ft 0¼in broad gauge when everywhere outside its region had adopted George Stephenson's 4ft 8½in standard gauge, so its direct successor the Western Region chose diesel-hydraulic locomotives as opposed to the diesel-electric types favoured elsewhere. Some of these, like the Class 52 Westerns and Class 42 Warships, turned in very impressive performances, while the North British Locomotive Company's Type 2 Bo-Bos often failed to impress, and the class had become extinct by 1971. British Railways decided to phase diesel-hydraulics out from the Sixties onwards in pursuit of standardisation, but not before much public money had been wasted. The last Westerns ran in British Rail ownership in 1977.

Needless to say, there are many stories of new diesels failing and having to be rescued by steam engines. Because of the 'one size fits all' policy of phasing out steam, many locomotives which would have been good for several decades, including new BR Standards, were withdrawn and scrapped after only a few years' service, to be replaced by inferior diesels.

It has been said that the Modernisation Plan failed because it merely tried to upgrade the existing railway so that it would leap ahead of road transport, rather than looking at the changing needs of customers in a changing world.

Steam locomotives were replaced by diesel types on a 'like-for-like' basis: just look at the similarity between the shape of a Class 20 and, say, a large GWR prairie tank. Large numbers of light-duty diesels such as the Class 14s, Class 20s and Class 24s were commissioned for local mixed-goods services, yet those who ordered them failed to see that the days of the pick-up goods, the traditional system by which freight wagons were collected from intermediate stations on branch lines and marshalled into one long train, were numbered because of fierce competition from the road hauliers.

In 1954, Britain was one of only seven out of 17 major European countries whose railways were not 'in the red'. The following year, it recorded its first working loss.

The haphazard stab at modernisation that marked the twilight years of steam did not, as everyone was led to believe, improve matters.

The railways' annual working deficit in 1956 was £16.5 million: by 1962 it had reached £100 million. Overall, the promised return on investment failed to materialise, the Leeds/Barnsley DMU services being one of too few exceptions.

The failure of the Modernisation Plan led to a distrust of British Railways' financial planning abilities by the Treasury, which was to haunt the nationalised railway for the rest of its existence.

STRIKE FORCE!

Many historians who have studied the decline of the British railway network and the switch to road traffic have said that the turning point was not necessarily the poor implementation of modernisation, overdue

dieselisation and electrification or growing competition from road hauliers, but the national rail strike of 1955.

During the 1950s, as the austerity years receded and the British economy boomed, trade unions became stronger. Backed by the threat of
strike action, unions found themselves able to demand better wages and
working conditions for their members.

Days after Anthony Eden's Conservative government won a General
Election victory, ASLEF, the Associated Society of Locomotive Engineers
and Firemen, the union representing train drivers in Britain, called a
strike over a pay dispute. A rise which amounted to around the price of
an extra packet of cigarettes a week was demanded.

The strike lasted from May 28 to June 14, and brought British industry
to a standstill, although locomen who belonged to the National Union
of Railwaymen continued to work. Nevertheless, British Railways still
managed to convey a quarter of its normal passenger traffic and a third
of its freight, but the damage in the minds of the public was irreparable.

The strike signalled a mass switch by both passengers and freight
customers from rail to road. They were forced to do so by necessity
during the strike, and in a world where road transport was now far
more commonplace than ever before, many customers did not return
after it ended.

The time-honoured pick-up goods services were hit hard in the aftermath of the strike. For example, Toddington station on the Stratford-
upon-Avon to Cheltenham route, which is nowadays the headquarters of
the Gloucestershire Warwickshire Railway, an award-winning heritage
line, had long been a main centre for the collection of fruit from the
orchards of the Vale of Evesham for transportation by rail, mainly to
London or the West Midlands. Once the strike was over, the fruit never
came back for rail delivery and from then on always went by road, as
it does today.

A compromise was eventually reached with the union, but the
dispute cost around £12 million in lost revenue. Five years later, the
British Transport Commission accepted the findings of a Government-
commissioned investigation into railway pay levels, the Guillebaud
Report, which led to higher wages and a shorter working week.

However, by then it was too late, for ASLEF had driven a nail into the coffin of the railways as they were. You cannot blame a union for fighting for better conditions for its members, but by the Fifties there was already widespread condemnation that their leaders were failing to exercise their power responsibly and judiciously. The abuse of power by both management and unions alike was satirised in the 1959 Boulting Brothers comedy film I'm All Right Jack starring Peter Sellers, Ian Carmichael and Terry-Thomas.

In this instance, the merits of the 1955 national rail strike were questionable: few predicted the severity of the outcome. Trevithick had by necessity turned from roads to rail a century and a half before, but now the balance was clearly and rapidly tipping back again.

The inability of the Modernisation Plan to claw back the promised £85 million a year, coupled with a desire to prevent the country ever being held to ransom again, saw government transport policy finally shift from rail to road.

CHAPTER TWO

Marples, motorways, a new master plan and the man to make it happen

THE OCTOBER 1959 General Election saw the appointment of Ernest Marples as minister of transport. Marples, a qualified accountant, joined the government in 1957 as Postmaster General, and introduced the subscriber trunk dialling telephone system which made redundant the use of operators on national telephone calls. He also introduced postcodes to the UK. On June 2, 1957, he started the first draw for the then-new Premium Bonds savings scheme.

He served as transport minister until October 16, 1964, during which time he introduced parking meters, yellow lines and seat belts.

Marples was undeniably a roads man: indeed, he had founded Marples-Ridgway, a construction firm that built many roads, and was to quickly demonstrate that he preferred expenditure on motorways to investment in railways. In 1959, he gave the green light for the first inter-city British motorway, the M1. Britain's first section of motorway, the eight-mile Preston bypass, the first part of the M6 to be completed, was opened on December 5, 1958. It was built after two years of work, without modern hydraulic machinery, and was officially opened by Prime Minister Harold Macmillan, whose car led a convoy along it.

Former bridge engineer Harry Yeadon, 86, later recalled: "People recognised the significance. It was a guinea pig for all the future motorways and a lot of innovation went into its design and construction." Indeed, it was a massive pointer, if there was one, to future national transport trends and policies. Motorways had first been introduced in Italy by Benito Mussolini in the 1920s and then in Germany in 1931, Hitler subsequently speeding up the autobahn development programme.

In Britain, Lord Montagu had formed a company to build a 'motorway like road' from London to Birmingham in 1923, but it was not until the Special Roads Act 1949 that the construction of roads restricted to specific types of vehicles was allowed, and the 1950s when the country's first motorways were given the government go-ahead.

When the Preston bypass was opened, it had solid shale either side instead of hard shoulders, and if you broke down and tried to change a wheel, the jack sank into the ground. But motorways would not remain that way for long.

The first section of the M1, between Junction 5 (Watford) and Junction 18 (Crick/Rugby) was opened by Marples on November 2, 1959 in a short ceremony that took place near Slip End, at Junction 10 south of Luton. It has been said that when cars waiting at the junction to be among the first to travel on the new road poured down the slip road, the recently appointed transport minister said: "My God, what have I started!"

Indeed, Marples expressed concern about cars not being driven in a safe manner, but it was not until 1965 that the 70mph speed limit on motorways was introduced.

To avoid a conflict of interest, Marples undertook to sell his controlling shareholder interest in his road construction company as soon as he became transport minister, although there was a purchaser's requirement that he buy back the shares after he ceased to hold office, at the original price, should the purchaser so require. However, it was later revealed that he had sold his shares to his wife.

It was therefore ironic that the man who held the future of the railways in his hands should be so closely connected with a major financial interest in road building. As transport minister, his first move was to impose tighter control over the British Transport Commission and call a halt to the excesses of the modernisation programme.

Early in 1960, the BTC was told that any investment project that involved spending more than £250,000 would have to be cleared with the ministry, the ultimate decision resting with Marples.

By then, there was a widespread feeling at Whitehall that despite the vision for the future that had been outlined in British Railways' Modernisation Plan, railways were an expensive and increasingly outmoded legacy from Victorian times, and why should the national network be propped up with large amounts of taxpayers' money when roads were being built to do the same job and more effectively?

The slow pruning of the most unprofitable fringes of the railway network had steadily continued throughout the Fifties. In 1953, 275 miles were axed, followed by around 500 miles between 1954-57, and just 150 miles in 1958.

However, the biggest shock in transport circles came when the closure of a complete system was recommended by a British Railways committee.

In May 1958 a report was finalised by British Railways. It concluded that the entirety of Midland & Great Northern Joint Railway (M&GNJR) was loss-making, and was largely duplicated by routes of the former Great Eastern Railway.

At the Grouping of 1923, the M&GN had been Britain's largest joint railway with 180 route miles, penetrating from the East Midlands at a junction with the Midland Railway at Saxby into East Anglia where the Great Eastern Railway had otherwise enjoyed a monopoly. It served Great Yarmouth, Norwich and King's Lynn. The M&GN system was formally operationally incorporated into the LNER in 1936, although it relied heavily on the LMS to provide the bulk of its longer-distance traffic, including many holiday excursion trains from the Midlands and the north.

Largely single track, in the years following nationalisation it had appeared increasingly vulnerable: a harbinger of doom was the withdrawal of all night goods trains after February 1953.

Early in 1958 there were rumours that closures were on their way, but many were left breathless when the full scale of them became apparent.

The whole system was listed among the 350 route miles nationwide to be closed in 1959, with the only sections to be left open for passenger traffic being Sheringham to Melton Constable and North Walsham to Mundesley. For the time being, goods trains only were allowed to continue to Rudham from King's Lynn, between Spalding and Bourne, and Spalding and Sutton Bridge.

One reason given for the closure was that the key West Lynn Bridge over the River Great Ouse needed major repairs to its structure, but many saw at the time, and still believe today, that this was more of an excuse than a reason.

At midnight on February 28, 1959, most of the M&GN system closed, apart from a few piecemeal sections like Cromer to Melton Constable. At 8am the following Monday, rail connections at Sutton Bridge were severed and lifting of the track to South Lynn began in earnest, followed by the demolition of West Lynn Bridge which meant that there could be no going back. The Yarmouth Beach station building was ripped apart, the site becoming a coach station, and by January 1960 the track had been lifted as far as Potter Heigham.

Much of the M&GN rail traffic was immediately transferred to those former GER routes.

The message to railwaymen was short, sharp and simple: if a complete system could be eradicated overnight, where would the powers that be stop in their drive to stem the losses at all costs?

It was not only on British Railways where steel wheels had been replaced by rubber tyres. In Britain's cities, the street trams which had brought cheap, fast transport in the early 20th century had by then all but been phased out, along with the slightly more versatile trolleybuses that had superseded them in many places.

London's trams ceased operation after July 5, 1952, with Birmingham closing its tramways the following year. The last closure was that of the Glasgow routes on September 2, 1962, leaving only Blackpool with trams. If trams could be replaced by buses, why could buses not do the job of the railways for people who could not afford a car?

In 1960, only one in nine families was said to own a car: that figure seems laughable by today's standards, but, coming three years after Prime Minister Harold Macmillan told Conservative party supporters in

Bedford: "Most of our people have never had it so good", it indicated the results of the 1950s postwar wave of prosperity. There were also around 1.9 million motorbikes at the time, again highlighting the prevalence of private transport as an alternative to the railways.

On March 10, 1960, at the start of the parliamentary debate on the previously mentioned Guillebaud Report on railwaymen's wages, Macmillan said: "The carriage of minerals, including coal, an important traffic for the railways, has gone down. At the same time, there has been an increasing use of road transport in all its forms.

"The industry must be of a size and pattern suited to modern conditions and prospects. In particular, the railway system must be remodelled to meet current needs, and the modernisation plan must be adapted to this new shape.

"Secondly, the public must accept the need for changes in the size and pattern of the industry. This will involve certain sacrifices of convenience, for example, in the reduction of uneconomic services."

His words were music indeed to the ears of the Road Haulage Association, but struck a discordant note that would reverberate throughout the railway industry in the years to come, to the anger of users and staff across the nation.

"A GRAVE FINANCIAL PLIGHT"

Around this time, a report compiled by the Parliamentary Select Committee stated that "there is no doubt that a large-scale British railway system can be profitable". It emphasised that the size and shape of the system must depend primarily on financial considerations, but government subsidies for essential but unprofitable services were recommended.

The committee added that direct profitability was not the only consideration. Because of the cost of road building and congestion on them, the national interest might require railway services which did not directly pay for themselves, but which might cost the country less than the alternatives. There were several routes for which the future might appear to be uncertain, but which might be removed from the 'closure list' if such recommendations were adopted.

It was clear, however, that if subsidies were to be paid, the case for their retention must be fully proven, the report said.

Meanwhile, an independent advisory panel chaired by industrialist Sir Ivan Stedeford had been appointed to examine the structure and finances of the British Transport Commission.

Among its members was Dr Richard Beeching, a physicist and engineer at Imperial Chemical Industries who had been recommended by Sir Frank Smith, ICI's former chief engineer.

Following the panel's recommendations, Marples presented a White Paper to Parliament in December 1960, calling for the splitting of the British Transport Commission into a number of bodies, with the railways being run by the new British Railways Board. It also set financial targets for the railways, which would lead to cuts.

The paper read: "Sweeping changes will be needed. Effort and sacrifices will be required from all. The public will have to be prepared to face changes in the extent and nature of the services, provided and, when necessary, in the prices charged for them. The taxpayer will have to face a major capital reorganisation as well as continue to carry a large part of the burden until the railways are paying their way again. Those working in these undertakings, if their livelihood is to be assured, will have to play their part in increasing productivity and enabling the labour force to be deployed so as to secure maximum efficiency in operation.

"The heart of the problem is in the railways. They are a great national enterprise and a vital basic industry. They employ half a million people and represent an investment of nearly £1600 million, which is growing by more than £100 million each year.

"A railway system of the right size is an essential element in our transport network and will remain so for as long as can be foreseen. The development of other forms of transport and new techniques now faces British Railways, like the railways in other countries, with problems of competition and adaptation to modern circumstances and public demand.

"The railways are now in a grave financial plight. They are a long way short (by about £60 million a year) of covering even their running costs. This is quite apart from the problem of meeting their interest charges, whether upon the price paid for the undertakings or upon the money since borrowed for modernisation and other purposes. These interest charges now total some £75 million a year.

"The practical test for the railways, as for other transport, is how far the users are prepared to pay economic prices for the services provided. Broadly, this will in the end settle the size and pattern of the railway system. It is already clear that the system must be made more compact. There must also be modernisation, not only of layout, equipment and operating methods, but of organisation and management structure."

The break-up of the BTC was facilitated by the Transport Act 1962. Despite brief encouraging figures around the turn of the decade, in 1961 the railways' annual loss on operating account reached nearly £87 million.

On March 15, 1961, Marples told the House of Commons that Dr Richard Beeching would become the first chairman of the new British Railways Board, from June 1 that year.

CHAPTER THREE

Cometh the hour,
cometh the Axeman

F EW MEMBERS of the general public had cause to know the name of Richard Beeching until that time. Beeching was born in Sheerness on the Isle of Sheppey, the second of four brothers. His father was a reporter with the Kent Messenger, his mother a schoolteacher and his grandfather on his mother's side a dockyard worker.

Soon after his birth, the Beechings moved to Maidstone. All four boys attended the local Church of England primary school, Maidstone All Saints, and won scholarships to Maidstone Grammar School. Richard was appointed as a prefect there, although while his three brothers loved cricket, he preferred to go for walks in the countryside.

Richard and Geoffrey Beeching both read physics at London's Imperial College of Science & Technology in London and graduated with first-class honours degrees. There, Richard completed a research doctorate under the supervision of Sir George Thomson, the Nobel laureate in physics who achieved fame through his joint discovery of the wave properties of the electron by electron diffraction, and who was knighted in 1943.

Richard Beeching remained in his chosen discipline, taking up a post at London's Fuel Research Station in Greenwich in 1936 and then, the following year, moving to the Mond Nickel Laboratories. There, he became chief physicist, carrying out research in the fields of physics, metallurgy and mechanical engineering.

He married Ella Margaret Tiley in 1938, and the pair set up home in Solihull. They had known each other since schooldays.

When he was 29, during the Second World War, Beeching was loaned by Mond Nickel to the Ministry of Supply and worked in the armament design and research departments at Fort Halstead. There, he had a rank equivalent to that of army captain and worked under the department's superintendent and chief engineer Sir Frank Smith, the former chief engineer with ICI. Sadly, his brother Kenneth was killed in the war.

When Smith returned to ICI after the war, his successor promoted Beeching, now 33, to deputy chief engineer with a rank equivalent to that of brigadier.

Beeching continued his work with armaments, concentrating on anti-aircraft weaponry and small arms, but in 1948 he rejoined his former boss Sir Frank Smith as his personal technical assistant at ICI.

Zip fasteners, not bombs and bullets, were now the focus of Beeching's attention. He also worked with paints and leather cloth, with a remit to boost efficiency and cut production costs.

During his time at ICI, he was appointed to the Terylene Council, the forerunner of the company's fibres division, the board of which he later joined.

In 1953 he accepted a posting to Canada as vice-president of ICI (Canada) Ltd and was placed in charge of a terylene plant in Ontario. Two years later, he came back to Britain as chairman of the ICI Metals Division on Smith's recommendation.

He was appointed to the ICI board in 1957, serving as technical director, and for a brief period as development director.

It was yet another recommendation by Smith, who had by then retired, that saw Marples appoint Beeching to the previously mentioned advisory group.

When he was given the job of chairman of British Railways, succeeding Sir Brian Robertson, Beeching was paid an equivalent salary to that which he received at ICI, £24,000 a year, said to be around £370,000 by today's standards. That was £14,000 more than the prime minister was paid, and 250% more than the head of any other nationalised industry received at the time. ICI gave Beeching leave of absence for five years to do the job.

Beeching's brief was simple: return the railways to profitability without delay.

In doing so, he would change the transport map of Britain forever and, for good or bad, create a new streamlined railway system out of the steam era network.

In May 1961, *The Railway Magazine* wrote in its leader column: "The appointment of Dr Beeching has aroused mixed feelings both inside and outside the railway service.

"Surprise and concern have been expressed because the choice did not fall on a senior railway officer who could have brought to the new board many years of specialised experience of the intricacies of railway administration.

"Dr Beeching lacks this qualification, but, as a member of the Stedeford Committee, he must be fully aware of the magnitude of his task. It may be that a man who has attained a high position in the scientific industrial world at a comparatively early age will prove equally successful in the railway sphere, and it would be unfair to prejudge the appointment.

With remarkable clarity of vision, the writer continued: "A noteworthy feature is that Dr Beeching's present intention to return to ICI after five years probably will cause him to be regarded in circles as a surgeon rather than a railwayman."

Ironically, on the same page, it was noted that the first section of the British Transport Commission's museum at Triangle Place, Clapham, London, was opened to the public on Wednesday, March 29, 1961. Apart from the then much smaller York Railway Museum, it was the first permanent exhibition in Great Britain entirely devoted to the history of transport by rail, road and water. Soon, much, much more would be consigned to railway history, not least of all a third of the UK's national network.

In his first year in office, while drawing up the legendary blueprint which would bring him overnight fame or notoriety, depending on your perspective, Dr Beeching gained a then-unique insight into at least one controversial railway closure — by helping to reopen it!

On April 1, 1962, he travelled on a railtour from London Bridge via Haywards Heath and Ardingly to Horsted Keynes, where the network still connected with the newly opened Bluebell Railway, behind Great Northern Railway J52 0-6-0ST No. 1247, the first ex-main line steam engine to be preserved by a private individual. There, he officially opened a new stop built by the Bluebell revivalists in the form of Holywell Halt.

The British Transport Commission had intended to close the loss-making Lewes-East Grinstead line from May 28, 1955. The cross-country route engineered by the London, Brighton & South Coast Railway served mainly rural areas and was largely devoid of passengers, but that did not stop local spinster and battleaxe Madge Bessemer, who normally travelled by private car, launching a campaign to keep it open.

At first she asked for help from the Society for the Reinvigoration of Unremunerative Branch Lines in the United Kingdom, but found the nostalgia-minded organisation to be of no practical help.

She then studied key documents from the line's history, and reread the small print in the Act of Parliament which had empowered its building. It required the owners to run four trains each day. Missed by the BTC, the determined Miss Bessemer had discovered a loophole.

Helped by local MP Tufton Beamish, she forced the BTC to reinstate the service "very begrudgingly" in August the following year. Madge, granddaughter of Henry Bessemer, who invented the process for converting pig iron into steel with his Bessemer Converter, said: "They have got to keep the law just like everyone else!"

However, British Railways complied with the letter of the law, but not so much with the spirit of it. While four trains a day were indeed reinstated over the line, they were mostly restricted to just a single coach, and they did not stop at Barcombe or Kingscote, because those two stations did not appear in the original Act of Parliament. Also, the services appeared to be deliberately timed so that they would be of little use, arriving at East Grinstead after the start of normal working hours and leaving before knocking-off time.

The 'Sulky Service', as it came to be nicknamed, kept the line alive while British Railways went to the time and trouble to obtain the necessary statutory powers for revoking the terms of the line's original enabling Act of Parliament.

Services were again withdrawn between Lewes and East Grinstead on March 16, 1958, but Madge Bessemer had by then attracted the ears of the national press, radio and TV to her cause. When the final train ran, the unduly large numbers of passengers and sightseers proved that the public at large really did care about rail closures.

On that last day, Madge met Chris Campbell, a part-time student at Carshalton Technical College who had many recollections of travelling on the line while spending school holidays with relatives. Inspired by her efforts to save the line, Chris, 18, wondered if there was anything that could still be done. Elsewhere, Martin Eastland, 19, a telecommunications engineering student of Haywards Heath, David Dallimore, a student at the London School of Economics, from Woodingdean, and Brighton-based Alan Sturt, 19, who was studying at the Regent Street Polytechnic, had kicked around the idea of setting up a Lewes and East Grinstead Railway Preservation Society.

The publicity machine was sparked off again in December 1958 by a chance remark made by Chris to a reporter on the East Grinstead Observer about the formation of the preservation society, leading to the headline: "Bluebell Line Sensation: May Be Run Privately."

Chris travelled on a Rambler's Excursion from London Victoria to Horsted Keynes on December 7, two days after the report appeared. At Horsted Keynes, his party of 15 walked south along the disused trackbed to Newick & Chailey station where they had lunch in view of Madge, who was picking flowers on the lineside opposite. It was then that Chris met Martin for the first time and decided to call a public meeting to officially launch the society.

The landmark founders' meeting was held on March 15, 1959, at the Church Lads' Brigade Hall in Haywards Heath. It was chaired by Bernard Holden because the students, all under 21, were minors in the eyes of the law at the time and legally barred from holding positions. Bernard, 51, a signalling assistant in the general manager's office at Liverpool Street, had been born in Barcombe station house where his father Charles was stationmaster.

The rest is history. Part of the line, between Sheffield Park and a point south of Horsted Keynes, reopened on August 7, 1960. The revivalists did not succeed in their original ambition to save the entire Lewes-East Grinstead route, but their Bluebell Railway slowly but surely grew to become a world market leader in preserved steam railways.

There were many more would-be Madge Bessemers in the decade that followed, but few would meet with even a hint of her albeit temporary success in the face of an unprecedented tidal wave of Whitehall negativity against rural railways.

As for Dr Beeching, he and his wife moved to nearby East Grinstead in the Sixties and he spent the rest of his life there.

Ironically, Holywell Halt subsequently closed, when the Bluebell Railway obtained permission to run into Horsted Keynes, and as a heritage line it thrives today.

CHAPTER FOUR

The times they are a-changing

So life was never better than
In nineteen sixty-three
(Though just too late for me) –
Between the end of the Chatterley ban
And the Beatles' first LP.

S O RAN the final verse of Philip Larkin's poem Annus Mirabilis, which homed in on the beginnings of what some might well consider the greatest decade of change in the history of western civilisation, one in which everything that went before would be reassessed and if found wanting, replaced. Everything, it seemed, was up for grabs in a new supersonic age promising unparalleled technical progress and personal liberty. Few saw it coming, although maybe they should have learned the lessons of the aftermath of the First World War and the 'lost generation', the youngsters who came of age during the conflict and who were afterwards determined that there would be no return to the old order.

As the gloom lifted from Britain with the passing of the years of austerity, with its ration books, shortages and National Service, there abounded a new-found affluence and with it a sense of freedom, which began with a yearning and evolved into demands and insistence.

Maybe better education of the masses played a liberating part, or perhaps it was the higher wages and better working conditions that the Fifties ushered in, or the advance of popular technology. The Fifties also brought TV into many people's homes for the first time, and while at first viewers' diet was limited to the BBC, the 'voice of the establishment', the emergence of ITV, the commercial channel funded by advertising and which could afford to pay the big stars of stage and screen to appear, saw TV sets appearing in ordinary homes across the country. Then there was rock 'n' roll, the 1955 social commentary film Blackboard Jungle, about teachers and unruly pupils in a US inner-city school, which sparked off a teenage revolution by itself. The film is best known for the single by Bill Haley & His Comets, Rock Around the Clock, which became an overnight hit and stayed at the top of the Billboard charts for eight weeks.

When shown at a cinema near the Elephant and Castle in south London in 1956 the teenage teddy boy audience started to rip up seats and dance in the aisles. Their actions sparked off a trend, with copycat riots taking place in cinemas around Britain wherever the film was shown. While the vandalism died down after a few months, Blackboard Jungle is viewed by many historians as the beginning of a period of visible teenage rebellion in the late 20th century, in which what was seen as the 'old order' was there to also be ripped up and torn down.

While Haley, who had started his career as a country and western singer, was quickly superseded as a teenage icon by the likes of Elvis Presley, Little Richard, Chuck Berry and Eddie Cochran, and in Britain, Cliff Richard and the Shadows, Lonnie Donegan and Tommy Steele, a rolling stone had been set in motion that, with the aid of Beatlemania in 1963, a fateful year for both Larkin and the railways, became an unstoppable social and cultural revolution.

The old order was also on its way out in the world of literature and censorship. The ban on DH Lawrence's novel Lady Chatterley's Lover ended in 1960 with an obscenity trial at the Old Bailey, when Penguin Books was prosecuted under an Act of Parliament introduced in 1959. This law made it possible for publishers to avoid conviction if they could show that a work was of literary merit.

With Lady Chatterley, one of the principal objections was the use of the f-word. Chief prosecutor Mervyn Griffith-Jones, however, scored a major own goal when he asked the jury if it was the kind of book "you would wish your wife or servants to read". By then, how many ordinary people kept servants? Was there one law for the middle and upper classes and another for everyone else?

Compare the publicity over the trial with the secrecy and deafening silence which was dished out to the British public during the Edward VIII abdication crisis in 1936. No details of the newly crowned king appeared in the British press while it was in full swing, thanks to the firm control of the newspapers by the establishment, yet at the same time every lucid detail appeared in the press on the far side of the Atlantic. It was only when Edward VIII announced his abdication so he could marry Mrs Simpson, as portrayed in the 2011 multiple award-winning film The King's Speech, that we Brits were permitted to know the basics of what had really been going on regarding our monarchy.

The Chatterley jury of three women and nine men returned a verdict of not guilty on November 1960, making the novel available for the first time to the British public. It has now long since been considered a literary masterpiece.

Walls came tumbling down in the field of politics. Sir Harold Macmillan, the British Prime Minister, who seemed to epitomise the status quo of the old establishment, resigned on the grounds of ill health due to a medical misdiagnosis of inoperable prostate cancer on October 18, 1963, during the Conservative Party conference.

In its final year, the credibility of his government had been permanently damaged by the Profumo affair. John Profumo, Secretary of State for War, had lied to the House of Commons about his affair with Christine Keeler, the reputed mistress of an alleged Russian spy.

To the rebellious youth of the time, the scandal appeared to represent the moral decay of the British establishment. Years later, I was told by journalists that the exposure of the affair by the British press was revenge for a D-notice gagging order used to suppress revelations about a senior aristocrat and his relationship with a soldier.

Indeed, in several ways it highlighted a new-found freedom of the press in the early Sixties' winds of change. Incidentally, homosexuality between men aged 21 and over was decriminalised in England and Wales under the Sexual Offences Act 1967, one of many more benchmarks in the sexual revolution that popularly typifies the Sixties. Following the resignation of 'Supermac', the Conservatives demonstrated that they 'just did not get it' as far as the mood of the public was concerned. They liked and wanted change and fast, but despite multi-dimensional moves away from what had gone before, the surprise successor to Macmillan was simply more of the same and visibly so.

Foreign Secretary Alec Douglas-Home took over as prime minister: known as The Earl of Home from 1951 to 1963 after he inherited his father's peerage, he gave it up to move from the Lords to accept the position of prime minister, using the Peerage Act 1963, which had been passed earlier to allow Tony Benn to disclaim his peerage as Lord Stansgate. The old wine was repackaged as Sir Alec Douglas-Home, and in his new identity he won a by-election in the safe seat of Kinross & West Perthshire so he could enter the Commons.

The Profumo affair had, however, so badly tarnished the Conservative government that it was incapable of saving, least of all by a 60-year-old aristocrat who in the view of the general public represented much of the past that they wanted rid of. By contrast, the Labour party was newly led in 1963 by Harold Wilson, a comparative youngster at 46.

At the Labour Party's annual conference that year, Wilson delivered a keynote speech on the implications of scientific and technological change, stating that "the Britain that is going to be forged in the white heat of this revolution will be no place for restrictive practices or for outdated measures on either side of industry".

In short, he promised a way forward into a new age of achievement and prosperity, one unshackled to the prevailing class system that was licking its wounds from the Profumo scandal.

Thirteen years of Conservative rule ended when Labour won the 1964 general election with just four seats, taking Wilson into No 10 Downing Street — and, seeking a bigger majority after 18 months, a second election in March 1966 returned Wilson 96 seats clear of his rivals.

TRANSPORT FOR THE SPACE AGE

Change was everywhere. City dwellers saw mass clearances of slums during the Fifties and Sixties, and the construction of new estates and high-rise tower blocks on greenfield sites to replace them, although successive generations would challenge whether these had brought about a marked improvement in social conditions for their working-class inhabitants. Town centres were redesigned: many old small shops were swept away for new department stores, as brushed concrete replaced Victorian red bricks.

Car ownership soared during the Sixties, and this by itself gave the individual the freedom to choose where they went, no longer limited to railway lines or bus routes.

At the other extreme of the modern transport spectrum, the Russian cosmonaut Yuri Alekseyevich Gagarin became the first human to venture into outer space, on April 12, 1961, setting the stage for the Cold War race to the moon which was won by the US when Apollo 11's lunar module touched down in the Sea of Tranquility on July 20, 1969, Commander Neil Armstrong and pilot 'Buzz' Aldrin setting foot on the surface the following day.

The concept of a space age had featured heavily in popular movies and sci-fi TV series during the Fifties and Sixties: it was widely seen as the new frontier in which imagination was the only limiting factor, and there were many who sincerely believed we would be making missions to Mars and maybe beyond by the end of the century.

Space rockets were not the only futuristic forms of travel being developed. On the Isle of Wight, an island since the last ice age, parliamentary powers for a railway tunnel beneath the Solent were obtained in 1901. The scheme failed to raise sufficient capital, was briefly revived after the First World War, but ultimately came to nothing.

Yet why build a railway under the sea if you can go almost as quickly over it?

On June 11, 1959, aero and marine engineering company and flying boat builder Saunders-Roe Limited, based at Columbine Works in East Cowes, demonstrated the Saunders-Roe Nautical 1 (SR-N1), the first hovercraft built to inventor Christopher Cockerell's design, under contract to the National Research and Development Corporation. A fortnight later, it crossed the English Channel from Calais to Dover.

The firm went on to develop more hovercraft, including the SR-N2, which began operations over the Solent in 1962, and the ASR-N6, which ran from Southsea to Ryde for several years.

Incidentally, a site on High Down, near the Needles Battery, tested Black Knight and Black Arrow rocket engines for the British intercontinental ballistic missile programme between 1956-71. The rockets later launched the Prosper X3 satellite, the only one successfully launched by a British rocket, from Woomera in Australia on October 28, 1971.

The hovercraft was widely seen as a great step forward, some believing it could do for transport in the 20th century what the steam locomotive had done in the 19th. In the wake of the success of the early hovercraft, inventors set to work adapting the air-cushion principle to land transport, including railways. Visions of futuristic monorails so often portrayed in the boys' comics of the day pointed to an era in which steam, diesel and electric locomotives, indeed anything that ran on two rails, would be yesterday's traction.

Air cushion technology offered lower frictional forces and therefore in theory could produce high speeds. The hovertrain concept was devised by English engineer Professor Eric Laithwaite of Imperial College, London, who experimented with linear induction motors and produced the first full-size working model of such a motor in the late Forties.

Paving the way in this field of research was the Aérotrain, an experimental high-speed hovertrain built and operated in France between 1965 and 1977. In England, a short test track for a tracked hovercraft rail system was constructed by Tracked Hovercraft Ltd at Earith near Cambridge, sandwiched between two of the fenland's biggest drains, the Old Bedford River and the Counter Drain.

Funded by the Government, a test vehicle, RTV31, was built. It was fitted with linear magnetic motors for forward motion, while a cushion of air powered from giant fans raised the vehicle off the track.

It reached 104mph from a standing start over a mile on February 7, 1973 — only for the project funding to be cancelled a week later by Aerospace Minister Michael Heseltine after it was considered to be too expensive for commercial use. Engineering firm Alfred McAlpine took over parts of the project, but it was finally abandoned in the mid-Eighties. No, it would not become the preferred transport of the brave new world of the Sixties' technocrat visionaries, but a static exhibit outside Peterborough's Railworld museum, and as far as this technology was concerned, Mars would have to wait.

Mankind was not only reaching for the sky and beyond in the Sixties, but also planning to take public transport beneath the sea.

On February 6, 1964, the British and French governments agreed a deal for the construction of a Channel Tunnel. The twin-tunnelled rail link between Britain and the continent, linking the two physically for the first time since the last ice age, would take five years, it was announced.

Unlike hovercraft and hovertrains, a Channel Tunnel was not a new idea, and had been first seriously mooted in 1802, only to repeatedly fall foul over concerns about British national security being compromised. However, in 1955, the defence argument was accepted to be no longer relevant because of the superiority of air power.

Despite the agreement, work on building the tunnel did not start for another decade, and was cancelled in January 1975 to the dismay of the French after Harold Wilson was returned to power.

Another agreement, the Treaty of Canterbury, was signed in February 1986 and work began again in 1988, the tunnel opening in 1994.

British Railways did, however, have one big futuristic trick up its sleeve, one that certainly inspired the imagination in a world in which the public was being told that steam was on the way out.

The iconic Blue Pullman came off the drawing board in the late 1950s, underwent its trials before the turn of the decade, and was then unleashed on the Birmingham Snow Hill-Paddington line, as well as on the Midland route to Manchester.

Branded with the classic Pullman hallmark of utmost quality, the new diesel trains offered meals at every seat, air conditioning, and a staffing level good enough to ensure that passengers would want for nothing. Indeed, it looked more towards the comforts and style associated with aircraft than traditional railway carriages.

A smoothness of ride was also assured by an all-new design of coach. As steam engines dwindled and more diesels appeared, the eight-carriage Blue Pullman was certainly a star turn for the hordes of schoolboy train-spotters on the lineside. However, their admiration was not always shared by those on board, who found out that looks were not everything — as many complained of a very bumpy ride.

When British Rail chose the London Midland Region's Euston-Birmingham New Street line, part of the West Coast Main Line, as the primary route between Britain's two biggest cities, as opposed to the Western Region's rival Paddington-Birmingham Snow Hill line, and decided to electrify it, the Blue Pullman's days were numbered. The former Paddington line was downgraded to a secondary route, and the Pullmans were despatched to the less lucrative Bristol and Cardiff routes. They were all withdrawn by 1973, and not one coach was saved for preservation, and no, they did not persuade sufficient car owners to switch back to rail travel as had been originally hoped.

By contrast, one of the biggest linear developments following the 1955 Modernisation Plan was the 25kV electrification of the West Coast Main Line from Euston to Glasgow, completed in stages between 1959 and 1974, the first length, Crewe to Manchester, completed on September 12, 1960, followed by Crewe to Liverpool, completed on January 1, 1962. The first electric trains from London ran on November 12, 1965.

Electrification of the Birmingham line was completed on March 6, 1967. Once electrification was complete between London, the West Midlands and the North West, new high-speed long-distance services were introduced in 1966, launching British Rail's highly successful Inter-City brand. This innovation brought hitherto-unknown journey times such as London to Manchester or Liverpool in two hours 30 minutes for the twice-daily Manchester Pullman. Services ran hourly to Birmingham and two-hourly to Manchester.

We often look back at the Sixties as a period whereby the public regretted the passing of steam trains in favour of modern traction. However, in the build-up to the launch of electric services from London to the West Midlands, Liverpool and Manchester in late 1966, British Rail produced souvenir items as part of a publicity drive.

Within a few weeks of going on sale, practically the whole stock of 50,000 penny blue and white 'London Midland Express' lapel badges, introduced to publicise the Euston-Liverpool-Manchester electrified services, were sold. Shoulder travel bags, bearing the legend 'Inter-City Electric' and on sale at principal stations for 15 shillings, also proved popular. So successful was the public response to the London Midland Region electrification exhibition train that it was taken on tour to the Southern Region, where third-rail electric on commuter lines from London has been the norm for decades.

Along with electrification came the gradual introduction of modern British Rail coaches such as the Mark 2 and, following the northern electrification scheme's completion in 1974, the air-conditioned Mark 3s. These carriages remained the mainstay of West Coast Main Line express services until the early 21st century.

On the route, line speeds were raised to a maximum 110mph. Hauled by Class 86 and Class 87 electric locomotives, the West Coast Main Line services were viewed as the nationalised railway's flagship passenger product, having the effect of doubling traffic between 1962 and 1975 after years of stagnation. This proved that if the public was given the right product, in the right location, and backed by sufficient capital investment, the railways' fortunes could be reversed.

The electrification of the route was accompanied by the total redevelopment of the Victorian stations along it and replaced with Sixties' designs built from glass and concrete, and lacking much of the ornamentation and style of their predecessors, placing functionality first. The redevelopment of Euston went as far as demolishing the famous Doric Arch entrance portal despite widespread opposition. Coventry, Birmingham New Street, Stafford and Manchester Piccadilly were, for better or worse, rebuilt.

However, by contrast, the Blue Pullmans were like so much in the Sixties, promising the earth yet ultimately delivering comparatively little that they had promised, although in fairness, lessons learned from their design paved the way for the introduction of the Inter-City 125 High Speed Trains in the Seventies, and these were so successful that they are still with us now.

Larkin's poem quoted earlier talked about: "A brilliant breaking of the bank, A quite unlosable game", and so it was in the Sixties, when it seemed that nothing could halt the march of progress, with innovation and invention lurking around every corner to surprise and delight us. Yet much of the optimism and positivity surrounding the era, or at least our popular image of it, ultimately turned out to be out of sync with reality, and failed to fully predict the medium and long-term implications of change that too often rushed off the drawing board and way ahead of itself.

It was in this most fertile of decades that one man, empowered by the government, would front a series of ground-shifting and hugely controversial decisions that he believed would finally yank Britain's entire national railway network out of the steam age of the Big Four so that it would serve the needs of the times in which 'liberated' mankind would take his first giant steps on the moon in 1969.

CHAPTER FIVE

The reshaping of British Railways

THE TRANSPORT Act 1962, which broke up the British Transport Commission and created the British Railways Board, set the scene for what was to quickly follow.

The new board was directed under Section 22 of the Act to run the railways so that its operating profits were "not less than sufficient" for meeting the running costs.

This clause marked a major first for British railway legislation and was a turning point for the system, for from then onwards, each railway service should pay for itself or at least show that it had the possibility of doing so. The days of mass subsidy, with profitable services supporting the unprofitable ones, and the taxpayer footing the bill if the overall figures did not tally in the right way, would soon be over, or so it was intended.

It was the Select Committee of the House of Commons on Nationalised Industries which had decided that the British Transport Commission should make its decisions exclusively on considerations of "direct profitability". Where decisions not based on self-sufficiency but "on grounds of the national economy or of social needs" had to be taken, the minister of transport would shoulder the responsibility.

No longer would there be a special case for the railways: they would have to compete in a free market in the same way as any other business. Section 3(1) of the Act stated that it was the duty of the British Railways Board to provide railway services with regard to "efficiency, economy and safety of operation".

The 1962 Act also introduced new legislation for the closure of railway lines. Section 56(7) demanded that British Railways gave at least six weeks' notice of its intention to close a line and to publish the proposal in two local newspapers in the area affected in two successive weeks.

Each notice would have to provide the proposed closure dates, details of alternative public transport, including services which British Railways was to lay on as a result of closure and inviting objections within the six-week period to a specified address.

A copy of the notice was also to be sent to the relevant Area Transport Users Consultative Committee, which would receive objections from affected rail users, and submit a report to the minister of transport.

The Central Transport Consultative Committee was a new body that replaced a similar one established under the Transport Act 1947 which nationalised the railways, and was intended to represent the railways' consumers. The Area Transport Users Consultative Committees were additional bodies set up to cover local areas.

It would be the job of the area committees to look at the hardship which it considered would be caused as a result of the closure, and recommend measures to ease that hardship.

The line closure would not go ahead until the area committee had reported to the transport minister and he had given his consent to it. Based on the area committee's report, the minister could subject his consent to closure to certain conditions, such as the provision of alternative transport services. However, the minister was not bound to follow any of the area committee's recommendations, and therefore there was no safeguard by which public feeling would take priority over policy.

In December 1962, *The Railway Magazine* reported: "The name of Dr Beeching is likely to live on in the Leicestershire village of Countesthorpe long after the current railway troubles are forgotten. It is reported that the parish council there has agreed to name a new thoroughfare off Station Road 'Beeching Close' because residents associate him with the closure of their railway station."

Countesthorpe station, just south of Leicester on the Midland line to Rugby, had closed in February 1962. While villagers there might have been irate, they would soon have like-minded bedfellows — to the tune of many millions. The nation had not seen anything yet.

THE DOCTOR PRESCRIBES THE MEDICINE

The biggest shock to the railway system was delivered on March 27, 1963, when Dr Beeching's report, The Reshaping of British Railways, was published. Seasoned railwaymen had seen traffic dwindle to a trickle or nothing on many lines and knew that closures were inevitable; however, the publication of a report detailing sweeping changes of the extent proposed was still received by many with horror.

To members of the ordinary public, who had no grasp of railway finances, and had accepted that the railways 'would always be there', Beeching would be immortalised as the man who took 'their' line away.

Dubbed the 'Beeching Bombshell' or the 'Beeching Axe' by the press, the 148-page report called for a third of the rail network to be closed and ripped up.

Out of around 18,000 route miles, 5000, mainly comprising cross-country routes and rural branches, should close completely, it recommended.

Not only were branches to rural backwaters listed for closure: this time, trunk routes were listed — the Somerset & Dorset Joint Railway system, the Waverley Route from Carlisle to Edinburgh, the Great Central Railway from Nottingham to Marylebone, along with passenger services on the Settle and Carlisle route.

Over and above all this, many other lines were to lose their passenger services and remain open for freight only, while intermediate stations serving small communities on main lines should close, with the aim of speeding up inter-city trains. A total of 2363 stations and halts were to be closed, including 435 under consideration before the report appeared, of which 235 had already been closed.

The proposed mass changes to the network would be implemented in a seven-year programme, the report recommended.

Basically, the report said that railways should be used to meet that part of the national transport requirement for which they offered the best available means, and stop trying to compete in areas where they were now ill-suited.

The report followed a key study initiated by Beeching into traffic flows on all the railway routes in the country.

This study, which had been carried out during the week ending April 23, 1962, two weeks after Easter, found that 30% of route miles carried just 1% of passengers and freight, and half of all stations contributed just 2% of income. Half the total route mileage carried about 4% of the total passenger miles, and around 5% of the freight ton miles, revenue from them amounting to £20 million with the costs double that figure. Clearly, the figures did not stack up, nor, it seemed, were ever likely to again.

From the least-used half of the stations, the gross revenue from all traffic did not even cover the cost of the stations themselves, and made no contribution to route costs, movement or terminal costs.

Regarding branch lines, figures showed it was doubtful if the revenue from up to 6000 passengers a week covered movement costs alone, and clearly money would be saved by withdrawing the service.

The report stated that overall, passenger traffic on a single-track branch line added around £1750 a mile to the cost of route maintenance, signalling and the staffing of stations.

Therefore, a passenger density below 10,000 could not be considered as economic, even where freight traffic absorbed a proportion of the route cost. Where there was no other traffic, 17,000 passengers per week might make a branch line pay its way.

Even the provision of railbuses — a cost-cutting measure introduced on many branches in the late Fifties as a key element of a drive to prune staffing levels and increase efficiency — demanded a passenger density of 14,000 a week, as against 17,000 a week with diesel multiple units.

Beeching stated in the opening to his report that "there had never before been any systematic assembly of a basis of information upon which planning could be founded, and without which the proper role of the railways in the transport system as a whole could not be determined".

Taken at face value, that claimed it was the first time that a detailed study of the economy of the nation's railways as a whole had been attempted, rather than the individual regions of British Railways (Western, London Midland, Eastern, Southern and Scottish) largely doing their own thing. Maybe if such a nationwide study had been attempted as part of the implementation of the Modernisation Plan, it would not have been implemented in such a haphazard, localised and floundering manner as it had been.

The Beeching report read: "Throughout these investigations and the preparation of this report the British Railways Board has had it in mind that its duty is to employ the assets vested in it, and develop or modify them, to the best advantage of the nation."

As we have seen, Beeching did not invent rail closures: a steady process of eliminating non-remunerative lines had been under way for decades. Indeed, several of the routes listed in The Reshaping of British Railways had already been proposed for closure by their regions: Beeching merely confirmed those decisions.

The closures of poorly used lines had fallen from 350 in 1959 to 175 in 1960, and even further to 150 in 1961. Yet in 1962, the year before The Reshaping of British Railways appeared, they shot up to 780. The Western Region, for one, which had embraced dieselisation, was making much publicity out of the improvements it was making, after years of closing branches serving rural backwaters.

In 1963, before the newly recommended Beeching closures could be implemented, a total of 324 miles were axed.

By taking a global view and applying the same criteria to all regions across the country, Beeching may be seen as merely streamlining the decision-making processes that had gone before, with a universal set of criteria. Not only that, it was Marples who employed him and instructed him — the doctor was "only obeying orders".

Much of the report proposed that British Rail electrify some trunk routes and eliminate uneconomic wagon-load traffic in favour of containerised freight traffic. The report — which claimed that the measures should eradicate the railways' deficit by 1970 — automatically sparked immediate outrage from many of the communities which would become disenfranchised by the rail network as a result of the closures.

However, the Conservative government, which accepted Beeching's report after it was debated in the House of Commons in April 1963, promised that axed rail services would be replaced by bus services, which would be much cheaper to operate.

The report said: "Today, rail stopping services and bus services serve the same basic purpose. Buses carry the greater part of the passengers moving by public transport in rural areas, and, as well as competing with each other, both forms of public transport are fighting a losing battle against private transport.

"Immediately prior to the war, in 1938, the number of private cars registered was 1,944,000. In 1954 there were 3,100,000, and in 1961 there were 6,000,000. By 1970 it is expected that there will be a total of 13,000,000 cars registered, equivalent to 24.3 per 100 of the population or 76 per 100 families."

Looking back, major flaws in the report may be seen as a failure to consider neither reduction of costs on loss-making services and electrification to countermand competition from road alternatives. Neither were subsidies considered or asked for, as Beeching intended that his slimmed-down railway network would eliminate its deficit within a few years. The report was debated by both the Commons and the country in the year leading up to a General Election. It might therefore seem surprising that such unpopular measures were introduced before an election rather than afterwards.

Yet while the Labour opposition led by Harold Wilson publicly said that it would reverse the Beeching cuts if elected, the Conservatives steamed ahead with the report's implementation. There appeared to be a general feeling that once protesters had been given their chance to vent their anger through initial newspaper headlines, there would be a growing general acceptance that closures were inevitable.

Marples approved the vast majority of closures which reached him for consideration, although the consultative machinery conveniently held back the first impact of the programme until the election campaign was well under way. The few he spared from the axe included important electrified commuter routes such as Manchester to Bury and Liverpool to Southport.

In February 1964, Marples made one concession — promising to close no seaside branch lines before October that year, so people could plan their holidays for the coming summer.

BEECHING'S 15-POINT TONIC

The Reshaping of British Railways identified 15 steps which needed to be taken to bring about the turnaround in fortunes envisaged by Beeching, as follows:

1. The discontinuation of many stopping passenger services.
2. The transfer of the modern diesel multiple-unit stock displaced to continuing services which are still steam hauled.
3. The closure of a large number of small stations to passenger traffic, eliminating loss-making stops which slowed down trains.
4. Improvement to inter-city passenger services and rationalisation of routes.
5. The damping-down of seasonal peaks of passenger traffics and withdrawal of corridor coaching stock held to cover them. In particular, this bode ill for branch lines serving holiday resorts, such as those on the London & South Western Railway's 'Withered Arm' system in Devon and Cornwall, where traffic levels boomed during the peak summer season but services were little used by locals during the rest of the year. The annual cost of providing the 6000 coaches for the summer season was £3.4 million, set against total revenue of just £500,000.
6. The co-ordination of suburban train and bus services and charges.
7. The co-ordination of passenger parcels service with the Post Office.
8. An increase in block train movements of coal by inducing the National Coal Board to provide train-loading facilities at collieries and the provision of coal concentration depots.
9. The reduction of uneconomic freight traffic by closing small goods stations and the adjustment of charges, in other words, the end of the traditional pick-up goods, with road hauliers ready and willing to fill the void.
10. The attraction of more sidings-to-sidings traffic by the operation of through trains at the expense of the system of forwarding of single wagons.
11. The study and development of the 'liner' train system.
12. The concentration of the freight sundries traffic on 100 main depots.
13. The rapid and progressive withdrawel of freight wagons over the

following three years.

14. The continued replacement of steam by diesel traction for main line services up to a probable requirement of at least 3750 to 4250 locomotives. At the time of the report, 1698 diesels were already in service and 950 on order.

15. The rationalisation of the composition and use of the railways' road cartage fleet.

PASSENGER SERVICES TO BE WITHDRAWN UNDER BEECHING REPORT 1963

Western England

» Avonmouth Dock-Bristol Temple Meads, *Filton J-St Andrews Road* 11/64
» Axminster-Lyme Regis, 11/65
» Barnstaple Junction-Ilfracombe, 10/70
» Barnstaple Junction-Taunton, 10/66
» Barnstaple Junction-Torrington, 10/65
» Bath Green Park-Bournemouth West, *BGP-Poole* 3/66
» Bath Green Park-Bristol Temple Meads, *BGP-Mangotsfield* 3/66
» Bere Alston-Callington, *C-Gunnislake* 11/66
» Berkeley Road-Sharpness, 11/64
» Bodmin Road-Bodmin North-Wadebridge-Padstow, *BN-Padstow* 1/67, *Halwill Jct-W* 10/66, *BR-Nanstallon Halt* 1/67
» Bridport-Maiden Newton, 5/75
» Bristol Temple Meads-Clifton Down-Pilning, *Pilning J-Severn Beach* 11/64
» Bristol Temple Meads-Patchway-Pilning *(local?)*
» Bristol Temple Meads-Portishead, *Parson Street-P* 9/64
» Bude-Okehampton, 10/66
» Calne-Chippenham, 9/65
» Chard Central-Chard Junction, 9/62 *(and to Creech Jct)*
» Cirencester Town-Kemble, 4/64
» Clevedon-Yatton, 10/66
» Exeter Central-Exmouth -
» Exmouth-Tipton St John's, 3/67

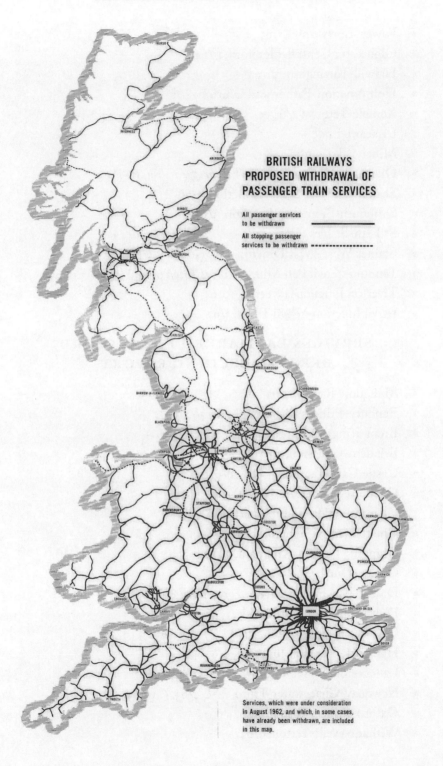

BRITISH RAILWAYS
PROPOSED WITHDRAWAL OF
PASSENGER TRAIN SERVICES

All passenger services
to be withdrawn

All stopping passenger
services to be withdrawn

Services, which were under consideration
in August 1962, and which, in some cases,
have already been withdrawn, are included
in this map.

63

» Fowey-Lostwithiel, 1/65
» Gloucester Central-Hereford, 11/64
» Halwill-Torrington, 3/65
» Holt Junction-Patney and Chirton, 4/66
» Kemble-Tetbury, 4/64
» Liskeard-Looe -
» Minehead-Taunton, 1/71
» Okehampton-Padstow, *O-Wadebridge* 10/66, *W-P* 1/67
» Seaton (Devon)-Seaton Junction, 3/66
» Sidmouth-Sidmouth Junction, 3/67
» St Erth-St Ives (Cornwall) -
» Staines West-West Drayton and Yiewsley, 3/65
» Taunton-Yeovil Pen Mill, *T-Yeovil Town* 6/64, *YT-YPM* 11/65
» Tiverton Junction-Tiverton, 10/64
» Yeovil Junction-Yeovil Town, 3/67

SERVICES EARMARKED FOR CLOSURE
BEFORE BEECHING REPORT

» Abingdon-Radley, 9/63
» Banbury-Princes Risborough, *(local)* 1/63
» Brent-Kingsbridge, 9/63
» Brixham-Churston, 5/63
» Castle Cary-Taunton, *(local)* 9/62
» Chalford-Gloucester, *(local)* 11/64
» Chard Junction-Taunton, 9/62
» Cheltenham-Kingham, 10/62
» Chipping Norton-Kingham, 12/62
» Coaley-Dursley, 9/62
» Didcot-Newbury, 9/62, *excursions until* 8/63
» Dulverton-Exeter St Davids, 10/63
» Gwinear Road-Helston, 11/62
» Hemyock-Tiverton Junction, 9/63
» Launceston-Plymouth, *L-Tavistock Jct* 12/62
» Newquay-Chacewater-Truro, *N-C* 2/63, *C* 10/64
» Oxford-Princes Risborough, 1/63
» Witham-Wells-Yatton, 9/63

ADDITIONAL SERVICES LISTED FOR CLOSURE AFTER BEECHING REPORT UP TO 1968

- » Bath Spa-Bristol (Temple Meads) (locals only) 1/70
- » Gloucester Eastgate/Central -Stratford-upon-Avon, *Cheltenham Spa (Lansdown Jct)–S–u–A* 3/68

Southern England

- » Alton-Winchester City, 2/73
- » Andover-Romsey, *Andover JCT-R* 9/64
- » Ashford (Kent)-Hastings -
- » Ashford (Kent)-New Romney, *Appledore–NR* 3/67
- » Bexhill West-Crowhurst, 6/64
- » Bournemouth-Ringwood-Brockenhurst, *Broadstone–Brockenhurst* 5/64
- » Brighton-Horsham, *Shoreham–Christ's Hospital* 3/66
- » Brighton-Tonbridge, *Lewes–Uckfield* 5/69, *Groombridge–T* 7/85
- » Clapham Junction-Kensington Olympia -
- » Eastbourne-Tonbridge, *Hailsham–Eridge* 6/65, *Hailsham–Polegate* 6/65, *Groombridge–Tonbridge* 7/85
- » Guildford-Horsham, 6/65
- » Portsmouth-Botley-Romsey/Andover, *Andover Jct-R* 9/64, *Eastleigh–R* 5/69
- » Ryde Pier Head-Ventnor/Cowes, Ryde St Johns-C 2/66
- » Three Bridges-Tunbridge Wells West, *TB–Ashurst Jun* 1/67, *AJ–Groombridge* 1/69

SERVICES WITH INTERMEDIATE STATIONS WITHDRAWN

- » Haywards Heath-Seaford (local)
- » Portsmouth-Netley-Southampton-Romsey/Andover (local)
- » Reading Southern-Guildford-Redhill-Tonbridge (local)

SERVICES EARMARKED FOR CLOSURE BEFORE BEECHING REPORT

- » Havant-Hayling Island, 11/63
- » Haywards Heath-Horsted Keynes, 10/63

» Selsdon-Woodside (Surrey), 5/83

ADDITIONAL SERVICES LISTED FOR CLOSURE AFTER BEECHING REPORT UP TO 1968

» Eridge-Hurst Green Jct –
» Fawley-Totton (light railway) 2/66

North London

» London Broad Street-Richmond -
» Croxley Green-Watford Junction, *CG–Bushey & Oxhey* 6/66
» Belmont-Harrow and Wealdstone, 10/64
» St Albans Abbey-Watford Junction -
» London St Pancras-Barking (local)

ADDITIONAL SERVICES LISTED FOR CLOSURE AFTER BEECHING REPORT UP TO 1968

» *Uxbridge Vine Street-West Drayton and Yiewsley, 9/62
» Greenford-West Ealing -

Midlands

» Banbury/London Marylebone-Leicester Central-Nottingham Victoria-Sheffield Victoria-York, *Aylesbury-Sheffield* 9/66 *but Rugby-Nottingham 5/69, Sheffield Victoria 1/70*
» Banbury-Woodford Halse, 9/66
» Birmingham New Street-Sutton Park-Walsall, *Castle Bromwich-W* 1/65
» Bletchley-Buckingham, *Buckingham-Verney Jct* 9/64
» Bromyard-Worcester Shrub Hill, B-Henwick 9/64
» Burton-on-Trent-Leicester London Road, 9/64
» Burton-on-Trent-Wolverhampton High Level, *Winchnor JCT-Walsall* 1/65
» Buxton-Millers Dale, 3/67
» Derby Friar Gate-Nottingham Victoria, DFG-*New Basford* 9/64
» Dudley-Old Hill, 6/64
» Dudley-Walsall, 7/64
» Dunstable North-Hatfield, 4/65
» Great Bridge-Swan Village, *Dudley Port-SV* 6/64, *Dudley-DP* 7/64

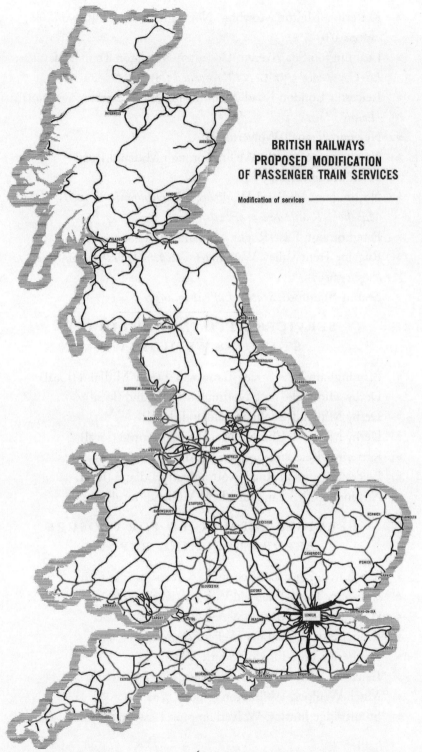

BRITISH RAILWAYS
PROPOSED MODIFICATION
OF PASSENGER TRAIN SERVICES

Modification of services ——————————

» Kettering-Melton Mowbray-Nottingham Midland, *local* 4/66, *express* 4/67

» Leamington Spa Avenue-Coventry-Nuneaton Trent Valley, 1/65, *LS-C reopened* 5/77, *C-NTV reopened* 5/87

» Leicester London Road-Melton Mowbray-Peterborough North - *Locals*

» Newport Pagnell-Wolverton, 9/64

» Northampton Castle-Wellingborough Midland Road-Peterborough East, 5/64

» Nottingham Midland-Worksop, *NM (Radford)-W* 10/64, *Mansfield-Radford reopened* 11/95

» Peterborough East-Rugby Midland, 6/66

» Rugeley Trent Valley-Walsall, 1/65, *reopened to Hednesford* 4/89, *to Rugeley* 6/97

» Seaton-Stamford, *Seaton-Luffenham* 6/66

SERVICES WITH INTERMEDIATE STATIONS WITHDRAWN

» Birmingham New Street-Tamworth-Derby Midland (local)
» Derby Midland-Trent-Nottingham Midland (local)
» Derby Midland-Sheffield Midland (local)
» Derby Midland-Chinley-Manchester Central (local)
» Kettering-Leicester London Road (local)
» Leicester London Road-Nottingham Midland (local)
» Nottingham Midland-Sheffield Midland (local)

SERVICES EARMARKED FOR CLOSURE BEFORE BEECHING REPORT

» Ashchurch-Evesham-Redditch, *E-R* 10/62, *E-A* 6/63
» Aylesbury Town-Sheffield Victoria (local), 3/63
» Hartlebury-Shrewsbury, *S-Bewdley* 9/63, *B-H* 1/70
» *Kidderminster-Tenbury Wells, *TW-Bewdley* 8/62
» *Kimberley East-Pinxton South, 1/63
» *Leicester Belgrave Road-Skegness, 9/62 *(excursions)*
» *Much Wenlock-Wellington (Salop), 7/62
» *Stourbridge Juntion-Wolverhampton Low Level, 7/62

ADDITIONAL SERVICES LISTED FOR CLOSURE
AFTER BEECHING REPORT UP TO 1968

» Ambergate South JCT-Chinley North Jct, *Matlock-Chinley NJ* 7/68
» Birmingham (New Street)-Redditch, *Redditch (Old)-(New)* 7/72
» Birmingham (New Street)-Worcester (Shrub Hill) –
» Trent (Long Eaton JCT-North Erewash Jct) 1/67
» Trent (Station North JCT-Trowell Jct)/Sawley JUN, *TSNJ-TJ*
  11/67, *TSNJ- SJ* 3/67

Eastern England

» Aldeburgh-Saxmundham, 9/66
» Audley End-Bartlow, 9/64
» Barton-on-Humber-New Holland Town -
» Braintree & Bocking-Witham (Essex) -
» Brightlingsea-Wivenhoe, 6/64
» Buntingford-St Margarets, 11/64
» Cambridge-St Ives-March, *C –St Ives* 10/70, *St Ives–M* 3/67
» Dereham-Wells-Next-The-Sea, 10/64 (*D-Wymondham* 10/69, *Kings
  Lynn-D* 9/68)
» Firsby-Skegness - *but Firsby* 10/70
» Firsby-Woodhall Junction-Lincoln Central, 10/70
» Grimsby-Spalding-Peterborough North, *G-Firsby* 10/70,
  Boston-PN 10/70, *S-PN reopened* 6/71
» Lincoln St Marks-Nottingham Midland -
» Mablethorpe-Willoughby, 10/70
» Maldon East and Heybridge-Witham (Essex), 9/64
» Marks Tey-Shelford, *Sudbury-S* 3/67
» Melton Constable-Sheringham, 4/64
» Mundesley-on-Sea-North Walsham, 10/64
» Romford-Upminster -
» Swaffham-Thetford, 6/64
» Westerfield-Yarmouth South Town, *Beccles-YST* 11/59

SERVICES WITH INTERMEDIATE
STATIONS WITHDRAWN

» Cleethorpes-New Holland Pier (local)

SERVICES EARMARKED FOR CLOSURE
BEFORE BEECHING REPORT

» Boston-Woodhall Juntion, 6/63
» *Grantham-Lincoln Central, 9/62 *(local)*, 11/65 *(all)*
» Immingham Dock-New Holland, *Goxhill–ID* 6/63
» *Palace Gates-Stratford, 1/63

ADDITIONAL SERVICES LISTED FOR CLOSURE
AFTER BEECHING REPORT UP TO 1968

» March-Wisbech East, *March–Magdalen Road* 9/68

North Wales

» Afon Wen-Bangor, *AW–Caernarfon 12/64*, *C–Menai Bridge 1/70*
» Amlwch-Bangor, *A–Gaerwen 12/64*
» Blaenau Ffestiniog-Llandudno -
» Chester General-Holyhead/Caernarfon (local), *see above*

South And Mid Wales

» Abercynon-Aberdare, 3/64, *reopened 10/88*
» Aberystwyth-Carmarthen, *A–Strata Florida* 12/64 *(flooding)*,
   SF–C 2/65
» Bala-Bala Junction, 1/65
» Barry-Bridgend, 6/64
» Bridgend-Treherbert, *Cymmer Afan–B 6/70*, *CA–T 2/68 on closure of*
   Rhondda tunnel, B–Maesteg reopened /92
» Caerphilly-Senghenydd, *S–Aber J Halt 6/64*
» Cardiff Clarence Road-Cardiff General, 3/64
» Cardiff-Coryton -
» Llanfyllin-Llanymynech, 1/65
» Maerdy-Porth, 6/64
» Morfa Mawddach (Barmouth Jct)-Ruabon, 1/65, *but Bala–*
   Llangollen 12/64 (flooding)
» Welshpool-Whitchurch (Salop) 1/65

SERVICES EARMARKED FOR CLOSURE
BEFORE BEECHING REPORT

» *Brecon-Hereford, 12/62
» *Brecon-Moat Lane Junction, 12/62
» *Brecon-Neath Riverside, 10/62
» *Cardiff/Barry-Pontypridd, *Cadoxton-Treforest* 9/62, *St Fagans-Tynycaeau JUN* 9/62
» *Cardigan-Whitland, 9/62
» Carmarthen-Llandilo, 9/63
» Dowlais Cae Harris-Nelson and Llancaiach, 6/64
» *Hirwaun-Merthyr, 12/62
» Pontypool Road-Aberdare High Level-Neath General-Swansea High Street, *PR-NG* 6/64
» Porthcawl-Pyle, 9/63
» Shrewsbury-Craven Arms-Llandovery-Pontardulais-Swansea Victoria/Llanelli, *P-SV* 6/64
» *Swansea High Street-Neath General-Treherbert, *Briton Ferry-Cymmer Afan* 12/62, *CA-T* 2/68

ADDITIONAL SERVICES LISTED FOR CLOSURE
AFTER BEECHING REPORT UP TO 1968

» Whitland-Pembroke Dock -

North West

» Bacup-Bury-Manchester Victoria, *Bacup-Rawtenstall* 12/66, *R-Bury* 6/72
» Barrow-Whitehaven -
» Blackpool North-Fleetwood, *F-Wyre Dock* 4/66, *WD-Poulton-le-Fylde* 6/70
» Bury Bolton Street-Manchester Victoria, *BBS-Clifton JUN* 12/66
» Buxton-Manchester Piccadilly -
» Carlisle-Penrith-Workington, *P-Keswick* 3/72, *K-W* 4/66
» Carlisle-Silloth, 9/64
» Carlisle-Skipton -
» Carnforth-Wennington — but *Morecambe-Wennington* 1/66
» Chester General-Liverpool Lime Street -

» Colne-Accrington-Bury-Manchester Victoria, *A–Ramsbottom* 12/66, *R–B* 6/72
» Crossens-Southport Chapel Street, *Preston–S* 9/64
» Earby-Barnoldswick, 9/65
» Etruria-Kidsgrove (Stoke Loop), 3/64
» Glazebrook-Stockport Tiviot Dale, 11/64
» Glazebrook-Wigan Central 11/64
» Greenfield-Stalybridge-Manchester Exchange - *but ME* 5/69
» Hadfield/Glossop-Manchester Piccadilly -
» Hayfield/Macclesfield- Romiley-Manchester Piccadilly, *H–New Mills* 1/70, *M–Rose Hill (Marple)* 1/70
» Lake Side (Windermere)-Ulverston, 9/65 *for extant excursion traffic*
» Lancaster Castle/Lancaster Green Ayre-Heysham, *LC–LGA* 1/66, *Morecambe (Torrisholme Js No1–No2)* 1/66
» Leek-Uttoxeter, 1/65
» Liverpool Exchange- Fazakerley-Wigan Wallgate -
» Liverpool Exchange-Southport Chapel Street -
» Liverpool Lime Street-St Helens-Wigan North Western -
» Manchester Central-Chinley-Hope-Sheffield Midland -
» Manchester Victoria-Horwich, H-Black Rod 9/65
» Manchester Victoria-Newton Heath-Middleton, *Middleton– Middleton JUN* 9/64
» Moor Row-Sellafield, *MR–Egremont (workmen's)* 9/65
» New Brighton-Chester Northgate-Wrexham Central - *Locals*
» Preston-Southport Chapel Street, 9/64
» Rose Grove-Todmorden, 11/65
» Royton-Royton Junction, 4/66
» Silverdale-Stoke-on-Trent. 3/64
» St Helens Shaw Street-Earlestown-Warrington Bank Quay, *StHSS–StH J* 6/65
» Stafford-Wellington, 9/64

SERVICES WITH INTERMEDIATE STATIONS WITHDRAWN

» Carlisle-Preston-Warrington-Crewe (local)
» Chester General-Crewe (local)

BUS SERVICES IN BRITAIN
ROUTES COVERED BY STAGE AND
EXPRESS SERVICES

» Chester General-Warrington Bank Quay-Manchester Exchange (local)
» Crewe-Shrewsbury (local)
» Huddersfield-Manchester Exchange (local)
» Liverpool Lime Street-Tyldesley-Patricroft-Manchester Exchange (local)
» Manchester Exchange-Tyldesley-Wigan North Western (local)
» Oxenholme-Windermere (local)
» Shrewsbury-Wellington (local)
» Stalybridge-Stockport Edgeley (local)

SERVICES EARMARKED FOR CLOSURE BEFORE BEECHING REPORT

» Alston-Haltwhistle, 5/76
» Cheadle (Staffs)-Cresswell (Staffs), 6/63
» Crewe-Wellington (Salop), *W-Nantwich* 9/63
» *Ellesmere-Wrexham Central, 9/62

ADDITIONAL SERVICES LISTED FOR CLOSURE AFTER BEECHING REPORT UP TO 1968

» Bamber Bridge Jct-Todd Lane Jct-Preston (East Lancashire side) 5/72
» Bootle Jct-Edge Hill, i.e. withdrawal of through services Southport (Chapel)-Euston /77
» Daisy Hill (Dobbs Brow Jct)-Blackrod (Horwich Fork JUN), 9/65
» Denton Jct-Stalybridge (via Hooley Hill) 1/68
» Denton-Droylsden 7/68
» Hadfield-Sheffield (Victoria)-Nunnery Jct: Withdrawal of electric services, Manchester (Piccadilly)-Sheffield (Victoria), remaining East Coast services to be diverted to Sheffield (Midland), *H-Penistone 1/70, Penistone-Sheffield 5/83, SV 1/70*
» Brindle Heath Jct-Dobbs Brow Jct-Crow Nest Jct –
» Liverpool (Exchange)-Ormskirk-Preston -
» Manchester (Victoria)-Rochdale/Oldham -
» Manchester (Victoria)-Rochdale-Todmorden –
» Preston (Todd Lane Jct-Lostock Hall Jct) 5/72

» Rochdale-Bury-Bolton-Wigan (Wallgate), *R (Castleton North Jct)-Bolton (East Jct)* 10/70
» St Luke's Jct-Loco Jct-Barrow Shipyard; Salthouse Jct-Loco Jct (workmen's) 7/67
» Warrington (Padgate JCT-Sankey Jct) 7/67

North East

» Bishop Auckland-Durham-Sunderland, 5/64
» Blyth-Newsham, 11/64
» Bradford Exchange-Batley-Wakefield, 9/64
» Bradford Exchange-Pudsey-Leeds Central, 6/64
» Church Fenton-Wetherby-*Harrogate*, 1/64
» Crook-Bishop Auckland-Darlington, *C-Etherley* 3/65
» Darlington-Northallerton-Harrogate-Leeds, *N-H* 3/67
» Darlington-Barnard Castle-Middleton-in-Teesdale, 11/64
» Darlington-Richmond, 3/69
» Driffield-Selby, 6/65
» Goole-Selby, 6/64
» Goole-Wakefield -
» Guisborough-Middlesbrough, *G-Nunthorpe* 3/64
» Harrogate-Wetherby-Leeds City, *W-Cross Gates* 1/64
» Harrogate-York -
» Hornsea Town-Hull, 10/64
» Huddersfield-Clayton West-Penistone, *CW-Shepley* 1/83
» Hull-Withernsea, 10/64
» Hull-York, *Beverley-Y* 11/65
» Knottingley-Leeds City, *Castleford Cutsyke J-Methley North J* 10/68
» Leeds Central-Castleford Central-Pontefract, *see above, P (Baghill)-P (Monkhill)* 11/64
» Leeds City and Bradford Forster Square-Ilkley-Skipton, *I-S* 3/65, also *Arthington-Burley-in-Wharfedale* 3/65
» Malton-Whitby, *M (Rillington)-Grosmont* 3/65
» Middlesbrough-Whitby-Scarborough, 3/65
» Monkseaton-Blyth-Newbiggin, 11/64
» Newbiggin-Newcastle-on-Tyne, *Newbiggin-Backworth, Hartley-Monkseaton* 11/64

» Newcastle-on-Tyne-Washington, *Pelaw-Durham* 5/64
» South Shields (Tyne Dock)-Sunderland, 6/65

SERVICES WITH INTERMEDIATE
STATIONS WITHDRAWN

» Bradford Exchange-Halifax-Huddersfield (local)
» Bradford Exchange-Mirfield-Huddersfield (local)
» Bradford Forster Square-Shipley-Leeds City (local)
» Doncaster-Leeds Central (local)
» Haltwhistle-Newcastle-on-Tyne (local)
» Hexham-Newcastle-on-Tyne (local)
» Leeds City and Bradford Forster Square-Keighley-Skipton (local)
» Leeds City-Cross Gates-Micklefield (local)
» Leeds City-Cudworth-Sheffield Midland (local)
» Newcastle-on-Tyne-Riverside-Tynemouth (local)
» Sunderland-West Hartlepool (local)

SERVICES EARMARKED FOR CLOSURE
BEFORE BEECHING REPORT

» Alston-Haltwhistle, 5/76
» Cheadle (Staffs)-Cresswell (Staffs), 6/63
» Crewe-Wellington (Salop), *Wellington-Nantwich* 9/63
» *Ellesmere-Wrexham Central, 9/62

ADDITIONAL SERVICES LISTED FOR CLOSURE
AFTER BEECHING REPORT UP TO 1968

» Bridlington-Scarborough -
» Barnsley (Quarry Jct)-Mexborough (No 2 Box) 1/70
» Penistone (Barnsley Jct)-Barnsley (Exchange) 1/70, reopened 5/83
» Methley North Jct- Castleford (Cutsyke Jct) (Goole trains to run
via Castleford Central) 10/68
» Mickle Trafford CLC Jct-Chester Northgate i.e. diversion of
trains to Chester General, via Mickle Trafford LNW Jct 10/69

Scotland
» Aberdeen-Ballater, 2/66

» Aberdeen-Fraserburgh, *Dyce Jct-F* 10/65
» Aberdeen-Inverurie -
» Aberfeldy-Ballinluig, 5/65
» Ardrossan-Kilmarnock, *Irvine-Crosshouse* 4/64
» Arrochar-Craigendoran *(locals)* 7/64
» Aviemore-Craigellachie-Elgin, *Boat of Garten-C* 10/65, *E-C-Keith JUN* 5/68
» Ayr-Dalmellington, 4/64
» Ayr-Kilmarnock, *A-Troon (Barassie)* 1/67, *Barassie-K* 3/69
» Ayr-Stranraer -
» Ballachulish-Connel Ferry-Oban, *B-CF* 3/66
» Banff-Tillynaught, 7/64
» Barrhead-Glasgow St Enoch -
» Carlisle-Hawick-Edinburgh Waverley, 1/69
» Carlisle-Riddings Junction-Langholm, *RJ-L* 6/64
» Coatbridge-Dumbarton, *Carmyle-D* 10/64, *Coatbridge-Rutherglen* 11/66, *Glasgow-Carmyle-Whifflet reopened* 10/93
» Comrie-Crieff-Gleneagles, 7/64
» Darvel-Kilmarnock, 4/64
» Dumfries-Castle Douglas-Kirkcudbright, *CD-K* 5/65, *Dunragit-Dumfries* 6/65
» Dumfries-Stranraer, *see above*
» Dunbar-Edinburgh Waverley *(local)*
» Dundee-Crail-Thornton, *Leuchars-St Andrews* 1/69, *St A-Leven* 9/65, *Leven-*
» *Thornton J* 10/69
» East Kilbride-Glasgow St Enoch -
» Edinburgh Princes Street-Carstairs-Lanark *(locals)*
» Edinburgh Princes Street-Glasgow Central (via Shotts and Holytown) -
» Edinburgh Princes Street-Kingsknowe, *Kinsknowe* 7/64-reopened 2/71
» Edinburgh Waverley-Musselburgh, *Joppa-M* 9/64, *Abbeyhill Jct-Piershill JUN* 9/64
» Elgin-Lossiemouth, 4/64
» Fraserburgh-St Combs, 5/65
» Georgemas Junction-Thurso -

- » Glasgow Buchanan Street-Stirling-Oban, *Crianlarich-Dunblane* 9/65
- » Glasgow Queen Street-Kirkintilloch, *Lenzie-K* 9/64
- » Glasgow St Enoch-Dalry-Kilmarnock (Lochwinnoch loop), *D-Elderslie* 6/66
- » Glasgow St Enoch-Kilmacolm, *Paisley-K* 1/83
- » Glasgow St Enoch-Paisley West, *Paisley West* 2/66
- » Hamilton-Strathaven/Coalburn, 10/65
- » Inverness-Kyle of Lochalsh -
- » Inverness-Wick -
- » Killin-Killin Junction, 9/65
- » Kinross-Alloa-Stirling, *K-A and locals* 6/64
- » Lanark-Muirkirk, 10/64
- » Maud-Peterhead, 5/65
- » Perth-Blair Atholl-Struan - *Locals* 5/65

SERVICES WITH INTERMEDIATE STATIONS WITHDRAWN

- » Aberdeen-Keith-Elgin (local)
- » Aviemore-Inverness-Elgin (local)
- » Berwick-upon-Tweed-Edinburgh Waverley (local)
- » Carlisle-Dumfries-Glasgow St Enoch (local)
- » Carlisle-Glasgow Central (local)
- » Fort William-Mallaig (local)
- » Glasgow Buchanan Street-Stirling-Perth (local)
- » Glasgow St Enoch-Lugton-Kilmarnock (local)

SERVICES EARMARKED FOR CLOSURE BEFORE BEECHING REPORT

- » *Beith Town-Lugton, 11/62
- » Berwick-upon-Tweed-St Boswells, *Tweedmouth-StB* 6/64
- » *Edinburgh Waverley-Duddingston-Morningside Road-Edinburgh Waverley, *EW-D-Portobello* 9/62
- » *Glasgow Buchanan Street-Coatbridge Central- Holytown-Motherwell-Hamilton Central, *(local)* 11/62

ADDITIONAL SERVICES LISTED FOR CLOSURE
AFTER BEECHING REPORT UP TO 1968

» Alloa (West Jct)–Larbert (Alloa Jct) 1/68
» Corstorphine–Haymarket West Jct 1/68
» Dunfermline (Touch South Jct)/Townhill Jct–Touch North
  Jct–Stirling (Alloa Jct), *DTNJ-TJ* 5/68, *DTSJ-SAJ* 10/68
» Grangemouth Branch Jct–Grangemouth 1/68
» Leuchars Jct–St Andrews 1/69

---

* Withdrawal already implemented

MAIN LINE STATIONS AXED TOO

The Beeching report proposed the closure of 2363 stations and halts, of which 235 had already been closed when it was published. Indeed, in the decade following the report, around 3000 stations and halts closed, around 50% of the network total.

The closures were not always on loss-making branch lines but on retained main lines too. Poorly patronised stations serving smaller communities were closed to passengers at first and shortly afterwards to goods, in order to eliminate the need for stopping trains and to speed up services in line for streamlining towards an inter-city network.

For example, on the West of England main line between Bristol Temple Meads and Exeter St David's, the route of Isambard Kingdom Brunel's Bristol & Exeter Railway, there are 22 disused railway stations, most of them closed in the 1960s. There are another 11 disused stations between Exeter St David's and Plymouth Millbay on Brunel's South Devon Railway route.

Indeed, Ernest Marples reported that regarding Flax Bourton station on the outskirts of Bristol, he received not a single objection to the notice of closure. Its derelict shell still stands alongside the main line today.

While for the affected communities, losing their main line station was as bad as having a branch line axed, if it meant having to drive 10 miles or more to the nearest station, shorter times for main line services made them more attractive to the public.

At Hele & Bradninch station between Exeter and Cullompton, passenger services were withdrawn on October 5, 1964 but public freight facilities remained until May 17, 1965, while a siding to the Hele Paper factory was used into the 1980s.

Despite the lack of trains, much of the derelict station survives today, the empty signalbox still standing at the north end of the southbound platform, the small stone booking office still on the platform next to the level crossing, and the goods shed opposite used by a garage firm.

The first stop to the south of Exeter was Exminster. It was closed to passenger traffic on March 30, 1964 and to goods on December 4, 1967, although only coal traffic had been handled for the previous 27 months. The loop sidings saw occasional use until 1985 and the signalbox was

closed on November 14, 1986. The signalbox has been moved for preservation at the Gloucestershire Warwickshire Railway, but the station
building very much survives in private hands as an architectural salvage
depot, fenced off from the main line.

It is easy to look at the map and wonder why the station is not
reopened to provide the now-sizeable community of Exminster with
the ability to commute by train into Exeter, but like so many stations
built by the Victorian pioneers, it stands a fair walk outside the village
down a narrow country lane, and it is debatable whether residents would
drive there just to ride three miles by train, or instead make the whole
journey by car. Indeed, this scenario highlighted one of the dilemmas
facing both Beeching and his successors.

CHAPTER SIX

The rationale and the results

T HE BEECHING report highlighted the former Caledonian Railway cross-country route between Gleneagles, Crieff and Comrie as a prime example of why lines should be closed, despite claims that loss-making branches nonetheless contributed revenue to the main lines they joined.

The rural route had 10 trains a day in each direction with an element of summer holiday traffic. Services were operated by diesel railbuses on weekdays only over a distance of 15 miles, with connections made at Gleneagles with main line trains to and from Glasgow and Edinburgh.

The stations on the route were Gleneagles, Tullibardine, Muthill, Strageath Halt, Highlandman, Pittenzie Halt, Crieff and Comrie. The report proposed that all stations except Gleneagles would be closed to passengers, in other words, the branch would be axed.

Explaining the rationale, the report said that around 340,000 passenger miles accrued to this service which accounted for 65,000 train miles a year. On average, this meant that there were only five passengers on board a train at any one time.

Earnings from the service were £1900 — just over a quarter of the train movement expenses of £7500. Station terminal expenses brought the total of direct expenses to nearly £11,000, less than a fifth of which was covered by the earnings of the service. "When track and signalling expenses are added — £8200 — the total expenses are 10 times as great as the earnings of the service," the report said.

Beeching acknowledged that passengers using the branch service in combination with other services, such as the main line trains, contributed more than £12,000 to their earnings.

One of the biggest criticisms made about Beeching closures is that he failed to take into account such contributions, and that many branches should therefore remain open as "loss leaders". While it was hoped that passengers inconvenienced by the loss of branch lines would merely drive to the nearest main line station to catch the train, history was to show that instead they decided to drive all the way to their destination, and as customers were lost to the rail network altogether.

In the case of Gleneagles-Comrie, it was estimated that withdrawal of the service would result in the loss of £9000 of contributory revenue from the branch.

However, the overall net financial improvement expected from withdrawal of branch line services was said to be nearly £8400, or more than two-fifths of the existing level of total direct expenses attributable to the services, the report said. The line was closed on July 6, 1964.

Another cross-country route listed in detail for the chop was the 23-mile former Great Eastern Railway line from Thetford to Swaffham, where again, the earnings from the service between the two towns covered only a tenth of the total direct expenses.

While the gross revenue accruing to other services contributed by passengers using the Thetford-Swaffham service as part of their rail journey totalled around £16,000, the estimated net financial improvement in revenue which would result from the withdrawal of the branch service amounted to about £29,000, more than four-fifths of the total direct expenses. So Swaffham, the junction for lines to King's Lynn, Dereham and Thetford via Roudham Junction, closed in 1968.

A third case study explained in detail was the North Eastern Railway's route from Hull to York via Beverley, a stopping service over a distance of 42 miles, serving a rural area between the cities of Hull and York, with some commuter traffic at each end. The stations served were Hull,

Cottingham, Beverley, Kipling Cotes, Market Weighton, Londesborough, Pocklington, Stamford Bridge, Earswick and York.

It was proposed to close all intermediate stations except Cottingham and Beverley. Nine trains ran in each direction on weekdays and mostly comprised diesel multiple units. On average, there were 57 passengers on each train.

The earnings of the service were £90,400, covering the movement expenses of £84,400. However, terminal expenses brought the total of movement plus terminal expenses to £107,500, so that earnings showed a shortfall of £17,100. It was estimated that withdrawal of the service would reduce track and signalling expenses by £43,300.

Overall, the earnings showed a shortfall of £60,400, equivalent to two-fifths of the total direct expenses of £150,800. However, because alternative services would be available after withdrawal of the service, £25,600 of the earnings would be retained.

It was estimated that passengers using the service as part of their rail journey contributed £37,700 to the revenue of other services. Because of the existence of services between Hull and York via other routes, only £4900 of this amount was expected to be lost. The total loss in gross revenue resulting from withdrawal of the service was estimated at £69,700, but the overall net financial improvement was expected to be £81,000, equivalent to more than half of the total direct expenses.

So the writing was on the wall for the route. While trains still serve Beverley and Cottingham as part of the Yorkshire Coast Line to Scarborough via Bridlington and Filey, the Beverley to York section fell victim to the Beeching Axe on November 29, 1965.

MINIMALIST OPERATIONS WERE NOT ENOUGH

It is often said that many Beeching closures could have been prevented if branch lines had been pared down to the bare minimum in terms of staffing levels, and operated by diesel railbuses. Indeed, looking at the number of people employed at even little-used stations back in the Fifties, from the stationmaster, signalmen, booking clerks down to porters, it comes as little surprise that many rural lines did not pay.

In the late Fifties, British Railways began to experiment with railbuses produced by a number of different manufacturers, such as Waggon und

Maschinenbau, Park Royal and Wickham, years before Beeching arrived. On February 2, 1959, a pair of AC Cars railbuses were introduced on the two branches that joined the Swindon-Gloucester main line at Kemble, the 4½-mile line to Cirencester Town and the 11-mile line to Tetbury.

Until then, patronage on both had been in decline. Passenger services on the Tetbury branch ran on weekdays only and consisted of six pull-push workings in each direction using auto trains. Two trains in each direction were mixed and these catered for most of the main freight traffic of coal and farm foodstuffs, as the afternoon freight train on Mondays to Fridays only ran if required. By 1958 the services had been reduced by one train and the pull-and-push sets had disappeared, while the freight levels had fallen so that only one of the two mixed trains ran as such. On the busier Cirencester branch there were nine up and 10 down trains, with two extra on Saturdays. Two of the trains each day were mixed.

With the introduction of the railbuses, services on the Cirencester branch were increased to 14 trains in each direction on Mondays to Fridays, with an extra two on Saturdays, while Sunday services remained unchanged at four in each direction. On the Tetbury branch, trains were increased from five to eight on Mondays to Fridays, with an extra working on Saturdays, but the branch remained without a Sunday service.

At the same time a new halt was opened at Chesterton Lane, near Cirencester, and on the Tetbury branch halts were provided at Church's Hill and Trouble House, a pub of the same name in the middle of nowhere. Culkerton was reopened as an unstaffed halt, using the existing platform, but the others had ground-level platforms 25ft long and 8ft 6in wide, built of old sleepers. An additional halt at Park Leaze, between Chesterton Lane and Kemble, was opened on January 4, 1960, when running schedules were slightly amended and an extra afternoon train provided.

The four-wheeled railbuses seated 46 passengers and were fitted with automatic doors and retractable steps for use at the halts. Cheap-day facilities were available from all stations and halts, and guards were supplied with Setright ticket machines similar to those used by many bus companies. They also carried mail and parcels. The experimental railbus services were successful and on the Cirencester branch more than

2500 passengers a week were carried in the first year. While the Tetbury branch carried only a tenth of this, the figure of 12,800 represented two-and-a-half times the annual number of passengers carried on the steam-hauled services.

Indeed, the Cirencester railbuses were often overcrowded with passengers on Saturdays. However, despite the early positive indications, sadly the receipts from both services did not justify their retention in the eyes of British Railways. Local pro-rail campaigners questioned the validity of British Railways' figures, in particular those for the Cirencester branch, but despite local protests, passenger services were withdrawn from both branches from April 6, 1964. When the Tetbury services ended on Saturday, April 4, the last down train was hampered by bales of blazing straw which had been laid across the rails.

There was also trouble at Trouble House Halt, both when steam on the Tetbury branch ended, and when the line closed altogether. When the last steam services had run on January 31, 1959, the demand for seats on the train known as the 'Tetbury Donkey' was so great that a brake van had to be added behind the 58XX 0-4-2T and its coaches.

As the train neared Trouble House Halt on the return trip, someone pulled the communication cord and the passengers alighted and went to the nearby Trouble House inn for half an hour until summoned back by the engine's whistle. Back at Tetbury, the passengers formed a procession headed by top-hatted mourners and marched through the town.

In 1964, a coffin covered with inscriptions, filled with empty whisky bottles and addressed to Beeching, was loaded by mourners in bowler hats at Trouble House Halt on the last advertised train to Kemble. There, it was transferred to the London train for delivery to the doctor. Incidentally, the name of the pub which stands alongside the A433 does not derive from drunken disorder or the like, but from a nearby patch of waterlogged, difficult-to-farm ground known as the Troubles.

On the following day a special steam pull-and-push train, worked by Collett 14XX 0-4-2T No. 1472, ran over both branches, and on the last down train on the Cirencester branch passengers were treated to free rolls and beer. An attempt was made to burn a 6ft effigy of the minister of transport, but the railway police intervened and so the demonstrators set it alight on the pavement outside the terminus.

The Tetbury branch was closed completely but freight lingered on the Cirencester branch until October 4, 1965.

The use of railbuses on the Dunmere Junction to Bodmin North branch in 1964 following the withdrawal of steam passenger services between Bodmin North and Wadebridge similarly proved insufficient to save the line.

Nevertheless, the railbuses had proved that rural lines could be made more attractive to the public, even if losses were not eradicated. So why did Beeching not prune more branch lines to basic one-engine-in-steam routes with unmanned stations and halts and operated by the bare minimum staff to keep them open?

The British Railways of 1961 when he took over was markedly different to the one he transformed over the following four years. Opposition to mass redundancies would have automatically come from trade unions single-mindedly protecting the rights of a multitude of very poorly paid workers, and moves towards wholesale rationalisation would have been quickly deflected as an unacceptable culture shock. By 1965, however, Beeching had reshaped that culture, and such economies might well have been possible on lines where the losses might have been reduced to acceptable levels. However, even he could not place the cart before the horse, and in any case, he had pointed out that reducing the cost of running trains by use of railbuses was not enough; the cost of providing the route itself was the key factor.

THE FIRST OF THE MANY

Ironically, among the first lines endorsed by Beeching for full closure was the Helston branch where, as we saw in Chapter 1, the Great Western Railway had pioneered the use of buses.

Local people saw closures elsewhere in the late Fifties and felt that the writing was on the wall for the line.

When the end for passenger services came on November 3, 1962, it was one of the first acts carried out by the new British Railways chairman, and pre-dated his 1963 report. However, the work involved in the compilation of the report would have included the Helston branch, which even dieselisation could not save from becoming the first of the Cornish branch lines to close.

In scenes that would in the next few years be repeated all over the country, local residents did everything they could in a desperate bid to try to save the branch, but many of them were already using cars as the main or only form of transport. A promise to improve the road between Helston and Redruth made at the time of closure was never carried out.

The first of the 1963 report closures involved the cessation of passenger services on September 9 that year between Newcastle Central, Usworth and Washington on the Leamside line, which itself was not closed as that stage. Indeed, out of 300 service withdrawal proposals contained in the Beeching report, this was one of only two, along with Stalybridge-Biggle which did not prompt objections.

The October 1963 edition of the industry newspaper Railnews reported the Newcastle-Washington closure as a peaceful affair, with the headline "So Quiet, The First Beeching Closure."

It would not remain so for long.

Seaside lines were particularly badly hit by Beeching. Because most people who rode on them were visitors and were neither regular passengers nor even resident in the area, there were few users on hand to campaign against their closure, or even to write a brief letter of objection to the Transport Users Consultative Committee.

So those branches to coastal resorts had the least chance of any effective voice being raised in their support. Occasionally, hoteliers, bed-and-breakfast establishment owners and traders protested that closures would ruin their livelihood, but their calls were dismissed as insignificant, especially as soaring car ownership would ensure that the same number of visitors came. However, in the case of many of Britain's traditional resorts, history records that it never did.

The background assumption in the corridors of power that rail passengers were by now a car-less minority whose numbers would diminish, whether or not Beeching's cuts went ahead, proved too strong for such fragmented and localised protests.

THE WAITING VULTURES POUNCE

A marked feature of the Beeching era closures was the haste in which closed railways were ripped up by demolition contractors so as to realise the scrap value as quickly as possible.

Sceptics, however, had a different view; they said it was evidence of a hidden agenda to get rid of railways so that they could never be reopened again in private hands, and compete with road transport.

Railway historian TWE Roche campaigned to save the GWR South Brent to Kingsbridge branch which closed on September 14, 1963. As a result of a letter printed in *The Railway Magazine* around that time, he received a large number of letters from as far afield as Ireland, Wales and Sussex expressing interest, pledging voluntary labour and some even giving money.

He wrote to British Railways and three local councils in the hope of forming a Primrose Railway Preservation Society, with the local authorities helping to operate it as a private venture.

On October 11 that year, he wrote to the divisional manager of the Western Region at Plymouth, asking what figure the British Railways Board wanted for the branch. The divisional manager acknowledged the letter on October 17, stating he would write again when in a position to do so.

On November 4, Roche was warned by a private contact that the track was about to be lifted.

Exhaustive inquiries led to confirmation on November 8, that the Civil Engineer's Department at Paddington was about to sign contracts for lifting that same day.

Roche protested, but he managed to obtain only a week's stay of execution.

He wrote: "I had arranged to meet the Joint Railways Committee of the three local councils in Kingsbridge on November 25, and duly did so, an officer of the Devon County Council being present. After a very long and considerate discussion they decided they could not proceed with the scheme in view of the uncertainty about the lifting tenders and the future of Brent, although it was quite evident that, had they been assured on these matters and had they had time to give the full financial facts adequate thought, the councils would have seriously considered taking over the line.

"It was fortunate they did not do so, for that very afternoon I encountered the first three of the contractors' men beginning to dismantle track in Kingsbridge station yard. Their contract, they told me, was to lift all tracks, signals, signalling equipment and steel bridges, but not granite bridges, station buildings or platforms or signalboxes. In the words of their foreman, very soon there would be nothing left at all.

"I feel that the extreme haste with which the lifting of the Kingsbridge line has been undertaken has robbed the South Hams area of the chance to retain a rail service which would have been of real social value to the local inhabitants as distinct from a purely tourist attraction."

Such scenes were repeated all over the UK. Barely had protesters time to gather their thoughts after a last train before their local railway was no more and there was nothing left to save apart from an empty trackbed. It seemed to all as if British Railways was hell bent on making sure that there was no going back.

Scrap sales in 1963 realised at least £20 million and included 4000 passenger coaches, 500 locomotives, 130,000 freight wagons, four ships and 250,000 tons of rails. In 1964, up to 100 steam locomotives were disappearing each week. Rail closures were, of course, by no means unique to Britain, Marples and Beeching. The ascendancy of motor transport was a global phenomenon which led at one stage or another to severe pruning of many countries' rail networks.

However, compare and contrast the situation in Britain with that of France, which also had an extensive rural network. Whereas it seemed that British Railways panicked to rip up tracks almost as soon as the last passenger left the station, across the Channel many closed rural lines were left in place for a decade or more before being ripped up.

Such a move was an insurance policy in the event that road transport might just yet not turn out as all that it was meant to be.

For me, the lifting of track from axed routes and in subsequent decades, the sale of strategic closed trackbeds for building development comprised the two greatest follies of the rail closures of the 1960s, whether Beeching's name was on them or not.

ERADICATION OF THREE TRUNK ROUTES

So far we have looked at the fate that befell branch lines. However, trunk routes would also be hit hard and fast and the biggest single Beeching closure was that of the Great Central's London Extension from Nottingham to Marylebone.

The rot of the Great Central set in during the late 1950s when vital freight traffic began to decline, and the route was neglected in favour of rival routes, such as the Midland Main Line which it largely duplicated.

In 1958, the route was transferred from the Eastern Region to the London Midland Region, where both management and staff still had loyalties to the old London Midland & Scottish Railway empire, and not a line which was long seen as a London & North Eastern Railway competitor.

Express passenger services from London to Sheffield and Manchester were discontinued in January 1960. That left just three daily 'semi-fast' London-Nottingham trains on the route.

In March 1963, just before the report was published, local trains on many sections of the route were cancelled and many of its local stations were closed. Yet there were those who still hoped that the route could be retained and improved for parcels and goods traffic.

Beeching had other thoughts, and decided that the Great Central traffic could easily be served by other routes linking London to the north.

This decision sparked widespread controversy, especially as in February 1964, as we saw earlier, Britain signed an agreement with France for the building of a Channel Tunnel. Back in 1899, the Great Central's extension to the capital had been built to the large Berne loading gauge in the hope that it would form a link to a Channel Tunnel, and it was ready and waiting for such use.

The 9th Earl of Lanesborough, Denis Anthony Brian Butler, had a letter expanding on this single point published in the Daily Telegraph on September 28, 1965. It read: "...surely the prize for idiotic policy must go to the destruction of the until recently most profitable railway per ton of freight and per passenger carried in the whole British Railways system, as shown by their own operating statistics.

"These figures were presented to monthly management meetings until the 1950s, when they were suppressed as 'unnecessary', but one suspects really 'inconvenient' for those proposing Beeching-type policies of unnecessarily severe contraction of services...

"This railway is of course the Great Central, forming a direct continental loading gauge route from Sheffield and the North to the Thames valley and London for Dover and France."

The sections between Rugby and Aylesbury and between Nottingham and Sheffield were closed in 1966 and the track lifted, leaving the section between Rugby and Nottingham over which diesel multiple units operated a skeleton shuttle service.

Nottingham Victoria station was closed in 1967, British Rail selling the lucrative city centre site for shopping redevelopment. As a result, trains from Rugby terminated instead at Arkwright Street station, which, ironically, had been closed in 1963. One platform was reopened to serve the six daily trains that remained.

The last train departed from Arkwright Street on Saturday, May 3, 1969. The station and viaducts carrying the railway were demolished around 1975 and the site is now occupied by houses.

Calls to save the Somerset & Dorset Joint Railway system also fell on deaf ears.

While its Bath to Bournemouth West main line was famous as the route of the 'Pines Express' from Manchester, its stopping trains were slow. In 1938, they were recorded as taking four hours to travel from Bath to Bournemouth. Meanwhile, the S&D's original main line from Evercreech to Burnham-on-Sea, relegated to branch status when the main line to Bath opened, took 70 minutes to cover just 24 miles.

The S&D main line crossed the Southern Railway's Waterloo-Salisbury-Exeter line at Templecombe, but connections between the two were poor, and if you lived along the S&D, it was far from an ideal way by which to travel onwards to London.

Like many rural routes listed for closure by Beeching, summer Saturdays saw a huge upsurge in traffic, with 13 long-distance trains using the line, 12 to Bournemouth and the other to Exmouth and Sidmouth, via Templecombe. Running non-stop over the Mendips, they took two-and-a-half hours to run from Bath to Bournemouth.

The rundown of the S&D system began in 1951 with the withdrawal of passenger services over the short length between Highbridge and Burnham-on-Sea and the closure of the branch from Glastonbury to Wells. In December 1952, passenger services were withdrawn between Edington Junction and Bridgwater, the branch closing altogether on October 1, 1954. Four of the smaller stations in Dorset were axed as an economy measure in 1956.

The watershed came when the line north of Templecombe was transferred from the Southern Region to the Western Region in 1958. Over the next five years, through trains from the north and the Midlands including the 'Pines Express' were diverted to other routes.

A champion of the railways prepared to take on Beeching was future poet laureate John Betjeman, famous for his writing about Metroland. Betjeman had been a leading figure in the battle to save the aforementioned Doric Arch at Euston, but is credited with helping to save the façade of St Pancras station, where a statue of him now stands at the new international terminus.

In summer 1962, Betjeman made Branch Line Railway, a BBC TV documentary on the S&D, riding on the branch from Evercreech Junction to Highbridge, asking, in vain as it turned out, Beeching to spare it from the axe.

When Labour came to power in 1964, winning two general elections, the new government promised to end railway closures. Nonetheless, Bournemouth West was closed in 1965, S&D trains being diverted into Bournemouth Central, and the vociferous campaign to save the line was lost in 1965 when Transport Secretary Barbara Castle confirmed the closure as outlined in the Beeching report.

The closure was set for January 3, 1966, but had to be postponed when one of the road operators withdrew his application for a licence to provide alternative road services.

An emergency four-trains-a-day service was introduced between Bath and Bournemouth, which lasted until the axe finally fell on both the main line and branch line, apart from three small isolated sections kept open for freight for a few more years.

Finally, Beeching described the Waverley Route between Carlisle and Edinburgh as "the biggest money loser in the British railway system". Already, both passenger and goods traffic was being lost to road, with passenger services on its branches being progressively withdrawn. The demise had its roots in the 1930s, during the Depression which hit freight loadings from Hawick and Galashiels.

By 1954, 80% of livestock from farms, traditionally carried by rail to market, had been switched to road, and by 1963, this traffic had vanished from the route. Road transport also took over the local woollen and tweed business. In the Sixties, the line had become more of a route for express rather than local freight.

Passenger services from Galashiels to Selkirk had been withdrawn on September 8, 1951, followed by Riccarton to Hexham on October 15, 1956 and the Kelso and Tweedmouth service on June 13, 1964. After the Kelso line closed to passengers, only the Carlisle to Edinburgh service remained.

Under Beeching's calculations, once the remaining freight trains and the two remaining St Pancras to Edinburgh services were rerouted on to alternative routes, only local passenger trains would be left, and along a route, the southern half of which was extremely sparsely populated, the economics of the route would never stack up.

In October 1966, British Railways posted closure notices at all stations on the line with the intention of withdrawing services from January 2, 1967.

Following early protests, a brief reprieve was given when the closure was postponed pending review. Nonetheless, on July 15, 1968, the Labour Minister for Transport Richard Marsh announced that the line would close on January 6, 1969.

The secretary of State for Scotland was among those who protested, including local MP David Steel, the future Liberal Democrat leader. Local people collected a petition and a delegation went to London in December 1968. However, as happened so often with Beeching closures, the views of local people were ignored. Marsh was persuaded by British Railways that the losses were too great.

The closure weekend provoked some of the most vociferous of all anti-Beeching protests, with banner-waving demonstrators at most stations. On January 4, British Rail ran a 'Farewell to the Waverley Route' special, while another was charted by the Border Union Railway Society. The society special, hauled by the now-preserved Deltic diesel D9002 *The King's Own Yorkshire Light Infantry*, carried a coffin bearing the inscription 'Waverley Line — born 1849, killed 1969 aged 120 years' and was addressed to the then Minister of Transport, Richard Marsh. The last passenger service on the line, which was also the final train to run over the entire route, was the 9.56pm Edinburgh to St Pancras sleeper on Sunday, January 5, 1969, hauled by Class 45 diesel D60 *Lytham St*

Annes. At Hawick, someone tampered with a set of points to delay the already-late train and a Clayton diesel, D8506, was sent in front of the express to 'prove' the route southwards.

At Newcastleton, the train was delayed again because the level crossing gates had been padlocked with more than 200 protesters led by local vicar the Reverend Brydon Mabon standing on the line holding placards with slogans like 'Stop the Great Train Robbery', 'No Trains No Jobs' and 'Don't Cut Our Lifeline'. The minister was among several arrests made — he was released only after the intervention of train passenger David Steel — and by the time the express reached Carlisle, it was two hours late.

The section from Newtongrange remained open for goods traffic as far as Hawick until April 28, 1969, the stretch from Lady Victoria colliery to Newtongrange lasting until December 20, 1971, the last traffic having been switched to road. The final section, Newtongrange to Millerhill, closed on June 28, 1972.

In 1969, a consortium calling itself the Border Union Railway Company was formed under the guidance of the late TV presenter Bob Symes (whose full name was Robert Alexander Baron Schutzmann von Schutzmansdorff) with the aim of buying the entire route and running trains using imported German Pacific steam locomotives.

That November, British Rail demanded a deposit of £250,000, and when the company asked for extra time, the reply was that four months would be given, but interest of £8000 a month would have to be paid.

Negotiations ended two days before Christmas. It seemed that British Rail had been placing every possible obstacle in the way of the revivalists, and many thought that the powers that were simply did not want a private operator running a main line. Most of the track was lifted by early 1972.

Bizarrely, after the track had been torn up, the parcels office at Hawick stayed open so that British Rail vans continued to carry parcels traffic by road.

CHAPTER SEVEN

The backlash and the back-pedalling

BACK IN 1935, when a protest meeting was held in a bid to stop the Southern Railway from closing the Lynton & Barnstaple Railway, a telling question killed the debate, like a pin bursting a balloon. The packed room was asked how many attendees had travelled by the railway that day. The lack of raised hands spoke volumes.

Many railway lines that closed in the Fifties died their deaths with barely a murmur. Others were marked by special enthusiasts' trains to mark the last day. When there were local opposition groups, it was too often a case of people who might have used the railway protesting too much about the fact it would soon no longer be an option. Joni Mitchell sang: "You don't know what you've got till it's gone" and in so many cases that principle applied to our branch lines. In many cases, people saw the closure notices as foregone conclusions.

However, the sheer scale of the Beeching cuts, coming directly in the wake of 780 miles closed in 1962 and another 324 in 1964, led to nationwide rather than localised anger, from rail users, local residents, civic representatives and the unions.

Protest marches were held, councils voted against closure, MPs were lobbied, accounts were disseminated to provide fresh arguments that certain lines could be made viable, but in most cases to no avail. In fairness, not every proposed closure or withdrawal of service listed in Beeching's 1963 report was carried through, but there were many other cases where local people felt that they had done enough in presenting counterarguments, only to be left with the feeling that they had fallen on deaf ears. Lord Stonham, the Labour peer who had been the only member of the party ever to be elected MP for Taunton, and later won the inner London seat of Shoreditch and Finsbury, launched a broadside against the Beeching report and its backers in a speech to the House of Lords on May 2, 1963.

Beginning by mentioning the minister of transport's statement that 25,726 jobs would disappear, he said: "…the whole difficulty, the whole acute public anxiety which undoubtedly exists throughout the country about the Beeching Plan is, in my view, attributable to what the noble Viscount (Lord Hailsham) called Mr Marples' flair for publicity: the terrific public relations job which has been done on the presentation of this Plan, and its blowing up out of all reasonable sense of proportion."

Commenting on Marples' statement to the Commons that the period ending in September 1964 "… will see the most intensive implementation of the plan on the assumption that closures will go as fast as anyone could reasonably expect," Lord Stonham said: "The precise mention of the number of jobs which are going to be lost indicates that the decision, insofar as it can be made, has already been made; and almost every word that the minister of transport says on this subject is proof positive that the minds of the government have been made up."

He raised the issue of the planned closure of rail connections to Stranraer, the ferry port for Northern Ireland, asking Lord Hailsham if he was "aware that 40% of the people who go on the boat to Larne in Northern Ireland go by rail to Stranraer; that the steamer's income increased to £286,000 this year from £200,000 the year before, and that Ayrshire County Council are afraid that if the rail link is broken they will eventually lose the steamer and the short sea route to Ireland altogether?"

He described Marples' promised consultation on the Stranraer line as "the kind of consultation that a condemned man gets when they ask him what he wants for breakfast before they hang him". Lord Stonham said: "Many of the figures in the Beeching Report are known to be wrong, although unfortunately none of them can be really checked."

He said that many of its provisions — the reduction in stopping and branch line services; closure of little-used wayside stations or their conversion to halts; reductions in passenger stock and wagons; great reduction in the number of marshalling yards, plus resiting and modernising; larger wagons, particularly for mineral traffic; complete reorientation of freight services to speed movement and reduce costs and provide direct transits for main streams of traffic and attract to the railway a due proportion of the full load merchandise traffic which would otherwise pass by road — had been spelled out in the British Railways 1955 Modernisation Plan. This was "faithfully copied" into the Beeching report — despite Marples' statement that there has been nothing like it before in the history of British Railways.

Lord Stonham said that unlike the Modernisation Plan eight years earlier, the report had "occasioned anger — anger cutting across party barriers; anger deeper and more widespread, in my opinion, throughout the country than almost any domestic issue during the last 20 years".

He asked why the only pleasant comment he had heard on the plan "is the advice to use Dr Beeching's face cream because it removes all lines."

He suggested that while the 1955 plan had been announced as being "not designed merely to make our railway system self-supporting: it aims at producing far-reaching benefits for the economy of the country as a whole and for the better ordering of its transport arrangements,"

Beeching was not allowed to spare a thought for the economy of the country as a whole.

Also, whereas the Modernisation Plan aimed to benefit the whole country, including the parts furthest away from the main industrial centres — like Scotland, Wales and the west of England — all of those areas would "have virtually ceased to exist" under the Beeching proposals.

Lord Stonham added: "In 1955 the same ideas were presented with wisdom as a means of rehabilitation, re-equipment and, in some cases, expansion. In 1963 it has been brutal surgery allied to mishandling so foolish as to appear deliberate." Crucially, he shifted the blame from the man whose name appeared on the report, and which has become synonymous with rail closures. He continued: "For this I blame the Government; certainly not Dr Beeching. Indeed, one can only blame such an outstanding technologist for having accepted his task with such limited terms of reference and thus inevitably producing an intellectual exercise in a vacuum; as any plan for the railways must be when it is conducted in isolation from other forms of transport and from the economic and social needs of the country."

A PENNY A WEEK 'WOULD STAVE OFF CLOSURES'

Lord Stonham called, in vain as it turned out, for a postponement on closures until it was known what they would cost the country and until the longer-term, fundamental question of the national cost relationship between road and rail was answered. He pointed out that in recent years, 340 branch lines and 4000 miles of track had been closed — saving the railways less than 1%, or two old pence in the pound of their total costs.

He said that the expected saving of £18 million a year by closing 5000 miles of passenger services was equivalent to just four days' defence expenditure. "Would an £18 million branch line subsidy be a worse way of spending money than the much larger business car subsidy?

This sum of £18 million a year means one penny a week for each one of us," he said. He also drew attention to the high summer patronage of closure-earmarked branch lines, when some of the doomed stations received 100 times their daily winter average of passengers, and predicted that the already-choked roads would have to shoulder this burden during holiday times if the closures went ahead.

He also questioned Marples' statement that if the railways attracted all the traffic they wanted from the roads after the implementation of the Beeching report, road traffic would fall by 2%. While the Beeching report proposed to cut 900 freight depots down to 100 larger ones, extra lorries would be needed, and they would all be in congested areas.

Lord Stonham criticised the minister for not having plans in place to widen and improve roads to handle the extra traffic before closing branch lines.

He said: "The closure of the marginal Peterborough-Grimsby line will isolate a large part of Lincolnshire, including towns like Skegness, which will be 23 miles from the nearest railway station. The roads are comparatively narrow and wind extraordinarily, and 150 miles will need straightening and widening. At £100,000 a mile, that means £15 million for only one area.

"In addition, it will put an enormous burden on ratepayers at the very time when they are losing income because people will not be going to the seaside resorts. How much it is going to cost on immediate works the minister does not know. My guess is that it well may be £1000 million, and as the estimates come in, that may well prove to be an underestimate. This cost alone is going to knock the £18 million a year silly. How can the closure procedure be started before this information is available?

"There are literally scores of what I regard as utterly daft proposals in this Plan. In the Rhondda, there is a two-mile railway tunnel under the mountains. It is proposed to continue the railway for freight but not for passengers. To get to the other side of the mountain by road entails travelling 40 miles and the roads round are not suitable for buses.

"Out of 195,000 miles of highways, there will be thousands of miles which will need major and costly improvements if they are to carry buses and lorries safely."

Lord Stonham described as "utter nonsense" the Commons statement by Marples that 100 extra buses would cover the 15,000 square miles of Scotland left entirely without railways.

"What sort of confidence does it inspire when he tells the doomed areas not to worry because he personally will have to approve every closure?" he said. "That is precisely what does worry them."

In the days before Lord Stonham's speech, a resolution passed by the National Council on Inland Transport at a conference which included representatives of 170 local authorities from all parts of Britain passed a resolution which stated that it was "appalled by the social and economic consequences of Dr Beeching's report and demands that it shall not be implemented until all the consequences and costs to the nation have been fully assessed."

THE COUNTRY IN UPROAR

The County Councils Association of England and every major authority in Scotland, Wales and the west of England followed up the resolution with similar demands.

Lord Stonham said: "This adds up to a unanimous and overwhelming demand from non-party organisations representing virtually the entire population. Any minister, in my view, would have to be either mentally subnormal or morally delinquent to ignore this overwhelming demand and the local knowledge and facts on which it is based."

Regarding public subsidies to railways, Lord Stonham accused the government of merely switching them to roads, so haulage "can profitably quote freight rates which put the railways out of business. That is the economics of Bedlam."

He said that taking into account road construction and maintenance which was rising to £250 million a year, the £230 million annual cost of accidents, £130 million spent on police signals and traffic control, the Road Federation's estimated cost of congestion placed at £500 million a year and damage to buildings at £100 million a year gave a total of £1210 million a year. While fuel duties and vehicle taxes brought in around half this sum, it revealed a net subsidy to road transport of more than £600 million a year — four times the railway deficit.

"In other words, the roads are a far bigger national lossmaker than the railways," he added.

Nonetheless, Lord Stonham said that he still saw "much to commend" in the Beeching report, particularly with the proposals to boost freight. "But they cannot succeed unless we see to it that they get the chance to compete (with road haulage) on equal terms," he said.

"We should ask Dr Beeching to look again, not at how easily he can close lines down, but at what must be done to keep them open.

"Give them a facelift: apply with goodwill the many methods whereby costs can be lowered by running modified services, rather than destroy them altogether.

"Use and foster the growing interest of many local authorities in their railway and their anxiety to increase its business.

"Jettison the idea, which our people will never accept, that they must holiday abroad because British Railways will make no provision for holidays in Britain.

"Before the war, students used to come from all over the world to watch and learn from British Railways. They will begin to come again if we call a truce to amputation, and, by infusing modern efficiency with the old spirit of public service, restore our railways to their former position as the envy of the world."

While several of the lines he mentioned were eventually spared the axe, and Skegness for one is still served by rail, most of his counterarguments against the Beeching closures fell on deaf ears.

History was left to judge how many of them were valid, balanced by the fact that despite Marples' personal interest in roads, the switch from rail to road and the growth in car ownership at the expense of railway branch lines was a global phenomenon by no means restricted to Britain.

By the time Labour replaced the Tories in office in late 1964, "Beeching Must Go" was almost a national war cry.

To add balance to Lord Stonham's criticisms of the Beeching report, it should be remembered that while it was a Conservative government that called for the network to be rationalised, it was to be the ensuing Labour government, a party long associated with verbal support for public transport, and which before it won the General Election in 1964 pledged to reverse the Beeching cuts, that nonetheless implemented most of it.

Lord Stonham went on to serve as a Home Office junior minister from 1964-67 in Harold Wilson's Labour government and as minister of state in the Home Office with responsibility for Northern Ireland until 1969, when he was appointed as a privy counsellor.

AN EXPERT'S VIEW

The Great Central Association, a corporate member of the National Council on Inland Transport, published a report by Professor ER Hondelink, MSc, MICE, MInstT, which argued that had Britain's roads been subjected to a Beeching-style study, the case for closing railways en masse would have quickly fallen through.

Prof Hondelink, a consultant to the United Nations Technical Assistance Service, said: "Dr Beeching's pronouncement that there is no sensible alternative to his plan must be challenged with the greatest vigour."

He said that the one-sided government approach had ignored "the identical but more complicated and more serious problem of overall economic road transport deficits" and outlined the position as he saw it as follows: "Roads provided, owned, maintained, administered and paid for by 1288 highway authorities, used by millions of transporters, individuals, groups and companies. Accounts legion in numbers, complicated and not easily analysed. Widespread research in other lands compared with position here point to the likelihood that overall deficit — ultimately borne by taxpayer and ratepayer — is far in excess of the railway deficit. It is certainly at least £300 million, may well be as high as £600 million.

"If a similar exercise were carried out on the roads and road transport sector, it is probable that the bottom would fall out of Dr Beeching's report."

The professor, who had just stood down as Director General of the European Central Inland Transport Organisation, and who clearly 'knew his stuff', said that many rail routes had been subjected to "calculated neglect and starvation" prior to closure, and that the additional burden on the highway authorities of transferring rail traffic to roads had been ignored.

As did many critics of Beeching, he stressed the importance of loss-making branch lines as feeders of traffic to the main line, and said other countries that had closed unremunerative branch lines had later reopened them.

He urged, largely in vain as it happened, the government to order the British Railways Board to probe road and other transport costs in the same way Beeching had addressed the railways, to postpone all closures until such studies had been completed and to immediately concentrate on making maximum and more economic use of existing equipment, while reducing staff by operational and administrative methods already in widespread use on continental Europe.

LABOUR'S BROKEN PROMISE

Under Harold Wilson's Labour government elected in 1964, the pre-election promise to halt the Beeching closures was not only quickly and conveniently forgotten, but also the closures continued at a faster rate than under the Marples transport regime.

In 1964, the first year that many of the Beeching recommendations took effect, 1058 miles were closed, followed by 600 in 1965, in the first year of the Wilson administration.

In December 1965, *The Railway Magazine* correspondent Onlooker, in pleading for a square deal for the railways after what he called a "year of frustration", commented: "The Reshaping report listed 267 passenger services to be withdrawn and 2363 stations and halts to be closed. Over 300 parliamentary constituencies were affected, yet not a single Conservative MP voted against its approval.

"Also, since changing sides in the House, not a single Labour MP has had the courage to remind the party's leaders about this unredeemed pledge.

"Back in their constituencies, however, they bay to a different moon. Whenever a public inquiry is held by the Transport Users Consultative Committee into a proposed withdrawal of a service, local MPs, whether Tory or Labour, line up to lead the objectors. As Hamlet might have said: 'Thus a three-line whip does make cowards of us all... and enterprises of great pith and moment, with this regard, their currents turn away and lose the name of action.'

"The root cause of Labour's betrayal of rail is not far to seek. There are 2,500,000 workers employed in the road transport industry, while the BR payroll barely reaches 500,000 — a ratio of five to one. Can a government deal fairly with a plaintiff's case when there are five bellicose defendants breathing down its neck?"

In 1966, another 750 miles were closed, followed by 300 miles in 1967, 400 in 1968, 250 in 1969 and 275 in 1970. Only then did the rate of closures rapidly fall off.

So while it is easy for subsequent generations to shift the blame for the axe on Ernest Marples, the road building minister who appointed Beeching the 'bogey man' and rubber stamped many of the closures that he recommended, it was the Labour opposition that despite its public vows to reverse the trend, stuck to much the same policy once elected, when it also found that it had to make the same hard decisions based on available criteria in the face of the soaring British Railways deficit which accompanied the growth in car ownership.

A seaside resort hit particularly hard was Whitby, where the closure of all three routes to the town was recommended. Local people widely expected the main route to York to be saved; however, in September 1964, just a month before the General Election, Marples surprised everybody by confirming the closure of both the routes from York and Scarborough but reprieving the line from Middlesbrough via the Esk Valley.

It was certainly an unusual choice. While the wonderfully scenic Esk Valley route serves several isolated villages, it was far from being the most direct link between Whitby and the main population of Yorkshire. Marples made his decision based on the importance of Whitby itself of retaining a rail service to connect it with the nearest large centre of population, the importance of the tourist trade to the port and the surrounding area and the extreme difficulty of operating buses over the Esk Valley roads, especially in winter.

As part of his campaign, the Labour candidate for Scarborough and Whitby produced a pledge signed by Harold Wilson himself that the remaining closures would not go ahead if his party won the election.

Within a month, Wilson was in Downing Street, ending more than 13 years of Conservative control, but had only a majority of four seats, and it was clear that Wilson would need to go to the polls again sooner rather than later to obtain a comfortable working majority.

How much the Beeching closures played in the downfall of the Conservative government as opposed to, say, the Profumo affair scandal and the general mood of modernisation and a desire for change, drawing a line under the 'old order' once and for all, could not be calculated. Yet Labour's victory was by no means a landslide in favour of those who pledged to stop the Beeching cuts; indeed, apart from the pledge, the closures barely featured in the election campaign.

Looked upon to redeem Labour's pre-election pledge with regard to Whitby, new Transport Minister Tom Fraser claimed that due to a technicality in the 1962 Transport Act, he was powerless to reverse his predecessor Marples' decisions, despite the fact that they had not yet been implemented. Neither did Wilson appear inclined to intervene with a state-controlled industry.

The word 'cop-out' comes quickly to mind, and instinctively begs the question — why does the electorate still heed election promises?

Yet there was no widespread uproar over the apparent U-turn. Maybe it was an indication that the new car-owning classes no longer had a reason to care about railways when they had discovered the new freedom that the open road gave them.

Also, many sections of the press were in support of Beeching's attempts to reduce the burden on the taxpayer by ridding the country of sizeable parts of a transport system which was by natural forces of supply and demand becoming obsolete. Indeed, *The Railway Magazine* had carried an editorial in its May 1963 issue which began: "Whether one agrees with all of 'the plan' or not, it has to be admitted that Dr Beeching's report is basically correct and backed by such a weight of carefully prepared evidence as to be almost unassailable. It has been described as brutal, brilliant and right."

After turning his back on the promises to Whitby, Fraser authorised 39 out of 40 outstanding closures across the country. It appeared to be nothing less than a case of a seamless join with the Marples administration.

To many, this 'carry on as before' approach underlined the fact that some form of large-scale closure policy was viewed as inescapable on both sides of the political fence in a rapidly changing and modernising world. Therefore from this point of view at least, it is surely unfair or wrong to blame one or two individuals, Marples and Beeching, who found themselves in the time and place where circumstances dictated that they had to grasp the nettle in the first instance.

The perennial question asked is — could the problems of declining demand for rail services and the soaring deficit combined with streamlining the network to ensure its survival have been approached in a different way than that outlined in the Beeching report, and if so, would more or fewer closures have taken place? Could overall losses have been stemmed or reduced to an acceptable level, maybe by pruning operating costs to bare bones and running lines on a skeletal basis, or would it have been a case of sticking a finger in the dyke and putting off the evil day when far more drastic cutting-back would have been inescapable?

A THERMOMETER IN THE WEST

One stretch of British road became immortalised by traffic jams in the mid-20th century, firstly as car ownership and leisure time boomed, and secondly, as more car journeys were needed to replace closed railway branch lines to holiday resorts — the Exeter bypass.

The West Country has always been Britain's choice destination for summer holidays, and Exeter was a hub both for journey by rail, with the Great Western and Southern rail lines from London meeting there, along with several of the main roads to both Devon and Cornwall.

By the 1920s, with the new car-owning middle class taking motoring holidays in the west, as opposed to travelling there by train, the city's streets were becoming overburdened, and several buildings had to be demolished for road widening and traffic lights first appeared in 1929. It was suggested that a new road should be built to take passing traffic around the town rather than through it.

Work began on an eastern bypass in the early 1930s, and the first section, from Bath Road west of Pinhoe to the Countess Wear roundabout, was completed by 1935. The section included the building of Gallows Bridge at Gallows Cross across the A30 London Road, with a slip road to allow traffic from London to join the bypass, and a roundabout where it crossed the road to Sidmouth at Middlemoor. Gallows Bridge was built from local red sandstone, and to the untrained eye, ironically looks every bit like a railway overbridge. Incidentally, the 'Gallows' recalled the place of execution at Heavitree where three Bideford women were hanged in 1682, when they became the last people in Britain to be documented as being executed for witchcraft.

In August 1935, the building of the final section of the bypass between Countess Wear, running across the River Exe and Exeter Ship Canal to join the roads to Dawlish Road, Torquay and Plymouth began. It included a new swing bridge over the canal specially to accommodate the huge volumes of holiday traffic. This final section was opened by Transport Minister Leslie Burgin on February 22, 1938. The minister said: "The people of Exeter need have no fear of the bypass for it is better to have willing customers who can reach the city than disgruntled tourists who are delayed on their journeys through being unable to pass through it."

However, the bypass generated more disgruntled tourists than ever before by the mid-50s, well before the great swathe of branch line closures began. Holiday specials still ran to the West Country resorts behind Great Western King 4-6-0s, but the motor car was rapidly seizing their crown, and queues on the bypass tailed back for hours at peak periods because it was not big enough to cope with the volume. Long queues returned to Exeter city centre as frustrated motorists tried to avoid the bypass.

In a bid to address the problems in the summer of 1959, a raised platform was built in the centre of the Countess Wear roundabout, from which a policeman could manually control four sets of temporary traffic lights.

By the mid-60s, rising car ownership combined with more resorts disenfranchised from the rail network saw 12-mile tailbacks on the Exeter bypass. By the summer of 1966 they were regularly making national news, as nearby the last rites were being read over branch line services. This situation, while individually notorious in terms of traffic congestion, may be viewed as a microcosm of the changing traffic patterns brought about by the great shift from rail to road, promoted by public demand and perpetuated by government transport policy.

The government's solution? Build more roads. In 1968, plans to extend the M5 south from Bristol to Exeter, bypassing the infamous bypass, were announced. It was completed in October 1975, and included a new bridge built by British Rail for the surviving branch line to Exmouth.

The section of the bypass between the Countess Wear roundabout and Dawlish Road still generates traffic queues, at rush hour.

CHAPTER EIGHT

Beeching HQ: an inside story

JOHN EDSER left the London School of Economics in 1960 with a degree in medieval history. Like many fellow graduates, he did not know precisely what to do next.

He joined the Southern Region as a trainee booking clerk and went through training school at Clapham Junction.

He passed out and was given his first job at the Surrey station near where he lived, Stoneleigh, which opened in 1932. Typical of many suburban stations of the day, it was built in a utilitarian concrete style. The ticket office is sited in the overbridge opposite the island platform entrance, and it was there that John spent a year from August 1960. It was an extremely busy station and he reckoned that in two or three days after the Christmas break the season ticket takings covered the salaries of all the staff and paid for any maintenance the station needed in the coming year.

He was then transferred to the goods office at Wimbledon. Back then, it had two busy goods yards and John learned much about freight handling.

A third transfer saw John move to the South West District Control Office at Woking. He took on the job of what was in other regions a controller, but at Woking he was officially listed as a trained supervision clerk, a level which was paid less than controllers, even though he performed the same functions.

He worked there as assistant to the man in charge of the Waterloo main line, booking trains and keeping statistics. There followed a slight promotion with an office relief job before there came a permanent post looking after the Woking to Portsmouth route and the Isle of Wight.

He fondly recalls the end of one night, when he received a call from Ryde St Johns signalbox saying that the early morning newspaper and mail train from Ryde to Ventnor behind one of the ageing London & South Western Railway O2 0-4-4Ts had derailed in the dark near Smallbrook Junction, after hitting a herd of cows on the line.

He was based at Woking during the winter of 1962/63, when the railways faced the most severe climatic conditions since 1947, and all the stops had to be pulled out to ensure that the country did not grind to a halt. "All I would say is that we did things then to keep the services running that would probably scare people today," John admitted.

"Everybody knew exactly what they had to do and everyone knew exactly how they had to do it. We kept a service going on most days, and after midday we ran almost a full service because by then all the snow had been scraped off the third rail conductor by the continuous passage of trains."

The thaw came in early March to the relief of all. For the railways, it was indeed a new spring, for the Beeching report had just been published, and it focused in the public mind the state of the railway network upon which people had depended for generations, and might soon no longer be relevant to many of them.

John had clearly impressed during his time at Woking, for in late May he was summoned to the chief clerk's office. He was informed, at short notice, that the British Railways Board had requested his transfer to its headquarters at 222 Marylebone Road, the former Great Central Railway Hotel a stone's throw from Marylebone station, a week later. "That is when I started a period of seven years at the BRB HQ 222 commonly known as the Kremlin," John said.

He was in at the deep end. No longer would he be planning how to cope with failures and emergencies such as cows on the line or the wrong kind of snow, but he would be part of the Beeching team helping to do what the report promised — reshape the British Railways network.

CARRYING OUT THE DOCTOR'S ORDERS

All that John Edser knew about his role inside 222 Marylebone Road was that he had to report to the Planning Office (Reshaping). At this time, the newspapers and TV were full of public comments about the Beeching report, many of them adverse. Again, it seemed that what had been happening on a piecemeal basis line by line for the past 12 years created a shockwave when a huge portfolio of recommended closures was presented in one fell swoop. John arrived there to be introduced to his new boss, Charles Haygreen, the planning officer (Reshaping).

Making up the last member of a three-man team was Chris Hubbard, who had joined the Great Northern Railway in 1923 and who had come to the British Railways Board in the chief secretary's department. He had dealt with closures for years before Beeching was appointed.

The job of the trio was to instigate the progress and implementation of nothing less than the whole of the Beeching closure programme — both the passenger and freight proposals. They were part of the Central Planning Unit that the British Railways chairman had set up.

The actual work on the ground was carried out by the regions themselves. It was the job of the Haygreen team to process the closures.

They had to co-ordinate all the statistics and then follow each closure recommendation through the posting of notices, the Transport Users Consultative Committee hearings, the lists of objections if there were any, the TUCC reports which were forwarded on to the Ministry of Transport, and the response of the minister.

If the closure proposal was accepted by the minister, the team issued the notice of closure and got on with the work of withdrawing services, setting dates for the last passenger and goods services and, where applicable, ensuring that alternative transport such as bus services were provided.

John said: "The basic work was done by the regions. We were to a degree a post office, but we all knew exactly what was going on right throughout the system.

"We also were liaising with the Ministry of Transport and there were quite a few meetings between us and the ministry just to see how things were going.

"There was no political pressure applied whatsoever.

"We were administrators and if there were certain problems on the ministry side as well as the railway side, we got together.

"What people didn't realise was that as well as the passenger closures, there was a huge system of freight station closures which did not have to go through any public procedures.

"As well as keeping statistics on the passenger side and progress reports, also all the freight station closures were reported to us on a weekly or monthly basis.

The Kremlin, probably like its Moscow counterpart, had a map room.

The centrepiece was an enormous map of the British Isles with the whole of the railway system marked on it.

One of John's jobs was to plot the progress of the freight closures. "We did it with big different coloured pins," he recalled. "Those proposed were posted in one colour and when they closed they went red."

The Central Planning Unit found itself at the roots of the British railway system of the future.

Processing the closures was only part of its work, although that occupied much of John's work in his first two years. The unit was eventually responsible for producing the Freightliner network, the first Freightliner ships, the Trunk Route Report of 1965, the 1967 Network for Development under Barbara Castle, and a lot of spadework which led to the 1968 Transport Act.

"It was a very, very interesting period and it was a great place to work because it was not hierarchical," said John. "If you imagine the pyramid structure of a big company, there are always tiny cells close to the top working on special projects. The Central Planning Unit was one of those.

"There were no offices between it and one of the board members, so in fact we were only two levels away from Beeching.

"In the unit I worked for, the board member was very much insistent that when the meeting about progress with the closure programme was held, those that actually did the work were present. So quite unusually for a very junior clerk or manager, I was at the meeting because I was actually doing it.

"Board members and chief officers used to sit around a table and on occasions I made presentations to them which was highly unusual in those days.

"It led to a very relaxed atmosphere which was good."

John was not there when Beeching was appointed, but colleagues said that his managerial style was a sharp contrast to the approach of Beeching's predecessor, the former British Transport Commission chairman General Brian Hubert Robertson, 1st Baron Robertson of Oakridge, GCB, GBE, KCMG, KCVO, DSO, MC, and who had at one time been the military governor of the British part of occupied Germany, who insisted on utmost formality. It was said that he refused to have a woman as a secretary.

Unlike Robertson, Beeching would sometimes go out of his office and walk down the corridors to meet people rather than summoning them to him. That might seem insignificant today, but such expressions of informality from the top man at first shocked senior management.

John said: "When he passed you in the corridor, he would say good morning or good afternoon. You would say good morning or good afternoon back. His attitude towards people at headquarters was certainly a step change from what had gone before."

Beeching did have a woman secretary who was equally as relaxed.

"One afternoon I went into his office to find his PA in tennis clothes, her feet on her desk, talking on the phone," said John.

"She wasn't the terrible female secretary that some people dreaded by any means. He also had an assistant, usually an ex-traffic apprentice, who had been picked out for further promotion. He definitely had a modern approach to people who worked for him."

"GET THE BIG ONES IN FIRST"

Some of the closures in the Beeching report were political dynamite. If his 1963 report had been followed to the letter, there would have been no rail services north or west of Inverness, and Wales would have lost its Central Wales Line. There would have been a huge and immediate backlash from Scottish and Welsh politicians if such lines, though clearly big lossmakers, were closed.

Surely Beeching cannot be criticised here. He was asked to identify lossmaking lines, and his report did just that. It was then left up to the Transport Users Consultative Committees to recommend keeping them open if there were grounds of hardship and the minister to make that decision on social or economic grounds.

The ministry was clearly geared up to rejecting the political non-starts in the Beeching record.

John recalls: "There was an extremely astute lady principal from the ministry, a Miss Fogarty, who was in charge of Wales and Scotland.

"She said 'please get the regions to put these big closures in first, because they are almost a racing certainty to be refused, and therefore, if we put refusals out quickly, people might think it was not going to be as horrible as they imagined under the original Beeching proposal.'

"That was political astuteness. We did so, and we got a lot of closure refusals."

Miss Fogarty also turned out to be an expert on railways in Britain's far-flung regions.

When querying the Beeching statistics on the Far North Line from Inverness to Thurso and Wick, one MP spotted variations in parcels from the small stations in the far north and queried it. Miss Fogarty, who had travelled on those lines, immediately had the answer. "It is easy. It is salmon going south to premium markets.

John said: "If, shall we say, McTavish was taking his van from the north-west of Scotland to Helmsdale, the salmon went to Helmsdale. If McGregor three days later was going from north-west Scotland to Thurso or Wick, the salmon went from there.

"She was able to tell them this straight off. She did not have to come to us and we did not have to go to the regions to find the answers. It saved a lot of time.

"She was obviously very bright because we heard she went into the cabinet office.

"Many of the Labour-controlled councils in the north were bitterly opposed to the closures and delayed replying to letters as long as they could. One in Lancashire proved extremely obdurate until our London Midland office found that the council had instructed their officers that anything to do with railway closures was to be immediately consigned to the bin and not be answered under any circumstances!"

The Far North Line did end up being saved, as was the Kyle of Lochalsh branch, the Central Wales Line and Llandudno Junction to Blaenau Ffestiniog. Also spared the recommended axe by Ernest Marples was the Darlington to Bishop Auckland section of the Darlington to Crook line, the Esk Valley Line from Middlesbrough to Whitby, Newcastle-Riverside-Tynemouth and the Bangor-Caernarfon section of the Bangor-Afon Wen closure proposal. The reprieve of the Bangor-Caernarfon line, however, did not last, for it was closed on January 5, 1970, near the end of the term of Harold Wilson's government. However, following the severe fire that damaged the tubular railway bridge over the Menai Strait on the Holyhead main line, the branch and goods yard were temporarily reopened for freight traffic from May 23, 1970 to January 30, 1972. Following closure all the track was removed and the station completely demolished. Ever since there have been repeated calls for it to reopen again.

Political considerations were through to be the reasons behind the saving of the Central Wales Line from Craven Arms to Llanelli. It passed through six marginal constituencies, and a General Election was looming.

Furthermore, it carried freight, serving the steelworks at Bynea and industrial areas such as Ammanford and Pontarddulais, linking them with the docks at Llanelli.

During engineering work, the line is still occasionally used as a diversionary freight route. Interestingly, in a bid to cut infrastructure costs, the line has been run under a Light Railway Order since 1972.

RUABON TO DOLGELLAU NEARLY SAVED

While the report recommended the retention of the Cambrian Coast Line from Shrewsbury to Pwllheli and Aberystwyth, the Ruabon to Barmouth cross-country route was listed for closure.

John Edser felt that this line, despite 'doubling up' with the Cambrian Coast Line, may well have ended up being saved after protests were received. It was a case of touch and go.

He recalled: "One surprise was that we got Ruabon to Barmouth for closure, on the grounds you only wanted one line across Central Wales. It was a bit dodgy."

The whole line was officially closed to passenger trains on January 18, 1965. Goods services between Morfa Mawddach and Llangollen ceased in 1964.

The line closed early, on December 12, 1964 following flooding. The section between Ruabon and Llangollen was subsequently reopened on December 17 for passenger trains until January 18, after which only freight services ran until 1968 when the line was closed completely.

The section between Llangollen and Bala Junction was abandoned following flooding, although a substitute bus service served the stations until January 18, 1965. The sections between Bala, Bala Junction and Dolgellau and from Dolgellau to Morfa Mawddach were reopened days later.

However, the track was lifted throughout the entire route by 1969. Two sections have since been opened as preserved railways, the 2ft gauge Bala Lake Railway in the early 1970s and the standard gauge Llangollen Railway which opened its first stretch in 1981. A 10-mile section between Barmouth Junction and Dolgellau is also used as the Mawddach Trail, a cycle route and bridleway. From time to time, calls for the route to be reopened throughout or in part are still made, but in vain.

SAVING BRAINTREE BUT NOT BOCKING

John recalled: "Basically we were a processing office.

"We would often find why things were going slowly because the TUCCs were area TUCCS and if they had a lot of closures they couldn't do them all at once, and so the programme tended to stretch out a bit. In some areas it went faster than others because they had fewer cases to deal with.

"There was laid down statutory procedure which had to be followed in every case.

"Once the TUCC reports had gone in, we became a bit more interested because we knew whether they had recommended closure or retention and all of the conditions that they might have applied, such as replacement bus services and things like that.

"Some regions fought closures to the nth degree. The classic case was the Braintree branch where the Eastern Region people in Liverpool Street fought tooth and nail against the closure.

"Hindsight is a great thing, but look at it today — electrified with a direct service and a very fine commuter service in and out of Liverpool Street.

"They could see the potential for Braintree and also to a lesser extent the Marks Tey-Sudbury line."

The Braintree branch is the northern half of the Maldon, Witham & Braintree Railway which opened in 1848. At Braintree & Bocking, it linked to the Bishop's Stortford-Braintree cross-country route, which opened in 1869 and closed to passengers in 1952. However, the Beeching report recorded that Bishop's Stortford handled more than 25,000 tons of freight traffic a year, and so the route was spared for the moment.

Faced with increasing competition from road transport, freight services progressively fell by the wayside, with Felstead closing on May 4, 1964, apart from the sugar beet siding, Rayne on December 7 that year and Takeley on December 18, 1966, when the Felstead to Dunmow section closed completely. Easton Lodge to Dunmow was closed on April 1, 1969, Braintree to Felstead on June 20, 1970, and finally Bishop's Stortford to Easton Lodge on March 1, 1972. A last enthusiast special ran from Bishop's Stortford to Easton Lodge and back on July 27, 1972, with most of the track taken up that autumn.

The case for saving the Braintree to Witham single-track line was made on account of the fact that the former was expanding as a commuter line for London. It was subsequently electrified at 25kV AC, and is thriving today. To the east, the first section of the Colchester, Stour Valley, Sudbury & Halstead Railway, the 12 miles from Marks Tey to Sudbury, opened on July 2, 1849 and was taken over by the Eastern Counties Railway on August 7, 1862.

Its successor, the Great Eastern Railway, opened a line from Shelford just south of Cambridge to Haverhill on June 1, 1865, extending it to Sudbury on August 9 that year. A branch from Bury St Edmunds was also completed, joining the Shelford line at Long Melford.

Cutbacks bit hard in the early Sixties, with conductor guards being introduced to collect fares on board trains while all stations became unstaffed apart from Haverhill and Sudbury.

Passenger trains on the route from Long Melford to Bury St Edmunds ended on April 10, 1961, with Bures, Cavendish, Bartlow stations on the main route from Shelford to Marks Tey closed to freight on December 28, 1964.

The twilight years saw two trains a day run between Sudbury and Cambridge, four between Colchester and Cambridge and six between Marks Tey or Colchester and Sudbury, with the same number making return trips, most services being operated by diesel multiple units.

In April 1965, British Railways Board applied for permission to end passenger services from the whole route between Marks Tey and Cambridge.

The closure move promoted local outrage, but went through, despite local councils showing some willingness to offer a subsidy… until the high costs became apparent.

All freight services were withdrawn on October 31, 1966, and passenger services between Sudbury and Cambridge ended on March 6, 1967, the track being lifted in 1970.

However, the protesters scored a partial and major victory in managing to keep the section between Sudbury and Marks Tey open, because of the fact that Sudbury was expanding and there was a potential growth in commuter traffic.

Further attempts were made to close the Marks Tey to Sudbury section, but it was given an indefinite reprieve after the 1974 energy crisis which led to the threat of petrol rationing, and has survived to this day.

An enthusiast-led group, the Stour Valley Railway Preservation Society, was formed on September 24, 1968 with the very over-ambitious aim of preserving all of the Sudbury to Shelford line.

However, the group's aspirations were soon whittled down to just the three miles from Sudbury to Long Melford, but even this proved beyond its grasp, as the funds to buy the section could not be raised.

In December 1969, the group established a headquarters at Chappel & Wakes Colne station on the Marks Tey to Sudbury section which was still open. British Rail gave the group a lease on the redundant goods yard, goods shed, signalbox and station buildings, a site which by then was largely derelict.

The group saw itself as playing a waiting game, establishing a presence and building up its resources until the line was officially closed, as many expected.

The enthusiasts bought the whole site from British Rail at auction in 1987, a year after it officially became the East Anglian Railway Museum. Four years later, it obtained a Light Railway Order to run passenger trains over its short running line.

If ever the Sudbury branch does become declared surplus to requirements, the museum will be ready to step in. However, it looks destined to remain as another Beeching recommended closure which got away.

In December 2006 the line was designated as a "community railway" by the transport minister, and is part of the Essex and South Suffolk Community Rail Partnership. It is now marketed as the Gainsborough Line, after the painter Thomas Gainsborough who was born in Sudbury.

During July 2005 the non-electrified line received around £3 million investment, which saw old track replaced with new continuous welded rail by 2007.

John said that there had been no strong case for adjoining lines, like Sudbury-Haverhill and the Cambridge route to be saved.

"You have to remember the Bury St Edmunds line had gone like a lot of East Anglian lines prior to Beeching.

"There were one or two cases like that where lines were shut when the regions had wanted to keep them. I can't think of specific examples now, but I know that it happened," he said.

TUCCS — GENUINELY DEMOCRATIC, OR RUBBER-STAMPING FOREGONE CONCLUSIONS?

The Transport Act 1962 paved the way for the Beeching report by making the statutory closures of railways easier than ever before.

The Central Transport Consultative Committee took the place of a similar body that had been created under the Transport Act 1947 and was intended as a consumer body to represent users of the railway.

In addition, Area Transport Users Consultative Committees were established to cover individual areas of the country. Their job was to make recommendations relating to the services provided by British Railways, but the minister of transport was not legally obliged to follow any of them.

Under the new procedures, British Railways was required to give at least six weeks' notice of intent to close a line and to publish this proposal in two successive weeks in two local newspapers. Such notices would give the proposed closure dates, details of alternative transport and would invite objections.

In many cases, objections were heard at a local inquiry. Rail users affected by a closure could also send their objections to the Area Committee who would then report to the minister of transport.

The Area Committee would consider the "hardship" which it considered would be caused as a result of the closure, and recommend measures to ease that hardship.

The closure would not then be proceeded with until the committee had reported to the minister and he had given his consent to the closure. Based on the report, the minister could impose conditions, such as the provision of alternative transport services, before the closure went ahead.

Sceptics have said that decisions were made before the local TUCCs held hearings, and that they were a cosmetic waste of time, simply there to appease the angry public.

John disagreed. "They were public hearings and all sorts of people were allowed," he said.

"The general public went to the hearings and there were obviously organised groups. Any man in the street in the area who had a point to make could go into the hearing and make it and it was listened to."

But was it ever taken on board? "That was a matter for the TUCC," said John.

To acquaint themselves with the holding of TUCC hearings, he and a colleague from the Central Planning Unit attended two by themselves, once the procedure for processing the Beeching closures had been set in place. However, they went incognito.

With an angry public in attendance, they did not want to distract the hearing by their presence and the last thing they wanted was to be identified as members of Beeching's planning team.

Not only were there fears of physical repercussions on the spot, but John said that they were simply there to observe proceedings so that they could personally become familiar with them, not to spy or report back to senior officers.

"I went to the Bexhill West branch closure hearing," said John. "It was held in Bexhill.

It was very local. All of them were specific to the line that was being closed.

"With the growth of cars on the south coast, people could get to Crowhurst without the train. It was basically used for two or three trains in the rush hour and the rest of the day you could count the number of trains on the fingers of one hand.

"I never met any TUCC members. We did not disclose to the TUCC that we had attended. "We were just there as members of the audience.

"If they had known there were people from British Railways headquarters, the audience could have given us a very rough time and we did not want to make the TUCC think they were under the watchful eye of Big Brother. We went there just to see what went on. It was a purely information-gathering exercise on how things worked."

The Bexhill West branch, built by the Crowhurst, Sidley & Bexhill Railway under the patronage of the South Eastern Railway, opened somewhat later in the day on June 1, 1902. It was a double track line running for just over four miles from Crowhurst Junction.

Protesters claimed that the timetables for the line, which was dieselised in June 1958, had been altered and disadvantaged commuters, while fares had been increased.

The minister gave the green light for closure, which happened on June 14, 1964. Yet again, one aspect about railway closures and local inquiries into them was the fact that often the loudest protesters used the line in question least of all and in many cases never.

John said: "Some of the more astute TUCCs, having held the hearings on the branch, used to ask 'how many of you have come here by train?'

"It produced some interesting answers."

THE LAST STEAM OF ALL ON BRITISH RAIL

The most obscure and remote rural branch lines that had not closed by Beeching's time invariably found their way into his report.

One very rural line that he did not list for the axe, however, was the 1ft 11¾in gauge Vale of Rheidol Railway which runs between Aberystwyth and Devil's Bridge in central Wales.

The line, which had opened on December 22, 1902, survived because someone in the London Midland hierarchy saw the success of the enthusiast-led preservation schemes that had successfully taken over other Welsh lines like the Talyllyn, Ffestiniog and Welshpool & Llanfair railways as tourist attractions, and realised that the Vale of Rheidol could do the same.

Following the highly unusual and eyebrow-raising decision by British Rail to retain the line running, despite the mass wave of closures of rural branch lines demanded by Beeching elsewhere, the corporate Rail Blue livery and double arrow logo being introduced on main line diesels were applied to the locomotives and carriages in 1967.

The LMR soon regretted the decision to keep the line open. Partially because it was still run by paid staff rather than volunteers, as on other Welsh narrow gauge lines, losses mounted, and in 1967 British Rail duly made plans to close it.

However, it was reprieved largely thanks to Transport Minister Barbara Castle, who visited it on July 1 that year.

Accordingly, after British Rail steam haulage — on the standard gauge national network — officially ended on August 11, 1968, the three GWR-built 2-6-2Ts on the Rheidol line carried on regardless.

However, under British Rail, maintenance suffered, and on May 26, 1986, trackwork came apart at a curve. A question was subsequently tabled in the House of Commons asking why British Rail was wasting its time on running a steam tourist line.

In April 1989, British Rail sold the line to the owners of the Brecon Mountain Railway, a tourist line near Merthyr Tydfil.

The Rheidol line was one of only two pieces of the operational national rail network to be sold to a private owner without interruption of regular passenger services. The first was the Paignton to Kingswear line, another former GWR branch which in 1972 was sold directly to Dart Valley Railway plc, which tried to carry on running the same services as under British Rail until economics dictated summer season running only.

With the best will of enthusiasts, even they could not stem the tide seen elsewhere. It is now known as the Dartmouth Steam Railway, and is phenomenally popular as a heritage line, but not running 'regular' services 365 days a year.

CHAPTER NINE

The whole world turns blue

Each of the 'Big Four' companies had its own corporate liveries for locomotives and rolling stock. British Railways tried to follow suit, but somehow struggled to get each of its regions to always agree.

The standard livery for most British Railway steam locomotives was black, while express passenger locomotives were painted in the Great Western colours of Brunswick green, with orange and black lining, irrespective of their 'Big Four' company of origin.

At one stage in the early Fifties, British Railways painted its express passenger locomotives in blue livery. Striking, yes, but practical, not at all: the livery was quick to show up dirt and grime at every available opportunity.

The livery met with a relatively early demise, but it was to remain, lurking around on a drawing board somewhere at British Railways HQ, ready for its moment again. That was to come with modernisation.

The first-generation diesel multiple units and locomotives by and large appeared in green livery too, as if they were trying to be steam engines by the back door.

As part of a plan to find a suitable corporate livery for the then-new diesel and electric fleet and coaching stock, several experiments were tried.

Class 31 diesel D5578 was painted in an unlined 'light electric blue' while sister D5579 took on a livery described as 'golden ochre'.

The first Class 52 Western class of diesel hydraulics, D1000 *Western Enterprise* appeared in a pale brown livery known as 'desert sand' livery when first delivered in 1961. Sister D1015 *Western Champion* was delivered in a slightly different golden ochre to D5579.

Several Westerns and some of the Class 42 Warships were outshopped in maroon livery, to match the standard British Railways coaching livery.

The 25kV electric locomotives built for the East Coast Main Line were originally painted in a paler but brighter shade of blue known as 'electric blue.'

Meanwhile, shortly after nationalisation in 1948, it was decided that all coaches should be painted in a two-tone livery of carmine and cream for corridor coaches, with all-over crimson very much a successor to the LMS carriage livery, being used for local, non-corridor stock, to give a traditional 'feel' while differing from any of the 'Big Four' company liveries. In the Fifties came a relaxing of this 'one size fits all' rule and the regions were allowed to revert to liveries of their choice, with the most independent of them, the Western Region, readopting GWR chocolate and cream, while the Southern Region reverted to malachite green.

Carriages were repainted as and when they came in for overhaul, leaving trains running with an assortment of liveries — a situation made worse when vehicles from different regions became mixed together.

It would need a businessman to insist that a new national corporate livery was needed in order to dispense with the untidy and often tatty appearance of such 'mixed' trains, one in which locomotives would match passenger stock.

That man was Dr Beeching.

He saw that while passenger numbers on the railways were declining, rival forms of transport were upgrading their identities and services in an effort to stay ahead of the pack.

He decided that if it was to stand any chance of a vibrant future, British Railways needed a major rebranding, from the locomotives and stock down to staff uniforms, station signs and even tableware, seat rest covers and official letterheads. The rebranding would highlight the improvements which had been made since the 1955 Modernisation Plan.

A new prototype train was to be produced, with improvements in internal equipment and decor, paving the way for future designs.

THE UNVEILING OF XP64

In May 1964, a train of eight new carriages, made up of three first-class corridor coaches Nos. M13407-9, two second-class corridor coaches Nos. M25508/9, and three open plan coaches Nos. M4727-9 rolled off the Derby production line.

Finished in a turquoise blue and pale grey livery with dark brown bogies and drawgear, the coaches were known as the Project XP64 stock.

The new coaches were designed to combine physical comfort and good appearance to a high degree, and give a smoother and quieter ride.

The improved smooth and silent running of the new trains was provided by the 'integral' method of building carriage frames, and a new carriage bogie, the B4 type, developed by the chief mechanical engineer's design staff. These developments aimed to save about five tons in the overall weight of each carriage.

The carriages were equipped with air heating and ventilation, improved sound proofing, 5ft-wide windows partially double-glazed, improved lighting, seats scientifically designed to be more restful, wider entrances with folding doors and wider steps designed to improve access, especially for passengers carrying luggage or children. Compact, easy-to-clean toilet compartments featured two illuminated mirrors, one fitted above the wash basin with an electric razor point nearby, and the other giving full-length reflections while the compartment also included a tip-up auxiliary seat.

Each of the three prototype first-class coaches had smoking and non-smoking compartments, and there were different decorations and colours for each one, making a total of six schemes.

At first, this new train was coupled behind a 'matching' Class 47 diesel, D1733. Its colour scheme was matched to that of the coaches and revolutionised the appearance of the British Railways fleet.

The body was painted in the carriage's turquoise blue with the addition of a red square panel on the drivers' cabs, to which was applied the new network logo of two fused arrows — but more on that later.

The final layout of the logo was still being decided at this stage, and was shortly afterwards removed from the locomotive.

Small yellow warning panels were applied to the ends of the loco-motives, and the numbers — two sets either side — were placed directly behind the cabs, and were in a new-style font. The bogies and underframes again matched the coaching stock's brown. Before widespread adoption, the shade of blue was slightly changed to a darker form, properly called 'monastral blue' and better known as 'rail blue'.

The XP64 coaches underwent demonstration runs between Marylebone and High Wycombe on May 28-29, 1964 and entered midweek service on the East Coast Main Line route between King's Cross and Edinburgh during the summer, made into a complete train by the addition of modern restaurant dining cars between the three first-class and one second-class coaches, with a standard second-class corridor brake at each end.

The previous year, the prototype British Railways Mk.2 coach, FK No. 13252, was built. British Railways' second design of carriage had a semi-integral construction, giving it more strength than a Mk.1 in the event of an accident, and the changed construction method overcame the serious corrosion problem point in the base of the Mk.1s, where they were attached to the underframe. Other changes of design, such as the window units, were also made to reduce maintenance costs.

The Mk.2s were introduced between 1964-66 and fitted with vacuum brakes, so they could run with Mk.1 stock. A subsequent variation, the Mk.2As, which appeared in 1967, was air braked only, and adopted many more features from the pioneer XP64 set.

FROM BRITISH RAILWAYS TO BRITISH RAIL

An exhibition entitled The New Face of British Railways was staged at the Design Centre in London from January 4-23, 1965, with the aim of launching British Railways' corporate identity programme. Everything was to be painted in monastral blue and pearl grey, set off by flame red.

From the outset, locomotives kept the small yellow front warning panels from the green livery era, until the British Railways Board's accident prevention service ordered that the yellow was to cover the entire front of the cabs in order to make locomotives more visible to trackside staff for safety reasons.

Everything seen and used frequently by the public, every station, sign, and piece of printed matter, was to be given a recognisable family likeness.

Dr Richard Beeching holds up a copy of his
report, The Reshaping of British Railways, which
immediately sent shockwaves through the UK rail
system when it was published on March 27, 1963. NRM

A poster being displayed in 1947 informing the public that Britain's railways were to be nationalised. NRM

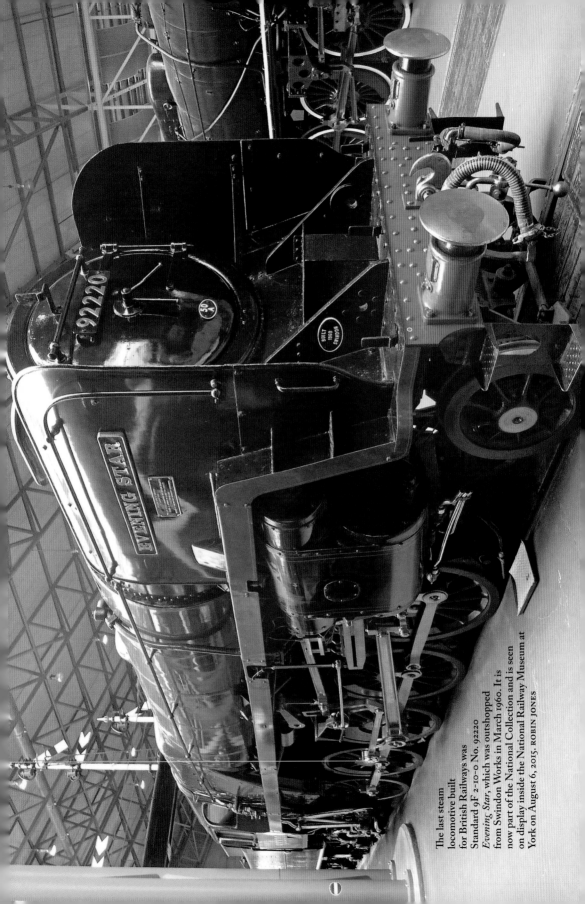

The last steam locomotive built for British Railways was Standard 9F 2-10-0 No. 92220 *Evening Star*, which was outshopped from Swindon Works in March 1960. It is now part of the National Collection and is seen on display inside the National Railway Museum at York on August 6, 2015. ROBIN JONES

The Northern Eastern Railway branch line north of Tow Law to Blackhill in County Durham lost its passenger service as early as May 1939. The line south from Tow Law to Crook closed on June 11, 1956. Many branches serving the Durham coalfield closed along with the exhaustion of the mines they had been built to serve. LNER A5 4–6–2T No. 69836 is seen with a passenger train at Tow Law in the early Fifties. BEAMISH MUSEUM

"Progress" was one of the classic British Railways posters used to publicise its 1955 Modernisation Plan. BRITISH RAILWAYS

A single green railcar in station waits at the GWR's Bromyard station, although there are far more weeds than passengers by then. It closed on September 5, 1964. GREAT WESTERN TRUST

The 1950s saw numerous rural branch line closures well before any railway staff or customers had heard the name Beeching. The final train from Gloucester to Ledbury is seen arriving at Barbers Bridge behind GWR Collett 0-6-0 No. 3205 on July 11, 1959. HUGH BALLANTYNE

Last summer: Midland 3F 0-6-0 No. 44231 passes the Midland & Great Northern Joint Railway signal bracket as it crosses the River Great Ouse at South Lynn with the 8am Chesterfield to Yarmouth Beach service on August 30, 1958. The M&GNJR became the first major system within the railway network to close, early the following year. HUGH BALLANTYNE

Dr Richard Beeching opened a new station nearly a year before his controversial report was published calling for 2363 others to be closed. He is seen unveiling the nameboard at the newly built Holywell (Waterworks) Halt at the Bluebell Railway on April 1, 1962. Two years earlier, preservation pioneer the Bluebell Railway had become the first section of nationalised standard gauge railway to be sold off for private use. Together with his wife Ella, and a bevy of press photographers, the doctor joined a railtour at Three Bridges which continued to the railway from London Bridge to Horsted Keynes via Ardingly, hauled by Captain Bill Smith's preserved GNR 0-6-0 saddle tank No. 1247. The electrified Ardingly branch was subsequently closed and lifted, but the Bluebell has long-term plans to rebuild it. BLUEBELL ARCHIVE

A scene of railway devastation soon to be replicated all over Britain: Pye Hill & Somercotes station on the Great Northern Railway's Pinxton branch in Nottinghamshire, which closed on January 1, 1963. MIDLAND RAILWAY TRUST

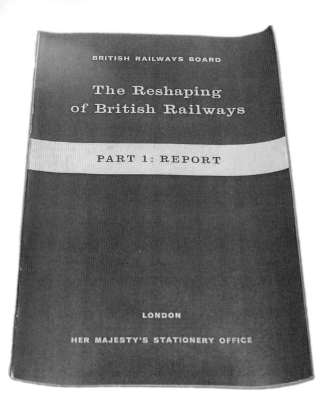

The Conservative government's transport minister Ernest Marples implemented many of the rail closures that Dr Richard Beeching recommended.

Dr Beeching's report The Reshaping of British Railways, a key document in British railway history. ROBIN JONES

An official British Railways notice, typical of those posted at stations across Britain, in this instance announcing the intended closure of the Waverley Route. BRITISH RAILWAYS

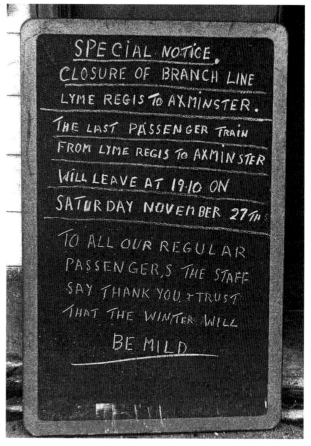

RIGHT: Yet another seaside branch bites the dust, in this case Axminster to Lyme Regis.

Leeds Holbeck (55A)-allocated Royal Scot 4-6-0 No. 46117 *Welsh Guardsman* awaits departure from Glasgow St Enoch on June 29, 1957, with the 'Starlight Special' for Marylebone. The station was closed on June 27, 1966 as part of the Beeching rationalisation of the local railway system and its 250 trains and 23,000 passengers a day were diverted to Glasgow Central. The roofs of the structure and the St Enoch Hotel that fronted the station were demolished, despite protests, in 1977. BRIAN MORRISON

The Hayling Island branch was closed by Beeching on November 3, 1963, even though it made a small profit. British Railways gave the reason as the cost of replacing the timber swing bridge which crossed the Langstone Harbour comprised an unreasonably large investment. HUGH BALLANTYNE

Doomed Dolgellau station on the line to Ruabon, as seen on July 1, 1967. GREAT WESTERN TRUST

A poster promoting the new electric services on the West Coast Main Line. BRITISH RAILWAYS

The closure notice at Evercreech Junction, the hub of the Somerset & Dorset system, on March 5, 1966. MIKE ESAU

The end of the Great Central route from London to the Midlands and the north: the last train departs from Nottingham's Arkwright Street station on May 3, 1969. DAVID HILLAS/CREATIVE COMMONS

Labour Transport Minister Barbara Castle continued with many of the Beeching cuts, but also introduced legislation facilitating the survival of loss-making routes that had social benefits. PASSENGER TRANSPORT EXECUTIVE GROUP

One of the shortest Beeching closures was that of the Barnoldswick branch in the West Riding of Yorkshire, which ran for just a mile and 64 chains from the main line at Earby. Watched by a small group of schoolboy linesiders, with, typical of the times, a 'last train' message chalked on its smokebox, BR Standard 2MT 2-6-2T No. 84015 is set to leave Barnoldswick with the last train on a dull September 25, 1965. The last coal train ran over the line on July 30, 1966.

HUGH BALLANTYNE

The last day of public services on the Somerset & Dorset Joint Railway system was March 5, 1966, when the Locomotive Club of Great Britain ran a special from Waterloo via Bournemouth. The northbound train hauled by Bulleid Light Pacifics No. 34006 *Bude* and No. 34057 *Biggin Hill* is seen making a photographic stop at Chilcompton for the benefit of those who sought to record the day for posterity. MIKE ESAU

A delegation of Waverley Route protesters in London in December 1968, with the future Liberal Democrat leader David Steel MP in the centre. NRM

A rare internal view of one of the Transport Users Consultative Committee line closure inquiries, in Huddersfield: photographs inside such hearings were generally banned by the Ministry of Transport. ALAN EARNSHAW COLLECTION

A Manchester march against the
Beeching cuts on October 13, 1963. NRM

During the electrification of the West Coast Main Line by British Railways, the GWR's Birmingham Snow Hill handled most of the rail traffic through the city, but overall, the Beeching closure programme in the 1960s took the view that Snow Hill station, seen here in the 1960s, was 'doubling up', and all services were switched to New Street and Moor Street. Long distance services through Snow Hill were cut in 1967 and the tunnel beneath the city centre from the south was closed to all traffic. The station was subsequently rebuilt under the West Midlands Passenger Transport Executive and reopened for southbound services in 1987 and northbound in 1995. BEN BROOKSBANK/CREATIVE COMMONS

Lincolnshire's Tumby Woodside station, mentioned in the song Slow Train by Flanders and Swann, which satirised the Beeching cuts. The station closed in 1970 and is pictured in 1981. Its canopy has since rotted away, but some of the crumbling brickwork is still apparent today. DAVID BURROWS

Epitome of the British Rail corporate blue and grey era: Deltic No. 55015 *Tulyar*, an example of one of the finest classes of first-generation British diesels, departs from Lincoln with a King's Cross-Skegness railtour on Sunday, August 13, 1978. BRIAN SHARPE

The mid-Sixties saw steam locomotives hauling rakes of blue and grey coaches intended for the diesel and electric era. In March 1968, Britannia Pacific No. 70013 *Oliver Cromwell* heads a rake of blue and grey coaches out of Carnforth. No. 70013 went down in history as one of four locomotives that hauled the legendary '15 Guinea Special' of August 11, 1968, the last British Rail steam-hauled train. Now part of the National Collection, it is based at Loughborough on the Great Central Railway. DAVE RODGERS

'Merry-go-Round' coal trains were one of Beeching's big success stories in the freight sector. This example is seen at Heck Ings in Yorkshire with Drax power station in the background. BRIAN SHARPE

BRITISH RAILWAYS BOARD

Route System Maps

CONFIDENTIAL

Here is the top secret 'Blue Book of Maps' correctly titled British Railways System Maps. Taking the format of a rail atlas, the book contained highly sensitive information about projected closure dates for coalmines and steel works, as well as railway lines. It shows that Harold Wilson's Labour government knew, for instance, about the life expectancy of collieries 20 years before Margaret Thatcher's Conservative government was criticised during the Miners' Strike of 1984-85 for closing them. The information contained in its pages was used to draw up the map of the national railway network that we have today. ROBIN JONES

Back in the Sixties, a train of brand new Freightliner containers painted in the operation's trademark livery is seen ready to roll.
BRITISH RAIL

Fresh dawn for steam: in 1969, four years after leaving British Railways, Dr Beeching was back – to reopen the line from Buckfastleigh to Totnes (which had closed before his time), as the Dart Valley Railway, a heritage line now known as the South Devon Railway. JOHN BRODRIBB

A train leaving Grimsby bound for Peterborough via the doomed East Lincolnshire line, via Louth and Boston, which has been criticised as one of the most short-sighted of the post-Beeching closures. A section of the route between Ludborough and North Thoresby has been rebuilt as a heritage line. LINCOLNSHIRE WOLDS RAILWAY

The UK rail network
showing closed lines in
red and those surviving
in the late 20th century
in black. NRM

Preserved LMS 'Black Five' 4-6-0 No. 45407 pulls into Kyle of Lochalsh station with the 'North Briton' railtour on August 5, 2006. Beeching recommended this beautiful line for closure, but today, mainland ports for the Isle of Skye are served by two rail lines, the other being the West Highland extension from Fort William to Mallaig which has also warded off closure threats. BRIAN SHARPE

Not only is the North Yorkshire Moors Railway, which occupies a line closed by Beeching, Britain's most popular heritage railway, but it has running rights over the Esk Valley Line, the only one of three routes to Whitby to survive the axe. On June 13, 2014, LNER B1 4-6-0 No. 61264 taking on the identity of scrapped sister No. 61034 *Chiru* stands at Whitby station. ROBIN JONES

Watched by Prince Philip and Scotland's First Minister Nicola Sturgeon, the Queen delivers her short speech at Tweedbank to mark the official opening of the Borders Railway and one of the biggest reversals of a Beeching cut, on September 9, 2016. It was at 5:30pm on the same day that she officially became Britain's longest-serving monarch, overtaking Victoria's record of 23,226 days, 16 hours and around 30 minutes. SCOTRAIL

Western Region 4-6-0 No. 7029 *Clan Castle*, the flagship of the Vintage Trains fleet, stands at Stratford-upon-Avon with a loaded test train on February 27, 2019. Under a new partnership with the West Midlands Rail Executive, the Tyseley-based Train Operating Company will use steam to promote the North Warwickshire line from Birmingham to Stratford, which, now marketed as the Shakespeare Line, twice survived closure attempts in the wake of the Beeching report and is now a vital commuter route. ROBIN JONES

GWR Collett auto tank No. 1453 and trailer W244W moves off from Sharpness with the 4.15pm service to Berkeley Road on September 26, 1964. The Sharpness branch closed to passengers in November 1964 and goods in January 1966, but the line serving Sharpness Docks was retained and is now being revived by enthusiasts as the Vale of Berkeley Railway. HUGH BALLANTYNE

One of the first applications of the new corporate livery was on British Railways ships: the hull was painted blue with a grey superstructure, while the black-topped funnel was red with the symbol in white.

The new corporate symbol, the finished double arrow, represented two-way rail service, and was simple enough to retain its impact when used in a wide range of sizes and materials. Formed of two interlocked arrows, it was nicknamed 'the arrow of indecision'.

However, it would become one of the most successful corporate logos in history, long outliving British Railways and its rebranding as British Rail from January 1, 1965, and is still in use today on road signs indicating the way to stations, station signs themselves, and on printed rail tickets.

The new logotype was drawn to suit modern typography and used the abbreviation British Rail, the brand under which British Railways would henceforth operate.

Most freight rolling stock was not affected by the new colour scheme, with the yellow livery of the road freight transport, together with the recently introduced freight symbol, retained.

The new, smart 'with it' (a classic mid-Sixties phrase) modern uniforms were to be in general use through the network from spring 1966.

By 1966 blue and grey coaches were appearing on steam-hauled trains as well as behind diesel and electric locomotives. The colour was all but universally adopted by the 1970s, with some maroon coaches still awaiting their turn in the paint shops.

Three classes of diesels, the 20s, 25s and the 47s, were still in production when the livery change was decreed. D8178 became the first Class 20 to be outshopped from the start in rail blue as opposed to being repainted in it; D7660 was the first rail blue Class 25 and D1953 the first Class 47. Incidentally one Class 20, D8048, appeared in rail blue livery with the double arrow symbols the wrong way round!

Deteriorating green liveries on many locomotives lasted into the mid-1970s. In November 1978, No. 47256 became the last Class 47 to be repainted into rail blue. Green Class 20s Nos. 20141 and 20147 were not repainted until July 1980 and may have been the last two locomotives to be reliveried.

Another aspect of the strict corporate image policy that marked a major break with that of the past was a ban on naming locomotives.

While the diesels that had been named in the early Sixties were left alone, everything had to have only a number. In 1968, the numbering system was streamlined by the introduction of Total Operations Processing System, or TOPS, a US-developed computer system for managing the locomotives and rolling stock owned by a railway.

Up to the introduction of TOPS, steam locomotives carried numbers up to five digits long, diesels had carried three or four-digit numbers prefixed with the letter D, and electric locomotives with the letter E, meaning that in theory, three locomotives could carry the same number.

TOPS needed similar locomotives to be numbered in a consecutive series so they could be treated together as a group. Under the system the first two or three digits were used to denote the class of locomotive or multiple unit. Locomotives were designated classes 01-98: diesel locomotives 01-70, DC electric locomotives 71-79, AC electric locomotives 80-96, departmental locomotives 97, steam locomotives 98, and British Rail's shipping fleet as Class 99. Around 500 diesel locomotives received TOPS numbers while still wearing green livery.

WAS RAIL BLUE A SUCCESS?

In time, everything was painted blue and grey. That may have been a great success in terms of corporate branding, but how did the general public view the new livery?

It was certainly a livery for the modern age, but was it the best choice of colour? While many were obviously impressed, there were those who felt it lacked warmth and the character of the old 'Big Four' and regional liveries.

For them, rail blue was, and still is, symbolic of an age of mass pruning and rationalisation: the ripping out of the steam era infrastructure and the paring of everything that could be down to the bare bone. Setting aside the many route and station closures under Beeching, what survived was visibly rationalised. The use of diesel multiple units eliminated the need for run-round loops at termini, and many surviving branch lines, which had already lost their goods yards, became little more than long sidings.

One big effect of the Beeching report was the reduction of several double track sections of railway to single tracks, such as the route from Bicester to Princes Risborough, the Kyle of Lochalsh Line from Inverness to Dingwall, and the London & South Western Railway's West of England Main Line west of Salisbury.

There were cases where road building schemes were given priority over railways to the point where routes were singled; a classic example is the Chester to Wrexham General line which has a dual carriageway bridge on the A483 over the railway where space was left for only one track. Such singling led to bottlenecks during the rail traffic resurgence experienced in Britain from the 1980s onwards.

Weeds grew amid the flagstones of platforms left devoid of passengers and track, and where many stations and halts remained in use, their Victorian buildings and expensive-to-maintain wooden canopies were pulled down and replaced with bus shelters, or in several instances no shelters at all. That begged the question — had modern man evolved to the point where, unlike his Victorian forebears, he was prepared to stand outside in all weathers waiting for trains?

British Rail adhered rigidly to the all-in-blue policy until 1976, when a few chinks of light in the wall appeared, with the introduction of the first Inter-City 125 High Speed Train and its modified form of the livery, with yellow from the front extended along the side of each power car, although the coaches retained the usual rail blue coaching stock colours.

Further variants followed, and with the sectorisation of the Eighties, different liveries altogether appeared, such as the Railfreight grey with yellow ends.

Privatisation in the Nineties wiped away rail blue, which is now confined to the heritage sector. Many modern traction enthusiasts who grew up with it adore it: for those who remember what went before, many see the all-pervading blue as a kind of anaesthetic and representative of a regime that purged the railways of everything that went before, regardless of any ill side-effects.

CHAPTER TEN

Beeching's second report and departure from the railways

I N TERMS of eradicating the British Railways financial deficit, Beeching's plan of 1963 failed. By axing nearly a third of the rail network, he achieved savings of just £30 million, yet overall losses were still running in excess of £100 million.

Despite the figures for savings he had promised in his report, as far as the given examples were concerned, the contrary was happening; the fact that loss-making branch lines acted as feeders to the main lines could not be escaped. Indeed, closing branch lines meant less traffic on loss-making main lines, which then became at risk themselves as a result.

Also, while many of the closed lines had recorded only a small operating deficit, they were still recommended for the axe. When it fell on them, the savings their closures contributed was a drop in the ocean to the overall scheme of things.

While the motorway network was expanding, the railway freight network was rapidly receding, with the closure of branch lines and the elimination of the pick-up goods. Rather than lorries taking goods to the nearest railhead for onward transshipment to another freight yard, where they would be collected again by lorry, it was easier, cheaper and far more convenient for a road haulier to do the job from start to finish. With the introduction of containerisation, this job was made easier for lorries. It is highly debatable as to whether Beeching placed sufficient emphasis on this aspect back in 1963.

The problem with sending freight by rail is that the end user ideally should also be rail connected. For instance, one of the biggest volumes of freight on the network comprised coal, taken straight from the mines to stations on every main and branch line, many of which would have a coal merchant based next door. Householders would be able to buy supplies of coal for heating straight from the rail yard.

However, this ceased to be the case when branch lines closed, and the supplier was cut off from rail access to markets. At the same time, coal was increasingly being replaced as a primary source of domestic heating by gas, electricity and oil, and more homes were being built or modernised with central heating. The emergence of natural gas by the Seventies as a mainstream form of domestic heating dealt a crushing blow for coal traffic.

As the railways expanded in the 19th century, heavy industry sprang up alongside rail lines, with goods being shipped in and out of private sidings. However, if the end user was not connected, road would be the only viable alternative. It is easy to ask today why this quarry or that foundry does not use rail, and increase environmental benefits, but it does not automatically make economic sense when the freight has to be offloaded from rail and on to road somewhere down the line.

Similarly, as stated earlier, Beeching appeared to assume that if a branch line was closed, passengers would simply drive to the nearest main line station. Most of them, it seemed, decided not to bother, and instead made the whole journey in their car.

Replacing branch line trains with theoretically more versatile bus services was far from an overwhelming success. Many bus routes were slower and less convenient than the trains they had replaced, while others simply ran between the closed railway stations, offering no advantage over the train.

Many replacement bus services only lasted a few years before they too were withdrawn due to lack of use, leaving large tracts of the countryside without public transport, and forcing people who had previously relied on it to buy cars.

THE TRUNK ROUTE REPORT: WORSE TO COME?

Less well known than The Reshaping of British Railways is The Development of The Major Trunk Routes, published in February 1965 as a follow-on.

Whereas the 1963 report dealt with closing economic lines and streamlining all of the remaining railway services including both passenger and freight for a viable future, the Trunk Route Report was not concerned with commuter services, heavy short-distance flows of mineral traffic or feeder services, but did what its title suggested and concentrated only on the choice of trunk routes to be developed.

It looked 20 years into the future to what traffic flows might be expected to be in 1984, "a period which is considered to mark the limit of a realistic and quantitative appraisal".

In its introduction, the report stressed that it was "not a prelude to precipitate action on a broad front", that is, more wholesale closures.

Instead, it was more of an ideas document, flagging up the potential of each trunk route and deciding how best to concentrate resources.

It stated that there were four principal reasons for the report: "Firstly, so that the selection of trunk routes can be subjected to constructive criticism; secondly, so that the next phase of development expenditure can be well planned; thirdly, so that any future proposals for trunk line closure, or diminutions of line utilisation, can be seen in a broader context; fourthly, so that commercial policies can be properly developed and customers be given a clearer view of the future."

However, while the report itself did not call for closures, Beeching's critics immediately pounced on the indication of around 3000 route miles selected for development.

What would happen to the routes that were not selected? Was this a roundabout way of saying that they would be a candidate for closure in the future? Coming so soon after the 1963 report, those who opposed further closures feared that it was a softening-up exercise, a harbinger of worse to come. Most strikingly when viewed from today's perspective, the routes not selected included the East Coast Main Line from

Newcastle-on-Tyne to Edinburgh. Instead, the Newcastle to Carlisle route was marked as being the preferred option to be developed.

The preferred route to the West Country stopped at Plymouth, not Penzance, sparking fears that Cornwall would be left without any railways at all.

In fairness to the sceptics, several routes marked by thin grey lines as opposed to thick black ones, those indicated for development, did disappear within a few years, and so these fears were proved to be grounded. Again, they included the Waverley Route from Carlisle to Edinburgh, plus the Southern Railway main line from Exeter to Plymouth, the Oxford to Cambridge line, the Great Central line from Nottingham to Marylebone, the Somerset & Dorset main line from Bath Green Park to Bournemouth West and the East Lincolnshire line from Grimsby to Peterborough, which is dealt with by a separate chapter as a case study. Also, Birmingham to Gloucester via Stratford-upon-Avon, in recent times the subject of calls for reopening as a diversionary freight route avoiding the Lickey Incline, was not indicated as a selected route. At the time, British Railways denied that the report was "a prelude to closures on a grand scale".

In short, the report envisaged a reduction of more than 50% in the existing network of 7500 route miles between the main centres of population and industry, by eliminating the duplication of major trunk routes. If this move was implemented, the railway could save £85 million a year on system maintenance and a further £100 million on new locomotives, rolling stock, signalling and other equipment.

Referring to the exclusion of certain lines from the plan for intensive development, the report said that it "does not necessarily mean that they will be abandoned in the foreseeable future, nor even that money will not be spent on some of them to improve their suitability for their continuing purpose.

"It is emphasised that the developed trunk lines will be supported by several thousand miles of freight feeder lines, and that clarification of the position with regard to trunk route development will facilitate decisions about the feeder network.

"It is also emphasised that the provision of capacity for commuter traffic into the main urban areas is the subject of separate consideration."

The report said that a choice had to be made between "an excessive and increasingly uneconomic system, with a corresponding tendency for the railways as a whole to fall into disrepute and decay, or the selective development and intensive utilisation of a more limited trunk route system".

It pointed out that the existing 7500 trunk route miles included 3700 miles of duplicated, 700 miles of triplicated and 700 miles of quadruplicated lines, all built as a result of the days of free competition between the railway companies of pre-Grouping days, with a two-thirds utilisation of the system's capacity.

It was proposed that trains should be grouped according to speed. Coal and minerals would move at an average speed of 35mph, oil and general merchandise at 50mph and passengers at either 50 or 70mph.

Trains of similar speed would be grouped rather than interspersed, and some use would be made of alternative routes for faster and slower trains, but 70% of all trains would travel at 50mph. At the time of the report, the average loading of double-track trunk routes was 40 trains a day each way, and the future loading of such a line might be expected to be between 140 and 200 daily trains.

The routes selected for intensive development would have a surplus capacity of about one third.

The report looked at duplicate routes, and chose what planners considered to be the best one.

For instance, the West Coast Main Line from Euston became the preferred option for traffic between London and Birmingham, London and Manchester/Liverpool, London and Scotland, with the Great Central line and Great Western line from Paddington through High Wycombe and Banbury to Birmingham rejected. History records that the West Coast line was eventually electrified throughout, a move supported by Beeching, the Great Central was axed and the GWR route from Paddington to Birmingham Snow Hill relegated to a secondary route from which any surplus infrastructure was eradicated.

For traffic between London, South Wales and the South West, the selected route was the Great Western line from Paddington through Reading and Swindon, dividing at Wootton Bassett for South Wales via the Severn Tunnel and Bristol via Bath. Rejected were the routes from Paddington through Newbury and Taunton and the Southern line from Waterloo through Basingstoke, Salisbury and Yeovil. Both of these are still with us.

For traffic across the Pennines: selected routes, the line from Leeds to Manchester via Hebden Bridge and the line from Sheffield to Manchester via Woodhead were chosen. Rejected were the lines from Leeds to Manchester via Diggle, from Sheffield to Manchester via the Hope Valley and from Derby to Manchester via the Peak. Interestingly, the Woodhead Route, which had been electrified in 1954 amid a blaze of national publicity, albeit to a non-standard system, was later closed in favour of the Hope Valley route.

A 4% annual increase in the level of trunk-route traffic over the next 20 years — a figure put forward by the National Economic Development Council — was used by the British Railways Board. It was also assumed that no major redistribution of population would take place, while the general spread of industrial activity in 1984 was also predicted to be the same.

The total volume of trunk freight movement was expected to double by 1984, but further falls in rail passenger travel were expected, particularly on stopping services on main lines. "Most of them are grossly underused and hopelessly uneconomic now and are likely to become more so in future because of road improvement and further growth in car ownership," the report said.

Whether the planners of 1964 got it wrong or right in general or specific instances is now a matter for historians. When we sit in judgment on Beeching and his team, however, we must ask — should British Railways have sat back and watched losses mount in the face of competition from a popular and more versatile form of transport to the point where the taxpayer would have demanded wholesale closures, or should they have taken reasonable steps to plan for the future as best they could from the data available in their time?

Yes, mistakes were made, but the overall goal was not to close the rail network down, but to transform it into one which could compete in a world of motor transport, offering clear advantages over the lorry, car and bus where it still could. The report said that air travel would hamper growth in long-distance passenger services, and that the railways did not expect to compete with the private car over distances of less than 100 miles where "the railways could not expect to retain a great part of this traffic by fare reductions".

Concentration on the provision of bulk transport over routes of heavy demand and over medium to long distances with frequent services at high speeds and a high standard of comfort was considered the answer to keeping fares at a competitive level. It was also expected that the railway's share of inter-city passenger traffic would fall by 1984.

"The railways must reshape and redeploy their assets and service, so as to concentrate on cheap bulk movement, if their decline is to be arrested and reversed," the report said.

The cost of providing the railway track and signalling per unit of traffic passing over it must be reduced to a level which enables services to be provided on a competitive basis, it was argued. The opportunity existed for expansion of the carriage of merchandise, oil and iron and steel, but only if such services were efficient and competitive. If such changes were made, then freight carriage could increase and the overall demand for rail transport over the trunk routes could show a considerable increase by 1984, even if passenger numbers fell off.

"If the railways concentrate on cheap bulk movement, their prospects as trunk carriers can be revived. The danger is that failure to change, to modernise and to concentrate, will cause the present decline to continue," the report said.

Progress in rail technology such as signalling would lead to greater efficiencies, but while the 1964 network of through routes was already under-utilised, the disparity between capacity and use would certainly increase, the report said. Greater utilisation of particular routes would also reduce the costs of sidings, stations and depots and materially increase the utilisation of motive power, train crews and staff.

Beeching knew that further rationalisation of the system would arouse widespread opposition, but felt it was the correct, if not the only way, forward.

"The real choice is between an excessive and increasingly uneconomic system, with a corresponding tendency for the railways as a whole to fall into disrepute and decay, or the selective development and intensive utilisation of a more limited trunk route system," the report said.

Regarding the indicated preference for the Newcastle-Carlisle route over the East Coast Main Line north of Newcastle, John Edser said: "I don't know why — that's the honest answer. Even we thought it was not a goer. I certainly found it peculiar."

FAREWELL TO THE DOCTOR — BUT
WAS HE 'STRUCK OFF'?

Two months before the Trunk Route Report appeared, it was announced in the House of Commons by Minister of Transport Tom Fraser that Dr Beeching was to leave British Railways the following May 31 and return to ICI, from which he had been seconded for a set period of time.

Accordingly, it would be left to others to develop and continue the reshaping work that he had started.

It has never been made clear as to whether Beeching went back to ICI as a director earlier than expected of his own accord, or if he had been pushed. He had always intended to return to ICI in rather less than the five years permitted by his contract.

In November 1965, Minister of Technology Frank Cousins told the House of Commons that Dr Beeching had been sacked by the government. Beeching, who in 1965 was rewarded for his years of public service by being made a life peer as Baron Beeching of East Grinstead in the Queen's Birthday Honours List, denied that he had been dismissed and had returned to ICI of his own volition.

The move surprised many, for in the months prior to the Fraser announcement, there had been widespread speculation that Beeching would accept a government offer to head a new board responsible for the coordination and integration of Britain's road and rail networks.

In 1964, Beeching had stated on several occasions that the true costs of carrying freight by road and rail should be determined as firmly as possible. He was backed up by statistics which showed that while the rail network was underutilised, road freight transport was not paying its full share towards the costs of the trunk roads it used.

Once the cost of each type of transport was established, then it would be possible to work out which was the best combination of both to provide the best service at minimum true cost. However, the rail unions were still smarting at the effects of the 1963 report, while road hauliers

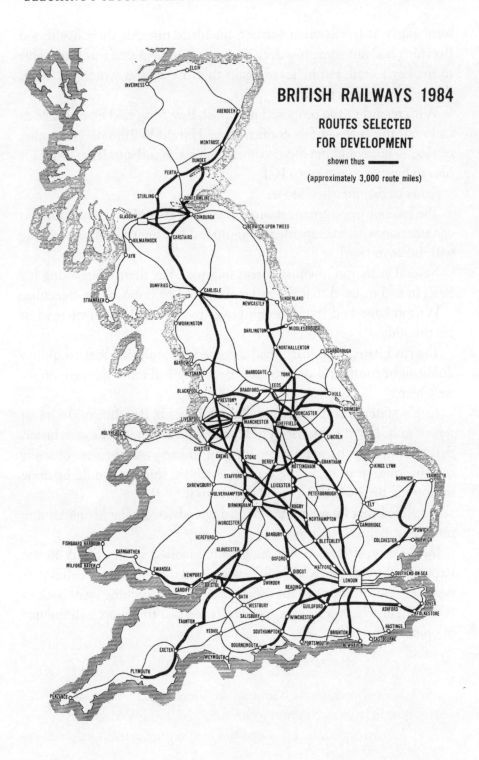

BRITISH RAILWAYS 1984

ROUTES SELECTED
FOR DEVELOPMENT

shown thus ▬▬▬▬

(approximately 3,000 route miles)

were angry at the axeman turning his blade towards their livelihood. Beeching had not come to a decision on the problem that was favourable to road or to rail, but believed again that the answer would be found through an in-depth study.

With regard to the proposed new post, Beeching said he was able to carry out the task — a fact confirmed by Harold Wilson on November 13, 1964 — but could devote no more than six months to it, in order for him to be able to return to ICI.

A major dispute then arose.

The Labour government wanted Beeching to undertake his study in conjunction with management and unions, but he insisted on working with his own team.

Several visits to Downing Street followed, but then Wilson dug his heels in and insisted that the assessors would be imposed on Beeching.

Wilson later said that Beeching was too pro-rail and anti-road in his thinking.

The road haulage industry had a powerful union side that would no doubt fight tooth and nail to stop Beeching inflicting damage on its well-being.

In his statement, Fraser said: "Since it is Dr Beeching's desire to return to ICI by the middle of next year, I have come to the conclusion that it would not be practicable for him to carry out the sort of study the government want, in the way in which we think it should be done, during the time which he could devote to it."

He added that he welcomed Beeching's advice during his remaining months at British Railways.

John Edser, who was only marginally involved in the Trunk Route Report as the closures were in full swing, said that he and his colleagues were never informed as to the exact reasons why Beeching went back to ICI early, or whether he was sacked. "It seemed to be just a difference of opinion," he said.

CHAPTER ELEVEN

Beeching's double freight success

D ESPITE THE criticism of the Beeching cuts that continue to this
day, the British Railways chairman has by way of contrast been
credited for doing much to haul freight carriage by rail into the
modern age.

Until well into nationalisation, freight not passenger journeys was
the principal revenue earner on Britain's railways.

Indeed, the first locomotive to be demonstrated in public by Richard
Trevithick in 1804 hauled a freight train. Again, the bulk carriage of raw
materials to and from the principal manufacturing regions and ports was
a primary factor in the decision to build Britain's first steam railways.

Freight trains and wagons manifested themselves in all shapes and
sizes, from the lengthy coal and iron ore trains to private owner wagons
with their firms' names emblazoned on the side to provide free advertising.

Up to the First World War, railways had an effective monopoly on
the transport of goods. By that time, the railway network had more
or less reached its maximum extent, and there were very few sizeable
settlements not connected to, or in reach of, a railway.

The thousands of stations formed a countrywide network for the movement of goods big and small, from parcels to deliveries of coal to the local merchant whose premises would be next to the goods yard, and the livestock of whole farms could be moved hundreds of miles from one place to another.

The pick-up goods became part and parcel of everyday life. A locomotive would trundle along a branch line with a mixed rake of wagons, maybe a milk tanker, a coal wagon or two, a cattle truck and box vans for sundry goods. At every station it would stop, uncouple and shunt a wagon on or off the train into or out of a goods siding. At bigger stations, a shunting locomotive would be in steam to do the job. Signalmen would be needed to control the short train movements and porters would be on hand to load and unload the wagons. There would also be a parcels office, and deliverymen waiting to take the goods on to their destination by road. Very, very labour intensive.

In the days of horses and carts, the ability to transfer goods to and from trains for rapid onward shipment was obviously a major advance over what had gone before.

However, once the horse and cart became superseded by a vastly more effective form of transport on the roads, chinks in the railways' monopoly appeared.

After the First World War, when a vast amount of army surplus lorries and vans appeared on the market, entrepreneurs began setting up their own freight haulage business, on a local level at first, but then spreading out further.

Eventually, the effectiveness of motor transport would pose the question — why take your goods to the local railways parcels office, go to the trouble of transferring them to the train, and then have to pay to have someone collect them at the other end, when a van or lorry can do the whole journey door to door, and often for a cheaper price?

To fulfil their legal obligation as a common carrier, the railways had to offer a collection and delivery service, even for small items, and found that they could not compete with private road haulage.

At nationalisation in 1948, British Railways inherited more than a million wagons, many of them small wooden-bodied affairs showing their age and lacking even vacuum brakes. The state-of-the-art technology at the time was a mountain of paperwork detailing every customer and every freight movement.

The aforementioned 1955 ASLEF strike proved a turning point in the minds of customers. They found they could survive without sending freight by rail, and after the dispute was settled, stuck with road transport, which offered door-to-door delivery at very competitive prices.

The pick-up goods system largely depended on the existence of a network with a vast system of branch lines, and a government willing to subsidise it with increasing amounts of taxpayers' money. As more and more branch lines were closed in the Fifties, more local freight had to go by road.

When passenger lines were closed, many people in British Railways thought that the passengers would simply get in their cars and drive to the next nearest station. They didn't — they drove the entire journey by themselves. Much the same trend occurred with freight.

In 1961, when Beeching was appointed, freight excluding parcels and mail was making an annual loss of £12.9 million. Taking on board the freight sector's fair share of overheads from the operation of the network, this figure would rise to £76 million. The Beeching report showed that it would be possible to close half of the freight stations and lose only 3% of gross receipts. He spelled it out bluntly. It was costing far more to run these stations than the railway could ever hope to recoup from freight.

That year, the carriage of general goods and sundries made a loss of more than £75 million. No private company could hope to absorb such losses, and there were those in government who held the view that the taxpayer should not have to foot the bill either. The writing had been on the wall for services such as pick-up goods long before Beeching came, and as road transport took more and more of the railway's freight traffic away in the late Fifties, all that was left was bulk haul traffic.

Another problem was the sprawling marshalling yards which delayed the sorting of wagons for onward shipment.

In the Fifties, the Chesapeake & Ohio Railroad had come up with the concept of the 'Roadrailer', a vehicle which could carry freight on both road and rail. In Britain, an experimental train of Roadrailers was built in 1960 and trialled on the Eastern Region, but it never entered revenue-earning service.

It did, however, sow the seeds for one of Beeching's greatest triumphs, the Freightliner system.

THE RISE OF THE CONTAINER

From Beeching's time onwards, the movement of bulk freight would slowly but surely come to be dominated both in Britain and elsewhere in the world by containerisation.

The basic principle is the loading of goods into a container in which they can be carried on various forms of transport, road, rail and ship, without having to transfer the freight laboriously from one to another.

The concept dates back to the days of horse-drawn tramways: in 1795, Benjamin Outram opened the Little Eaton Gangway which carried coal in containers on wagons. The containers could be transferred from the railway to the adjacent Derby Canal.

The Liverpool & Manchester Railway had wagons carrying four timber boxes which carried coal from the Lancashire collieries to Liverpool, where they were transferred to horse-drawn carts by crane. It is said that Richard Trevithick contemplated the idea of using containers on ships.

By the start of the 20th century, many railways were using closed container boxes for transfer between road and rail. In the Twenties, the size of such containers was standardised by the Railway Clearing House.

RCH containers were five or 10 feet long and made of wood, but could not be stacked. Early containers, both the RCH standard van and open containers and the later demountable tank containers, were handled at the goods yard using the standard hand-powered yard crane or in larger yards by small mobile cranes.

The RCH standard 'van' containers had lifting rings on the roof, attached to side straps leading down to the floor. The RCH open containers and the demountable tank containers had lifting rings fitted to their upper sides. These containers were lifted using a heavy ring with four chains attached. Small hooks on the ends of the chains were fitted into the lifting rings on the container and the big ring was then slipped on to the crane hook itself for the lift.

On the east coast of the US, in 1929 Seatrain Lines began carrying boxcars on its ships plying between New York and Cuba. In the Thirties, the Chicago Great Western Railway began transporting road freight trailers on flat wagons in 'piggy back' fashion, and by 1955, around 25 railroads had followed suit.

That year, former trucking company owner Malcom McLean and engineer Keith Tantlinger developed the modern intermodal container. It was not an original idea as such; during the Second World War, the US Army had used containers to speed up the loading and unloading of transport ships. However, the new challenge was to develop a container that could be carried by rail and transported securely on ships.

British Railways had looked at container trains before Beeching, but did not take the subject seriously until 1963. Yes, Beeching saw the urgent need to cut out the dead wood and eradicate freight services which would never make a profit, but at the same time, he did not want to prune railways merely to boost the more versatile road traffic, but to identify areas in which the railways could do a more efficient job with bulk loads and compete once more.

Gone were to be the slow and costly pick-up goods on rural branches. Instead, the primary image of rail freight would be liner trains carrying containers and travelling across the country at the speed of express passenger trains.

Shildon wagon works began building a prototype liner train in October 1964; Beeching had originally intended the first container train services to be running by the end of that year. At this point, the unions intervened. The National Union of Railwaymen objected to the liner trains on the grounds that private hauliers would be able to collect and deliver freight at the proposed new terminals.

A working compromise allowed test runs to be carried out with trains carrying empty boxes in summer 1965.

Then the unions raised the issue about guards. A container train did not need a guard's van, and British Railways planned to have the guard sitting in the rear cab of the diesel or electric locomotive pulling it. The unions refused, and at first won the day.

As a result, the first liner trains ran with a guards van either coupled behind the locomotive or in the traditional place at the back of the train. To reach a solution, British Railways even modified a 10ft container to turn into a guard's brake to be carried on the last wagon. In trials the occupants had a bumpy ride and were even injured when flung across the container when the train took curves at speed. It was then agreed that the guards could travel in the rear locomotive cab as originally intended.

THE DAWN OF FREIGHTLINER

The first tests of liner trains carrying revenue-earning loads took place on November 15, 1965. Up to the last minute, the National Union of Railwaymen was still arguing the point about the private hauliers, and it was agreed that during these trial runs, only railway hauliers would be allowed to operate inside the terminals.

The first train left London's Maiden Lane terminal at 8.05pm for the 391-mile trip to Glasgow's Gushetfaulds depot. Hauled by a Class 47 diesel, it comprised 13 Freightliner wagons with 39 containers, and a dynamometer car to record the results.

It marked the start both of two weeks of experimental running and of Freightliner. It seemed from the outset that here was a winner. One train covered the journey 51 minutes ahead of time. With feats like this, it was found to be easy to deliver the goods to customers by 6am the next day.

The first week saw just 30 containers of commercial traffic carried, with TVs, cookers, washing machines, food and beer on board.

The service quickly expanded. In 1966, 27,000 containers were carried. By 1969, this had risen to 400,000.

Special handling equipment had to be installed in the new Freightliner terminals. Fourteen US-designed Drott Travelift Portable cranes were initially bought, but were superseded by Loughborough-built Portal electric rail-mounted cranes once traffic had soared.

On October 31, the King's Cross to Aberdeen Freightliner became the first to run over the East Coast Main Line. The following year, a Stratford to Sheffield service began. In 1967, a service from London to Belfast and one from King's Cross to Felixstowe was launched.

Transport Minister Barbara Castle officially opened the first Welsh terminal in Cardiff on June 8, 1967.

August 1967 saw the Royal Family use Freightliner to shift their luggage and office equipment to Balmoral in a single container. The same month saw a record 700 tons of steel carried on the South Wales to London steel Freightliner, serving the Fords of Dagenham and Vauxhall plant in Luton among other customers.

At first, British Railways concentrated on liner trains to service the needs of the domestic market, and ignored the potential worldwide market. The first containers were therefore 8ft tall, complying with Britain's loading gauge which is smaller than that of many other countries.

However, once Freightliner considered the burgeoning global market, the size of the containers was increased to 8ft 6in tall from 1966. The idea was that containers worldwide should be of the same size so that they could be carried on any railway, regardless of its track or loading gauge, making them totally interchangeable.

The first of two 4000-ton container ships, *Sea Freightliner I*, was launched at South Shields on December 2, 1967, for use on high-capacity services between Harwich and Zeebrugge. A second, *Sea Freightliner II*, followed on March 15, 1968. More were to follow.

In 1968, the Geneva-based International Organisation for Standardisation published its standards for containers. To accommodate the higher boxes, British Rail had to spend millions on extending clearances on its Freightliner network. That year, livestock was carried by Freightliner for the first time, when 48 cattle were taken from King's Cross to Aberdeen.

Freightliner offered customers a highly developed complete transport system, with large capacity containers, specially designed wagons and new transfer equipment providing low cost, express freight train services between exclusive road-rail terminals.

It combined the advantages of rail trunk movement over medium to long distances with the flexibility of road transport for door-to-door distribution.

As a 'best of both worlds' package, it was Beeching's solution to the demand for improved transport of general merchandise traffic.

British Rail's marketing described Freightliner as "a high-speed conveyor belt over the trunk routes of Great Britain" which provided "in every respect the essential qualities of economy, reliability, speed and safety with the advantages of lower charges, faster trains, all-weather reliability, security and protection from damage and door-to-door service".

In May 1968, Freightliner weekly container loadings rose above 5000 for the first time. By 1970, the Freightliner network was all but complete, with 23 depots in Britain and one in Dublin, and Freightliner was by now taking deep sea containerisation seriously. By the following year, it was moving 100,000 TEUs, Twenty Foot Equivalent Units, the standard measurement for containers, of deep sea traffic. This helped Freightliner record its first profit in 1971.

One of the most profitable Freightliner terminals was set up at Dudley, on the site of the old Dudley Town station from which passenger services had been withdrawn under Beeching. Down the road in Birmingham was one of the least profitable, Birmingham Lawley Street. Bizarrely, in 1989, after eight years of trying, Freightliner closed Dudley down in favour of Birmingham.

Privatisation affected Freightliner like all parts of British Rail. In 1995 it was bought out by its own management as a stand-alone company.

In 1999, it set up its Freightliner Heavy Haul arm alongside its established container operation. Heavy Haul began by running railway infrastructure trains moving ballast and track materials but later expanded into other bulk loads including cement, coal, aggregates, specialist minerals, waste and scrap metal. Heavy Haul became a limited company in 2001.

Freightliner, now Freightliner Group Limited, then set up two more subsidiaries — Freightliner Maintenance Limited, to concentrate on the repair and maintenance of traction and rolling stock, and Freightliner PL Sp. z o.o., which began operations in Poland in 2007, when the state railway system passed out of government control. The Polish subsidiary was set up to deal with high volumes of coal traffic, mainly in the Gdansk-Warsaw corridor and southern Poland.

The Freightliner Group Ltd was in 2008 bought by Arcapita, a holding and real estate company based in Atlanta, Georgia, which is in turn owned by the Bahrain-based Arcapita Bank.

In 2008 the new owner decided to expand into Australia, and set up Freightliner Australia Pty Ltd, which began hauling bulk cotton in New South Wales in July 2009, and later expanded to exporting coal in the Hunter Valley.

A worldwide success story indeed, and one that grew out of Beeching's determination to make rail freight pay once more, despite the dominance of road transport.

John Edser explained: "Beeching had said that the movement of easily handleable things over long distance at high speed was something that the railways do well.

"It was developed to run at 75mph from the start. Back in the Sixties, that was unheard of. He obviously saw that this would be a good thing for rail freight and he was right.

"It was for trunk haul only between major centres. Beeching realised that one of the things about rail freight was transfer costs, either at either end or in the middle. You cannot avoid them unless you run private siding to private siding.

"It was Beeching who had the germ of the idea, but it was the Central Planning Unit that developed it at Freightliner.

"It was going on at the same time as the Beeching closures, in the Freight Operating Section which was completely separate from the one in which I worked.

"When Freightliner started, it was the beginning of the world container revolution in worldwide shipping. It started in America in the late Fifties, and so many people saw the potential worldwide.

"It was like Topsy, it grew and grew. It not only spread over the British system but it spread over the world."

John is justifiably proud of the fact that unlike many previous forms of rail freight workings, Freightliner has been able to adapt to the changing needs of the market.

He said: "One of the big things that affected rail freight was the rise of the out-of-town business park because there were no rail connections, and the business carried on there was more high tech or complex and did not need bulk supplies.

"But Asda and Tesco are now using Freightliner as part of the supply chain.

"This is years away from Beeching, but it goes to show how change in the logistics industry has worked."

John Edser wondered if the Great Central line which, as we saw in Chapter 6, was among the major trunk routes closed on Beeching's recommendations, might have been saved if Freightliner had got off the ground earlier.

"The problem was that until lots of ports had facilities for containers, it was a limited market.

"We didn't suddenly say 'yes, we have a Freightliner network that is running all over the country running 300 trains a day'.

"The fact is that over the last 40 or 50 years it has taken off as the way to send things round the world.

"Whether a use could have been found for the Great Central depended on how quickly the Freightliner network would have grown."

The Great Central route, as a backbone of England linking London to major manufacturing towns, and having less traffic than other routes, might well have found a second life as a freight artery. Sadly, it was not to be.

ON THE MERRY-GO-ROUND

The second big freight innovation of the Beeching era was the merry-go-round coal train. Known as MGRs, they are permanently assembled block trains of hopper wagons which can both load and unload while moving at low speed. The basic concept was that the wagons could operate in a non-stop loop from collieries to power stations, without stopping or shunting, on specially designed track layouts.

Intended to deliver bulk loads of coal to power stations, the merry-go-round system was drawn up with the aid of investment from the Central Electricity Generating Board and the National Coal Board into new power stations capable of accepting the trains and loading facilities.

Under Beeching, British Railways designed an all-new wagon with air brakes and a capacity for 32 tons of pulverised coal. The prototypes were two 32-ton units built at Darlington and tested in 1964, after which several large batches were constructed at the nearby Shildon wagon works. Ashford Works also built one small batch of 160 wagons in 1965. The wagons were fitted with continuous air brakes and ran on roller bearings.

Eventually more than 110,000 were built. They comprised the largest fleet of air-braked wagons built for British Railways.

The merry-go-round train locomotives were fitted with Slow Speed Control, a type of electronic speed control which enabled the driver to engage the system so that the train could proceed at a fixed very slow speed under the loading and unloading facilities. The system was originally fitted to some Class 20s, Class 26s and Class 47s. Some Class 37s and all Class 50s later had the equipment fitted, as did all members of classes 56, 58, 59, 60 and most recently, 66.

The merry-go-round system was tested at West Burton Power Station in Nottinghamshire, but the first deliveries of coal using the system were made to the then-new Cockenzie Power Station near Edinburgh in 1966.

It was estimated at the time that the 80 MGR hoppers needed to supply Cockenzie would replace up to 1500 conventional wagons: Beeching set out to provide a leaner, more streamlined and efficient railway, and here was the proof of his intentions.

Cockenzie was built to use around three million tons of coal a year in order to generate 1.2 gigawatts. The first coal supplies went to the station from a 3125-ton bunker at the National Coal Board's then-new Monktonhall Colliery between Dalkeith and Musselburgh.

It later took supplies from Bilston Glen Colliery and the Newbattle Preparation Plant, also in the Lothians coalfield.

At the colliery, the trains ran underneath the coal bunker, from which hoppers filled five wagons simultaneously, each with exactly 32 tons of coal, in 60 seconds.

Loading was wholly automated, with a single operator at a console controlling the delivery into wagons from the 88ft-high bunker.

A system of colour-light signals required the driver to stop his train within six inches of predetermined marks.

On arrival at the power station, the trains run at an automatically regulated speed of half-a-mile an hour over hoppers into which the coal is dropped without the train stopping. Door-opening levers and safety devices on the wagons are operated by lineside devices.

The Cockenzie trains of 1966 consisted of 28 wagons each and made five round trips a day over the six miles between Monktonhall and the power station. In one day, the train had a capacity to move 4500 tons.

Back in the steam age, large numbers of sidings were required both at the pithead and at the power station. In an operation of the scale of that at Monktonhall, at least 250 acres of shunting sidings would be needed. However, with the MGR system, only four acres were required.

Power stations built to handle the new MGR traffic were Aberthaw, Drax, Didcot, Eggborough, Fiddlers Ferry and Ratcliffe. Many of the older power stations were eventually converted to MGR operation.

Once in regular service, MGR trains were operated in rakes of up to 35 wagons, mainly hauled by Class 47 diesels. The Class 56 diesels were designed with these services in mind and took over most of them from 1976 onwards, later being joined by Class 58s and 60s.

The decline in the British mining industry from the Eighties onwards made many of these wagons redundant.

The automatic door opening and closing equipment located on the approach to and from the bunker in the power station became nick-named 'Daleks'. New wagon types introduced since privatisation have increased tonnage and have air-operated doors that have exterminated the need for such release mechanisms.

John Edser said: "Beeching is always regarded as being concerned with passenger trains, but we owe both Freightliner and merry-go-round to him.

"People did not see the freight revolution he undertook because they were more concerned as to whether their local passenger service survived or not, not the fact that suddenly the rattle of a train of 16 21-ton coal wagons rumbling by was to be replaced by 25 45-ton hoppers.

"Merry-go-round was also a big environmental gain, although people didn't see it in those terms at the time.

"Not all the power stations could take it. At the start of MGR, if you could count collieries on the fingers of one hand which could take MGR, you were lucky.

"It took an enormous investment on the NCB side as well as British Railways. There was an advantage to both, but if you had been to a pre-MGR colliery, the screens were low and the curves were tight. On some of them you couldn't have pushed an MGR train through even with the screen at the proper height because there was not enough line out the back."

CHAPTER TWELVE

Rethinking Britain's rail strategy

Beeching was replaced as chairman of British Railways by a figure from within the rail industry, at the much lower salary of £12,000. Stanley Raymond had joined the Western Region as divisional manager in 1962 and had impressed with his hard work to reduce soaring losses.

In a paper read to the Institute of Transport in spring 1966, Raymond said: "The problem is to decide how essential and how convenient, and what are the rules under which the railway services are to be provided."

With regard to Beeching's Trunk Route Report, he said that since its publication, a detailed examination had been made of the feeder services that would be required to sustain the proposed 3000-mile trunk route system and this, together with a reconsideration of some of the original proposals in the 1963 report, would add up to 9000 route miles which, along with the commuter services which needed separate consideration, would form the framework of the modern railway which the British Railways Board "now believes should be developed in the national interest".

While he far from condemned the Beeching closures, it became apparent that it was now seen that the steamroller set in motion by the doctor should stop.

Stanley Raymond said: "It seems clear that substantial sections of the nation are not ready to face up to the consequences of the streamlining of the railways to the full extent required by present legislation to enable the railways to eliminate their deficit. While the stage of saying 'this is the end of closures' can never be reached, because of the rapidly changing industrial scene and technological advance, it is feasible to establish a watershed and show a network of routes, services and facilities that substantially should remain for the foreseeable future.

"Such a network might involve closing 2000 or so route miles over which passenger services now operate, most of which has already been announced, and a further 1500 or so miles which carry freight traffic only. This would leave the 11,000/12,000 route miles of trunk and feeder lines already referred to.

"This network would be much greater than the 8000 route miles which, at one time, were in mind."

He echoed Beeching when he said that to the maximum extent possible, stopping passenger services would be removed from the main lines enabling the railways to concentrate on the operation of through and limited-stop fast passenger services between main centres of industry and population. "Fast and reliable freight services would be operated over this new streamlined network to link all main industrial areas and ports and give proper road/rail interchange facilities," he said.

Talking about urban commuter lines, he said that passenger services within the principal conurbation areas of London and the South East, Manchester, Liverpool, Glasgow, Birmingham, Tyneside and Teesside, West Yorkshire and Cardiff performed a unique function for the community. "It is now generally accepted throughout the world that suburban operations of this kind cannot be performed profitably on a commercial basis," he said. "Nor is there any form of transport yet devised to replace the function of the suburban railway services.

"The great transport issue today is not the old one of road v rail, but the new one of public transport v private transport, and what is the level of public transport which the nation requires and is prepared to pay for?

But a balance must soon be struck and decisions made as to the future size and shape of the railway system so as to give a degree of stability to the industry and allow railway management to concentrate more on their prime task of running trains and providing a service."

He said that the changes and service cuts made under Beeching "were essential to sweep away the clutter of the past so that clear decisions can be made for the future".

But again, he reiterated that it was now time to bring the rail closures to an end and determine what railway network should be set in stone, even if it meant subsidising lines for social reasons.

"We are now rapidly approaching a watershed and it will be in the best interests of the nation and of the industry if that watershed is determined, the remaining doubtful services eliminated, and energies devoted to making the substantial system that remains efficient and a national asset.

"But it must be emphasised that the system outlined will still have the capacity to provide a large element of standby transport for the users of private transport when it suits their convenience. This standby transport capacity will have to be paid for. It is essential that the preoccupation with the deficit and the administrative and planning work connected with the reshaping and streamlining should not monopolise the efforts of management."

THE BARBARA CASTLE YEARS

On December 23, 1965, Barbara Castle was appointed as transport minister. She became famous for introducing the breathalyser to tackle the rising problem of drink-driving, and also made the 70mph motorway speed limit permanent. She was behind legislation that ruled that all cars had to be fitted with seat belts.

Furthermore, she oversaw the closure of around 2050 miles of railway lines both under the Beeching plan and also routes that the doctor had not prescribed, such as Buxton to Matlock, and so her appointment was in that respect far from a U-turn. However, under her 1968 Transport Act, she importantly introduced a new social factor into legislation regarding such closures, and a further 3500 miles were given the possibility of a reprieve.

Castle recognised that while many services earmarked for closure were unremunerative, they nonetheless played a vital social role and if they closed, the communities they served would suffer hardship.

Her first role in the government had been as the first minister for overseas development, and she was only the fourth woman in history ever to hold a position in a British cabinet. She had hoped to win a bigger seat in the Cabinet, and at first did not want the transport portfolio (she could not even drive) but Wilson told her that he needed a 'tiger in the tank' in that department, quoting the Esso petrol advertising slogan of the day.

However, once appointed, she quickly warmed to the challenge.

While realising that the car was now king and would stay so, she wanted to see a new integrated transport policy that not only accepted that fact but would breathe new life into public transport, particularly in urban areas where congestion was making its mark. That would have to include, as Stanley Raymond had stated following the departure of Beeching, subsidies to commuter lines.

She said: "I refused to be a King Canute trying to force people on to railways which could not take them where they wanted to go.

"If the private car had brought the boon of mobility to millions of people, which it clearly had, then that boon should be available to everyone. We must collectively face the consequences and deal with them through new arrangements which reflected the new facts."

Despite some successes of modernisation such as the Freightliner container trains, British Rail could not make its still-enormous freight system pay its way, when faced with stiffening competition from lorry transport.

Castle tried to introduce balance by having road hauliers soak up more of the expense they imposed on the roads. She also improved road haulage safety standards, by introducing the tachograph which limited drivers' daily hours, a move by which the left-winger aroused deep anger from the trade unions.

A new National Freight Corporation would encompass Freightliner and British Rail's remaining road freight services to create a streamlined competitive single unit, again provoking the fury of the Transport & General Workers Union.

While railway closures rolled on at a very high rate, she saved several individual routes including branch lines: York to Harrogate, Manchester to Buxton, Oxenholme to Windermere, Exeter to Exmouth and in Cornwall, the Looe branch and the St Ives line.

With regard to the latter two, Barbara Castle called Beeching's plans 'slaughter of the innocents' and described St Erth to St Ives as the most beautiful coastal journey in the country.

The Looe branch was saved because of the difficult winding roads serving the resort. Mrs Castle said: "In spite of the financial savings to the railways, it just wouldn't have made sense in the wider context to have transferred heavy holiday traffic on to the roads which couldn't cope with it.

"Nor would extensive and expensive road improvements have been the answer. At St Ives, these would have involved destroying the whole character of the town. At Looe, they could not have avoided long delays in the holiday season. It would have been the economics of Bedlam to spend vast sums only to create greater inconvenience."

In a similar vein, part of the Bere Alston to Callington branch was saved, because of the hilly terrain at the point where the rivers Tamar and Tavy meet and the circuitous road routes. The branch was truncated at Gunnislake, and the section of the Southern Railway's Plymouth-Exeter main line which was lifted in 1968 was retained as far north as Bere Alston. A new station was built at Gunnislake in 1994.

She also spared Hope and Edale stations on the Manchester-Chinley-Sheffield line, which served in the Peak District National Park. However, at the same time, she allowed the controversial closure of the Buxton-Matlock route to passengers: since the early Seventies, revivalists under the banner of Peak Rail have been trying to rebuild it.

As minister, Barbara Castle tackled the problem of financing the railways, and wrote off more than a billion pounds of British Rail's debt, something while Marples did not do and which Beeching could not. She introduced the means by which both national and regional government would be able to subsidise loss-making parts of the network that nonetheless provided wider social and economic benefits.

Section 39 of the 1968 Act introduced the first government subsidies for such lines. Grants could be paid where three conditions were met.

Firstly, the line had to be unremunerative. Secondly, it was desirable for social or economic reasons for the passenger services to continue, and thirdly, it was financially unreasonable to expect British Rail to provide those services without a grant.

The Act saved several branch lines from closure, but some, like the aforementioned Waverley Route and the Barnstaple-Ilfracombe line, still did not qualify under criteria and were axed as Beeching intended. Indeed, the Varsity Line that linked the university cities of Oxford and Cambridge saw services withdrawn from the Oxford-Bletchley section and the Bedford-Cambridge section at the end of 1967, even though the line had not been listed for closure in Beeching's 1963 report.

By the time the 1968 Transport Act had been passed, many lines and services and railway lines that would have qualified for subsidies had already been closed, making it a case of shutting the stable door after the horse had bolted.

While this approach was a marked change from the Beeching report of 1963, in fairness the doctor had never been given a social factor remit of this type, and had been told to make whatever moves he saw fit on a financial basis to eliminate the railways' rapidly worsening deficit. From that viewpoint, it might be considered unfair to criticise Beeching's findings in themselves, as opposed to the implementation of them by Marples.

Castle's approach to subsidising railways has continued to this day.

Yet it was not only railways that were by now suffering financially. The remaining private bus companies, some of which had put the branch lines out of business, were also struggling against rising car ownership. The 1968 Act placed more of the national bus network under the National Bus Company, formed from January 1, 1969, by merging the bus operating companies of the government-owned Transport Holding Company with those of the privately owned British Electric Traction Company Limited, a large nationwide conglomerate, while fuel subsidies were increased and a fleet replacement grant introduced. Licensing for mini-buses was eased and a rural bus grant introduced.

For the cities, the Act legislated for integrated public transport networks to be set up: the Greater London Council would take over London Transport and elsewhere, new Passenger Transport Executives would be set up. These would have wide-ranging powers to integrate local road and rail services, running local buses and harmonising with British Rail on commuter fares and services.

The Marples-era weighting towards road building was eradicated with the capital grant regime adjusted so that public transport, as well as roads projects, could benefit from 75% capital grants. It was not just railways facing route closures in the Sixties. Their predecessors, the canals, were also being prepared for mass pruning.

As a point of clarification, it is often assumed that railways killed off the canals. This was certainly true in some cases, but the inland waterway network lived on alongside the railways until well into the 20th century.

It was the big freeze of 1962/63 which by and large sounded the death knell for large-scale freight traffic on canals, when barges were left frozen into position for several weeks.

In 1967, the government wanted to close canals to save money, but Barbara Castle managed to stave off the threat. She kept closures on the 1400-mile network to a minimum while reclassifying canals into commercial and leisure categories, recognising that pleasure boating was on the up. She said that her approach promised new hope for those who love and use our canals, whether for cruising, angling or just walking on the towpath, or who want to see stretches of canal in some of our unlovely built-up areas, developed as centres of beauty or fun.

Both the Conservative opposition and trade unions fought hard against the bill for the 1968 Act, with Enoch Powell even telling the House of Commons that it was "evil".

Despite around 2500 amendments and a record 45 committee sittings, Castle refused to water down her proposals, and her stance made her, according to opinion polls, the most popular minister in Wilson's government, which for various reasons had by then lost much favour with the public.

REDRAWING THE RAILWAY NETWORK

With the railway network, virtually all of the system is based on lines built in the 19th century, mostly between the 1830s and 1860s, when the economic make-up of the country was very different.

The early trunk routes stood the test of time because they linked conurbations. The first inter-city line was George Stephenson's Liverpool to Manchester Railway. There followed the Grand Junction Railway linking it to Birmingham, engineered by his one-time protégé Joseph Locke, and the London & Birmingham Railway, built by Stephenson's son Robert. Isambard Kingdom Brunel joined in with his Great Western Railway from London to Bristol. Such routes were wholly logical and have easily stood the test of time: none were included in the Beeching report.

At the opposite extreme are railways built for a particular purpose which has long since disappeared. A classic case is County Durham, which is criss-crossed by so many defunct routes that had been built to exploit the local mineral wealth. When the mineral resources became exhausted, the mines closed and the branch line serving it was no longer needed for freight, so passenger services quickly evaporated.

The great trans-Pennine route between Barnard Castle and Tebay opened on July 4, 1861 with intermediate stations at Lartington, Bowes, Barras, Kirkby Stephen, Ravenstonedale and Gaisgill and became a vital artery for freight traffic. Coke produced in County Durham ovens went to Cumbria for ironmaking at Barrow, Maryport, Millom and Workington works. In return, the superb quality haematite ore of the Barrow area was despatched to the east coast where it was mixed with the poorer Cleveland ore.

With the rapid growth of freight traffic, much of the Stainmore route was doubled in stages between 1867-74. By contrast, passenger numbers were always low, so much so that several of the smaller stations were unable to run at a profit for decades. Only bulk loads of freight made the line viable.

The decline of freight over Stainmore set in after the First World War, firstly as more foreign ore was imported for the County Durham iron-works, and then as the demand for Durham coke in Cumbria dropped.

Diesel Multiple Units entered service between Darlington and Penrith on February 3, 1958, and promised greater speeds over Stainmore summit.

However, despite them boosting passenger revenue, British Railways announced in December 1959, before Beeching, that it intended to close the entire Stainmore route between Tees Valley Junction and Merrygill, a mile east of Kirkby Stephen East, and from Appleby East to Clifton Moor.

Despite a two-year public campaign to keep the route open, the Minister of Transport announced on December 7, 1961 that the closure would go ahead from January 20, 1962.

The Railway Correspondence & Travel Society ran a steam-hauled special, 'The Stainmore Limited' that day, and it formed the final train between Darlington and Penrith over the Stainmore route, arriving back at midnight. The two locomotives heading it were British Railways Standard 4MT 2-6-0 No. 76049 and Standard 3MT 2-6-0 No. 77003.

Tracklifting across the Stainmore summit began almost at once, and all services between Barnard Castle and Bishop Auckland ended in June 1962. The line between Darlington and Barnard Castle remained open as part of the branch to Middleton-in-Teesdale, a prime target for Beeching's cost-cutting. The route between Darlington, Barnard Castle and Middleton was closed to passengers on November 30, 1964 and to freight on April 5, 1965, with the track lifted shortly after closure.

Sadly, the great metal viaducts on these were demolished for scrap, including Belah, at nearly 200ft higher than any other in England, Deepdale, and the viaduct across the Tees at Barnard Castle.

It remains a fair question to ask — even today, who would want to travel from Darlington to Penrith on a daily basis? Could you fill diesel multiple unit services on such a route?

All over the country, much the same could be said about country routes that closed. Take any of them at random and ask — how many people would travel from A to B on them on a regular basis, from Wadebridge to Port Isaac Road, from Bourton-on-the-Water to Andoversford, from Shrewsbury to Bridgnorth, if a cheaper, more regular and convenient and faster alternative was on hand, or even at all? By contrast, in cities, there again is an argument for rapid transit linking suburbs to the centres to reduce road traffic congestion.

TOP SECRET: THE 'BLUE BOOK OF MAPS'

Many country lines were laid in the 19th century on a purely speculative basis, in anticipation that settlements would mushroom alongside the stations. In many cases this did happen, but in others it did not.

Other routes were built to compete with a rival railway company: once nationalisation had taken place, there was no longer any competition and no need for doubling up. An ideal solution would be to draw the railway map of Britain, to start over from scratch. That is exactly what John Edser did in his role at the Central Planning Unit.

In British Railways headquarters, there was a large outline map of Britain. John and his senior colleagues had to fill it in. Obviously there would be the main centres of population. Then there would come the major industries, such as coal mines, steelworks, power stations, along with ports and harbours. Smaller but key industries would then be added.

The map would fill up, slowly but surely, dot by dot. Finally, the lines would be joined linking them all. These would be the railways. Of course, it goes without saying that this did not mean that they would rip up all of Britain's railway lines and start again.

What it did mean, however, was that the lines drawn by John and his team showed where there was a need for rail transport: where a route could support high volumes of freight and would be in demand for passenger services.

Where the lines on the map corresponded with existing rail routes, they would be safe.

There was in reality never any threat to the trunk routes such as London to Bristol or Glasgow to Edinburgh, but taking on board many of the lessons learned by the Trunk Route Report, the exercise did identify where railways were needed to serve the needs of the present, not the distant past, and by the best estimates of 1966-67, the future.

You will not find it in railway bookshops. It is not even in the search engine research facility at the National Railway Museum. In fact, few people know about its existence — yet the 'Blue Book of Maps' was central to this redrawing of the British railway network.

Compiled during 1966-67 from highly confidential data provided by key industries, such as the National Coal Board, British Steel, the Central Electricity Generating Board and so on, it contains essential information for the plotting of future traffic flows.

At first glance, the book looks like just another atlas of British Railways, or one of the maps from the Beeching report of 1963 sectioned and bound into book form.

It is far, far more than that. Red dots indicated a freight-only line; a red dot with a black circle round showed a line that only served private sidings and green dots a passenger-only line. Other lines were uncoloured but if any line had a figure beside it, it indicated the likely life of the line in conjunction with any of the industries/passenger flows/ potential or actual private sidings along it.

It has to be remembered that at this time there was an explosion in all areas of road transport and British Rail's share of these markets was plummeting. Many of the lines that were given a limited life are booming today with frequent passenger services that were unimaginable at the time. Then, such information was beyond doubt hugely sensitive, and could well have the power to bring down the government of the day. In the case of the railway lines, but when working to a schedule to redraw the map of the system, a best estimate was needed to work to. In the event, most of the dates for rail closures, some of which had not been listed by Beeching, were blindingly accurate. Even more sensitive was the information given by the National Coal Board which had to be added to the maps. It included dates predicting the closure of mines up to 20 years into the future. John did not know how the information was compiled by the NCB, nor did he have any involvement in gathering it.

However, such information was essential for the planning of the rail network. What was the point of investing in a railway serving a mine which had only five years' life left in it? Presumably the NCB had teams of geologists and other mining experts to assess the extent of viable mineral reserves left in each mine before drawing up a list of such dates. There was almost certainly no hidden agenda in providing such estimates, but would the public have seen it that way? The dates were never made public.

Mining and steelmaking in the mid-Sixties were still a major employer in many parts of Britain, and whole settlements, big and small, just like Consett, depended on it. If mines closed, families were left destitute. At the time, there was a Labour government in power. What would have been the political reaction if it had published the life expectancies of the mines? Mining communities were hard-core Labour territory, where ordinary people probably did not care a bit about the Profumo scandal in faraway London, but would have been outraged beyond belief had they seen what would have been a threat to their livelihoods, not to mention the power of the trade unions.

The data pre-empted the miners' strike of 1984/85 by nearly two decades. Had one of the maps found its way to the National Union of Mineworkers then or before, it could well have been political dynamite. The Thatcher government of the day was loudly blamed for the mine closures of the Eighties, yet the life expectancies of collieries were known about during the time of the Labour government, the Blue Book shows.

Even today, nearly half a century on, the book has not been published.

Yet however unpalatable the facts it contained might have been, how else could the British Railways planners have plotted the way ahead, to devise a new rail system as envisaged by Beeching, and one which would benefit the country as a whole?

Not to have been supplied with such data would have been a wholly irresponsible situation. Nonetheless, the Central Planning Unit was ordered to keep the strictest confidence about its contents.

John said: "All we asked for was a list of mines and their potential and we got a list of three, short, medium and long term. What the coal board made their decision on we don't know."

The NCB data was not infallible. John pointed to the case of Firbeck Colliery near Worksop, a top-notch pit producing a vast amount of coal, and certainly not a short-term closure prospect.

"It suddenly shut in 1968," said John. "The problem was a type of coal which looks beautiful but has the consistency of granite reinforced by steel. It would tear the teeth off a cutter.

"They ran into it in three out of four big seams and turned a highly profitably colliery into a big loss.

"In the Thirties, they built a branch line and triangular junction to serve it, but suddenly it was gone. Nobody predicted that."

John remembered: "The colleague and myself who carried out a lot of the basic research and assembled the map for the 1968 Network bemused many of the more traditional HQ managers.

"We had this huge blank map of the British Isles and began to plot major ports, areas of industrial activity, inter-city flows, coal mines (with NCB potential lives) power stations and the odd locations with major traffic flows.

"On quite a few occasions they asked 'but you haven't got any railways on it' and were a little surprised when we said 'when we know where they are needed — we will put them in' — i.e., what we both knew was the logical approach.

"I am rather proud that, in pretty basic terms, that network is the one we have today."

THE NETWORK FOR DEVELOPMENT

The 'Blue Book of Maps' was far from being the sole source of information for the master plan that was being drawn up as the basis for the Network for Development plan published in May 1967 by Barbara Castle in her role as minister of transport.

John recalled: "A lot of thought was given to planning.

"We plotted a raft of economic activity and consulted with all major industries about their future plans.

"We consulted with a terrific range of bodies around the country. We added potential customers and at the last drew in the railway lines.

"It was the next stage in development. In May 1965, after the Trunk Route Report, there was a Railway Feeder System report. In March 1967, exactly the same time as the Network for Development was published, there was an Integral Freight Plan.

"It was not all about passenger lines by any means."

In short, the Network for Development document formed the basis for the 1968 Transport Act.

It took a giant step forward from the Marples/Beeching era in that it offered subsidies for loss-making lines where a social need was proven.

As before, lines which were paying their way like the main trunk routes and some secondary lines would be saved.

However, those routes that did not fit one of these two criteria could be candidates for closure.

It comes as a surprise to learn that one of the first railway lines marked on the new map of Britain's railways by John and his colleagues was one of Britain's most obscure: Norfolk's Middleton Towers branch.

This three-mile spur, the remnant of the 26½-mile Lynn & Dereham Railway which linked King's Lynn with East Dereham, is still very much with us today.

The Lynn & Dereham Railway opened in stages between 1846 and 1848 and later became part of the Great Eastern Railway.

It was closed to passenger and freight services on Saturday, September 7, 1968, but the section from King's Lynn to Middleton Towers was saved.

John explained: "We put that in because it was turning out two or three trains a day from the quarry it served. The glass people around Pontefract and Doncaster said it was the only place where in England they could get the sand they wanted.

"There were one or two special lines which we drew in early like this.

"Another was the freight flow Redhill to St Helens for the Pilkingtons glass factory. The quarry near Redhill next to the Redhill avoiding line produced very high quality glass sand. The rail traffic from it has now gone."

"As a general rule, we did not draw in any new railway lines.

"You did not invent new lines. You said 'if we have to have a link between Liverpool and Manchester and Newcastle, we've got the lines to do it.'

"In that respect, we had a pretty good idea of what it was going to look like when we set out.

"To a degree, yes, we did redraw the railway map of Britain."

John recalled: "Work on the Trunk Route Report and Network for Development and everything in the Central Planning Unit was, for the 1960s, with the small team working together, done in a very relaxed atmosphere with very little 'rank distinction'. That was easy with only six or eight of us — me very much the junior.

SOCIAL CONSIDERATIONS BEFORE STEMMING LOSSES

As approved by Barbara Castle, the Network for Development plan is the basis of today's network. "There have been few additions and few closures since 1967," said John.

"You had lines like Mickle Trafford to Chester Northgate which basically involved a simple diversion, with not much harm, and no services really destroyed. You did not have to have two stations in Chester. There were things like that."

The Network for Development plan marked a subtle but strategic sea change in policy. The Beeching report had been about which lines paid their way and which ones did not, a case of pure economics.

The key next stage brought in a strong social element, as described above. From now on there would be a far greater chance, in theory at least, of saving a rail route if social need could be proven. In the foreword to the report, by Mrs Castle and Stanley Raymond, the policy was outlined:

"In recent years the railway system has been progressively contracted as uneconomic services have been withdrawn and lines closed. In addition, services have been concentrated on fewer centres in the same cities and localities and the number of duplicate routes has been reduced. "Early in 1966 the government agreed with the Railways Board that the network must now be stabilised if management and staff are to concentrate on providing the best possible service to the public.

"Such a system must not only provide for freight and passenger services which are commercially sound, but must also meet the needs of social and regional policy as decided by the government."

They said that the system was designed to provide a network of main trunk routes selected for special development, linking the main centres of population, industry and commerce; secondary lines feeding the trunk network, including some to be developed for carrying particularly heavy flows of freight; certain commuter routes in and around the main cities and conurbations, and certain lines essential to the life of remote areas.

The introduction emphasised that the basic railway network shown would still be "a very substantial system".

It continued: "It will make provision for a number of services which are important to the life of the community but which cannot in money terms pay their way.

"The government has decided that the board should be relieved of the financial burden of these services and the ministry and the board are now undertaking a joint review to determine how the costs can be properly calculated and allocated."

That, however, did not mean an end to closures.

"The best possible use must however be made of the lines which are to continue in being and the network must be developed to enable it to carry the traffic efficiently. The government will therefore provide finance for new worthwhile projects, including the continued modernisation of traction, rolling stock, track and signalling, which can be justified on a proper economic basis.

"Although investment will be concentrated on the main trunk routes, work will also be carried out on the other routes to make them an efficient and economic part of the country's transport system.

"The government and the board believe that, with the other measures being taken to improve productivity and morale, this new network shaped to meet modern needs will enable the board to provide a continually improving and more efficient service to the community."

THE DEPARTURE OF BEECHING'S SUCCESSOR

Barbara Castle's success as transport minister led to her being moved to the role of minister for employment before the bill was completed, but not before British Rail chairman Stanley Raymond was forced to resign in late 1967 following a disagreement with her.

He received a settlement of £28,000 as he was contracted to serve until 1970. Raymond, later Sir Stanley Raymond, was replaced as British Rail chairman by Sir Henry (Bill) Johnson, who had joined the London & North Eastern Railway and rose through the ranks to become general manager of the London Midland Region in 1958 and its chairman from 1963-7. He took charge of the electrification of the Euston to Manchester and Liverpool line, and the development of the new Euston station.

Railway finances improved under Johnson, largely as a result of the 1968 Transport Act, in which the government promised grants to prop up loss-making passenger services where they were providing a public service.

InterCity, started in 1966 as a branded operation of high-speed trains linking major cities, expanded, and in 1969, work began at the Derby Research Centre on the Advanced Passenger Train.

He took charge of the commercial development of surplus railway land, which realised £20 million a year for British Railways in the Seventies. He made progress towards improving industrial relations and despite the cutbacks which continued under Labour, he was popular with railway staff, many of who saw him as one of their own.

He was appointed CBE in 1962, knighted in 1968, and was made a KBE in 1972, the year after he stepped down from railways.

The map shows the basic rail network which the government and the British Railways Board believed in early 1967 was required for the future.

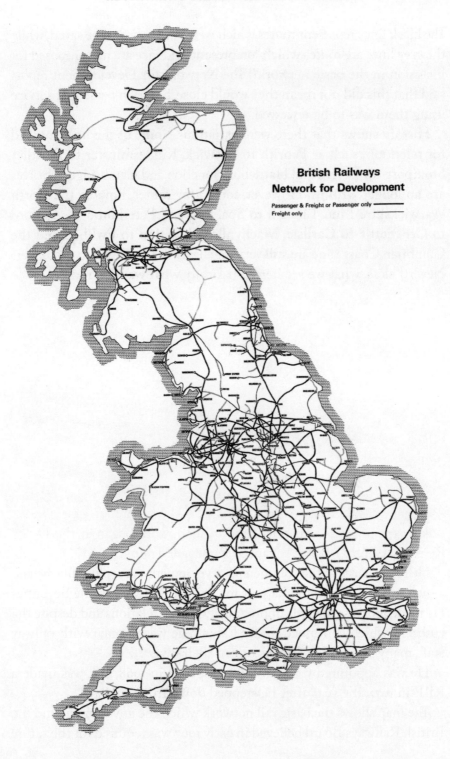

**British Railways
Network for Development**

Passenger & Freight or Passenger only ━━━━━
Freight only

The black lines represent routes which were earmarked to be saved, while the grey lines are routes which "on present evidence are not proposed for inclusion in the basic network". The Network for Development report said that this did not mean they would close, but each passenger service using them was to be reviewed.

History shows that there were variations. Some of the lines marked for retention, such as Penrith to Keswick, Kidderminster to Bewdley, Stourport-on-Severn and Hartlebury Junction and Cambridge to St Ives are no longer with us. However, some grey routes, notable the North Warwickshire Line, Lincoln to Spalding and Peterborough, Ashford to Ore, Settle to Carlisle, Machynlleth Junction to Pwllheli and the Cumbrian Coast Line are still very much with us and open to passengers. Nevertheless, what we see here is basically what we have today.

CHAPTER THIRTEEN

The end of mass closures

B Y THE early Seventies, the map of the British Rail network looked very much as it does today. In 1970, 275 miles were closed, followed by 23 in 1971, 50 in 1972, 35 in 1973 and none in 1974. By then, all the blatant lossmakers for which there were no social arguments to keep open had gone, and it was becoming increasingly clear that closures were having a negative impact.

The small amount of money saved by closing a line was outweighed by the increasing road congestion and pollution from motor vehicle exhausts.

One shock closure on January 5, 1970 which stood out from the rest was that of the 1500V DC electrified Woodhead Route between Sheffield and Manchester. The electrification had been completed in 1955 when the upgraded line was opened in a blaze of publicity.

Its controversial closure just 15 years later, and for which Beeching was in no way responsible, came after it was decided that the alternative Hope Valley line through Edale would stay open instead for social and network reasons, and would accommodate all Manchester-Sheffield passenger traffic. The Woodhead Route's Class 77 locomotives for passenger traffic were sold to the Netherlands Railways.

The line remained open for freight, mainly coal trains from Yorkshire to Fiddlers Ferry power station near Widnes which required a switch to diesel haulage for the final stage. However, a downturn in coal trade and a need to replace the ageing Class 76 locomotives led to the trans-Pennine route's closure east of Hadfield, with the last train running on July 17, 1981. Hopes of reopening the line quickly ended when most of the line east of Hadfield was lifted in the mid-1980s, but there are still regular calls for the powers that be to have second thoughts, despite the conversion of part of the trackbed to a cyclepath.

In October 1973, members of Organisation of Arab Petroleum Exporting Countries declared an oil embargo in response to the decision of the US to resupply the Israeli army during the Yom Kippur war.

Provoking fuel shortages in Britain, just as the 2011 Libyan crisis has seen the price of fuel at the pumps soar, the embargo lasted until March 1974, but by then had shown that it was folly to rely on road transport alone, and what was needed was an energy efficient and adequate public transport network.

One of the last Beeching closures was that of the GWR branch from Maiden Newton on the main line to Weymouth to Bridport.

Initially closure had been staved off because the narrow roads of the locality prompted a subsidy from Dorset County Council. However, the final trains ran in May 1975.

In the north of England, the Haltwhistle-Alston branch in the Pennines had survived Beeching's closure recommendation because of the lack of an all-weather road as an alternative. It lingered on until May 3, 1976 with the last train running two days earlier.

By the mid-Seventies, with the last of the Beeching closures out of the way, the network had shrunk to 12,000 miles of track and 2000 stations, around the same size it is now.

One Beeching closure was not enacted until 1985. It was the line from Eridge to Tunbridge Wells, which had been earmarked for the axe along with services from Brighton to Tonbridge.

Tunbridge Wells West station was itself listed for closure in 1966, but subsequently reprieved. However, services on the line were restricted to shuttles between Tonbridge and Eridge with a few through trains to Uckfield.

By the early 1980s, the track and signalling needed to be replaced. British Rail decided that the cost of keeping the line from Eridge to Tunbridge Wells Central station open by Grove Junction did not justify the cost of £175,000. Despite public objections, the line closed from July 6, 1985. It was believed though that Tunbridge Wells West station was the last on British Rail to have gas lighting.

A SERPENT FROM SERPELL

Apart from the years 1978-80, when passenger numbers grew in successive years, the overall decline which had begun in 1957 continued.

Rock bottom was reached in 1982 with the lowest number of passenger journeys of the second half of the 20th century, possibly as a result of a rail strike over rostering arrangements, the lowest level of passenger miles, and the lowest level of passenger revenue since 1968.

Revenue had decreased steadily from £2300 million in 1970 to £1800 million in 1982, while costs had risen from £2500 million to £2700 million. The passenger deficit was £933 million.

Meanwhile, car ownership was at an all-time high and continuing to soar year by year.

It was probably inevitable that a Conservative government headed by Margaret Thatcher which was marked by a drive towards self-sufficiency would re-examine the rail network sooner than later.

That year, one was indeed commissioned, and produced by a committee chaired by Sir David Serpell KCB CMG OBE, a senior civil servant who had worked under none other than Dr Beeching. However, even by the standards of Beeching's junked Trunk Route Report of 1965, its recommendations began at brutal and became worse from there.

In short, the Serpell Report, correctly named Railway Finances, offered the option of reducing the 10,370 route miles of the UK network down to a skeletal network of just 1630 miles.

The bulk of the report, published in January 1983, examined in depth the state of British Rail's finances in 1982, while its second part considered a series of options and variations of them for the network as it might appear in 1992.

The first option would be to aim for a commercial network, in which the railways as a whole would make a profit. To do that, route mileage would have to be cut by a staggering 84%, and annual passenger miles by 56%. That would leave London-Bristol/Cardiff, London-Birmingham-Liverpool/Manchester-Glasgow/Edinburgh, and London-Leeds/Newcastle as the only main line left.

This plan would keep some of the London commuter lines in the Home Counties, but all others would close.

The loss-making passenger sector would be subsidised by profits from the freight sector.

The second option was almost identical to the first, apart for making provision for the cost of tackling road congestion caused by rail closures. If the overall cost to the nation of closing a railway line was greater than saving it once road congestion had been considered, it would be kept. This second option would still cut route mileage by 78%, and annual passenger miles by 45%, keeping most of the London commuter lines.

The third option took a different tack, by offering various ways to cut the annual deficit through specific targets. One of these would have kept the existing network virtually intact, apart from the worst of the loss-making routes and closing many smaller stations. Listed among the 1% of the network that would close here was the Westbury-Weymouth line. Overall passenger miles would have been cut by only 4%.

Another target suggested was to cut the annual deficit to £700 million, by closing more loss-making services such as the Tarka Line from Exeter to Barnstaple, Trowbridge-Melksham-Chippenham line, the Norwich to Cromer and Sheringham branch, the Central Wales Line and the Cambrian Coast Main Line west of Shrewsbury.

An ever harsher target would be to reduce the deficit to £500 million a year. That would have seen the elimination of all lines in East Anglia apart from the line to Norwich, all routes in Wales apart from the valley lines north of Cardiff, all rural routes in Scotland, all lines in Devon and Cornwall other than the GWR main line to Exeter; the Salisbury-Exeter line, the trans-Pennine line; and most local routes east of the East Coast Main Line. This would have slashed route mileage by 39% and yearly passenger miles reduced by 15%.

A fourth option would dispense with the overriding financial restraint, and keep routes serving communities with a population greater than 25,000.

The Serpell Report was immediately pounced on by rail supporters, who said that it did not consider improvements to rail services as a means of attracting passengers.

Indeed, it was labelled as a 'second Beeching' because of its focus on closing secondary routes.

Matters were made worse by the fact that Transport Minister David Howell, who had commissioned the report, sat on it for a month after receiving it, during which time parts were leaked to the press, generating anger and fear among commuters and the rail unions.

The government blamed British Rail for the leaks, which a grateful Labour Party in opposition under Michael Foot made much of. With a general election looming, many Conservative MPs became nervous.

The popular British Rail chairman from 1976-83 Sir Peter Parker said that he found Serpell 'as cosy as a razor blade'. He exploited the report's suggested closures to persuade the train drivers' union ASLEF to call off a threatened strike that would have shut the rail system. Serpell, then 70, who had become permanent secretary at the Ministry of Transport in 1968, even endured personal abuse from a guard on his train home to Devon.

Largely because of the report's extremely harsh first option, it met with so much fierce resistance from many quarters that it was quickly abandoned, and there were no changes to the network made. However, it nonetheless reflected the way in which some in high places were thinking, and pre-empted the following years, in which British Rail was often accused by the unions of trying to cut costs and close lines by introducing 'Serpell by stealth'.

The Serpell Report led to the end of Howell's ministerial career, many believed, for after the Conservatives' crushing victory in the April 1983 election, Thatcher dropped him from the cabinet.

However, passenger numbers improved through the mid and late Eighties, reaching a 20-year high in 1988, and with privatisation on the horizon in 1993, the Serpell Report was consigned to history.

Serpell decided to retire for good, and moved to Dartmouth, ironically the only town in Britain with a station that famously has never had a railway running into it, for it was built on the opposite side of the river from the rail terminus at Kingswear, to which it was linked only by ferry.

He died on July 28, 2008 at the age of 96.

MARPLES' MOONLIGHT FLIT TO FRANCE

And what of Ernest Marples, the transport minister who, rather than Beeching, made the ultimate decision to close a third of Britain's railways?

Road builder Marples, who had spent his younger days working as a miner, a postman, a chef and an accountant, becoming an army captain during the Second World War, was elected to Parliament as Conservative MP for Wallasey in 1945 and became Postmaster General in 1957. He retired from the House of Commons at the February 1974 general election. Three months later, his public service was rewarded when he was made a life peer as Baron Marples of Wallasey.

In early 1975, before the end of the financial year, Marples fled without warning to the tax haven of Monaco, by the night ferry with his belongings packed into tea chests, after fighting off a reassessment of his financial assets.

It was said that he had formulated a plot to remove £2 million from Britain through his Liechtenstein company. He claimed he had been asked to pay unpaid tax dating back three decades.

After he had gone, discarded clothes and possessions were found scattered over the floors of his Belgravia home.

The late Fleet Street editor Richard Stott, when investigating Marples' flight to France, was told by him: "You are the worst journalist I have ever met. The most aggressive man I have ever met in my life."

The comment, of which Stott was immensely proud, was highlighted in the programme for the journalist's memorial service at St Clement Danes in the Strand on July 30, 2007 after he died at the age of 63.

The government froze Marples' remaining assets in Britain for the next 10 years, but most of his fortune had by then been squirrelled away to Monaco and Liechtenstein. He never returned to Britain, and spent the rest of his life in his French chateau at Fleurie, where he owned a vineyard, dying on July 6, 1978 in the Princess Grace Hospital Centre in Monaco.

It has since been claimed that when the late Lord Denning investigated the security aspects of the Profumo Affair in 1963, he told Prime Minister Harold Macmillan that a similar contemporary rumour, one

Far worse than Beeching: how the UK rail network would have looked had the Serpell Report of 1982 been implemented.

GLASGOW EDINBOURGH

NEWCASTLE

LEEDS

MANCHESTER

LIVERPOOL

BIRMINGHAM

CARDIFF LONDON

PLYMOUTH

concerning Marples, appeared to be true. Journalists claimed that the story was suppressed and was omitted from Denning's final report, but we will probably never know whether there is any truth in such claims.

CHAPTER FOURTEEN

Great Beeching survivors

WHILE BANNER-WAVING protesters who gathered outside stations on the last day of services on their local line may have felt that they were wasting their breath against a government 'one size fits all' policy, that the consultation procedures were purely academic, and that the Labour government which pledged to reverse the cuts reneged on that promise after it won two General Elections in 1964, several lines were reprieved sooner or later.

On March 3, 1964, nearly a year after the publication of the Beeching report, Marples announced that he had refused consent to closure in two cases — the Central Wales Line between Craven Arms, Pontardulais and Llanelli (now marketed as the Heart of Wales Line), and the Ayr-Kilmarnock line in Scotland. He did, however, agree to the closure of the southernmost branch of the Central Wales Line between Pontardulais and Swansea Victoria, from June that year.

Regarding the Central Wales Line, Marples said he had taken on board the fact that it served several towns and villages in central Wales, some of which had no other public transport and few of which had even a daily bus; it also provided a cross-country link between Swansea, west Wales and the north of England. He did accept that some stations and halts were all but unused and told the British Railways Board that he would be prepared to consider their closure.

Regarding Ayr-Kilmarnock, Marples endorsed the finding of the Scottish Transport Users Consultative Committee, but said he might reconsider in another 12 months.

Marples said that the railways' annual operating loss had been reduced by about £17 million in 1963, and that progress was being made, but unremunerative passenger services listed by Beeching were costing the taxpayer at least £30 million in annual subsidies, a heavy burden which had to be reduced.

Marples said: "That is far from being the case. Most of my consents are not just 'yes', they are 'yes, but...'".

Some of his consents had no conditions except maintenance of existing bus services; others were consents with special requirements for extra bus services; others were consents deferred to give time for road improvements; and yet others were consents with the proviso that warning must be given if British Railways wished to take up the track.

Marples said that he was taking into account all important factors, including social considerations, the pattern of industrial development and possible effects on roads and road traffic. "They also show that in every case, I have accepted the Transport Users Consultative Committee's view on hardship almost entirely," he said. "This shows how much I rely on them. I have also nearly always accepted their proposals for extra services to relieve hardship, and sometimes I have gone further than they recommended.

"We look at everything that has a bearing on each proposal — buses, roads, traffic, regional development, commuting needs, holiday travel. All the facts are brought to an official working party, on which all government departments with relevant responsibilities are represented. They report to me, and I consider each case personally."

Marples' decision on the Central Wales Line came despite observations made by the Transport Users Consultative Committee that between Llandovery and Craven Arms, only the stations at Knighton and Llandrindod Wells were taking more than £5 a day in receipts. Yet the TUCC also said that the withdrawal of services would cause considerable hardship.

Nevertheless, the line was reduced to single track during 1964/5 as an economy measure. A second closure threat appeared in 1967, but the line was again reprieved, on social grounds. Sceptics said that Harold Wilson saved it from closure because it passed through six marginal constituencies.

British Rail continued to seek economies despite receiving a subsidy to operate the line, and in 1972, produced a stroke of inspiration, one which might have saved many other lines in the Beeching report. It successfully applied for a Light Railway Order under the 1896 Act for the section of the 78¾-mile section of the line between Craven Arms and Pantyffynnon, even though the line speed is 60mph and not the required 25mph. However, the order still allowed many operational procedures to be simplified and so produced economies.

The future of the line was again thrown into question in 1987 when the Glanrhyd bridge near Llandeilo collapsed after heavy flooding, and an early morning northbound diesel multiple unit plunged into the swollen River Towy, killing four people. The Carmarthen-Aberystwyth line had been closed in 1965 following serious flood damage because the cost of repairs was deemed uneconomic, but in the case of the Central Wales Line, by then there was unanimous support for the line to be saved.

THE SETTLE AND CARLISLE LINE

Following the closure of smaller intermediate stations in the 1960s, the Beeching report recommended the withdrawal of all passenger services from one of Britain's most scenic and best-loved routes, the Settle-Carlisle Line.

The Beeching recommendations were shelved, but in May 1970 all stations apart from Settle and Appleby West were closed, and local passenger services cut to two trains a day in each direction, leaving mostly freight.

The 'Thames-Clyde Express' from London to Glasgow Central via Leicester was withdrawn in 1975, and night sleepers from London to Glasgow using the route followed the year afterwards. A residual service from Glasgow to Nottingham survived until May 1982.

It was clear that the line and its viaducts and tunnels were suffering from lack of investment, and deterioration might yet do the job of the

Beeching Axe. During the 1970s, most freight traffic was diverted on to the electrified West Coast Main Line. As a countermeasure, Dalesrail began operating services to closed stations on summer weekends in 1974, promoted by the Yorkshire Dales National Park Authority to encourage ramblers.

Yet by the early 1980s, the route handled only a handful of trains per day, and there were those who heard the cogwheels turning in British Rail's mind from afar. In 1981 a protest group, the Friends of the Settle-Carlisle Line, was set up to campaign against the line's closure even before it was officially announced.

Between 1983-84 three closure notices were posted up by British Rail, which was determined to shut the route. While the Beeching threat had been staved off, this time BR saw no need for the line which had lost its freight, through passenger services and had a very limited local service. BR also considered Ribblehead Viaduct to be in an unsafe condition, and used it as the key reason for closure, stating that its repair or replacement could cost more than £6 million.

Freight ended in 1983, although more enthusiast steam specials were by then running over it.

As the threat of closure hung over the line, passenger use underwent a resurgence, as packed Class 47-hauled trains carried people wanting to travel the line for one last time. Annual journeys were recorded at 93,000 in 1983 when the campaign against closure began, and had shot up to 450,000 by 1989.

Plans were even drawn up in 1987 to sell the line off to a private bidder. However, 22,000 signed a petition against closure, and eventually, on April 11, 1989, the recently promoted Conservative Transport Minister Paul Channon announced that the closure notices had been withdrawn. In 1991, work began on repairing Ribblehead Viaduct.

The decision was the right one. While it may be easy to justify closing a line because of the current viability, how often are future traffic flows predicted, or how far can they be expected to be foreseen?

Much freight now uses the Settle and Carlisle route due to congestion on the West Coast Main Line, and includes coal from the Hunterston coal terminal in Scotland taken to power stations in Yorkshire, and gypsum from Drax Power Station carried to Kirkby Thore. Significant engineering work was needed to upgrade the line to carry such heavy freight traffic and additional investment made to reduce the length of signal sections.

The line is also used as a diversionary route from the West Coast Main Line during engineering works, while eight of the stations closed in 1970 were reopened.

In 2009 a bronze statue of Ruswarp, a collie dog belonging to Graham Nuttall, the first secretary of the Friends of the Settle-Carlisle Line, was unveiled on the platform of the refurbished Garsdale station. It is there to mark the saving of the line by people power, and the fact that Ruswarp is believed to be the only dog to sign a petition against a rail closure originally proposed by Beeching, or any other for that matter.

CHAPTER FIFTEEN

It never should have closed!

THAT PHRASE has been heard time and time again over the past half century in connection with railway routes that were axed before, during and after Beeching. In recognising that the future of British Railways lay in an inter-city network, one of the key planks of rationalisation was to eliminate routes which 'doubled up'. If small towns and villages served by intermediate stations were no longer of primary or even secondary consideration, then why have two routes running from cities A to B when all the traffic could be concentrated on one, making it more viable and worthy of investment for the future?

Once you have accepted this principle, then you have to make the choice between the two or more routes to be closed. A classic example is Plymouth-Exeter: do you retain Isambard Kingdom Brunel's South Devon Railway sea wall route, one of the costliest stretches of Network Rail to maintain because of the constant threat from the sea on one side, or cliffs on the other, on the Southern Railway main line via Okehampton and Tavistock?

The GWR had become concerned about Isambard Kingdom Brunel's South Devon Railway sea wall route — in so many ways a nature-defying feat of engineering in itself — before the Second World War, and had begun buying land for a diversionary route inland. If the sea wall route had to be closed, it had the capability of running trains over the Teign Valley line between Newton Abbot and Exeter. However, nothing was ever done about building the replacement route.

The clear choice was passenger returns. The sea wall route runs through the sizeable towns of Dawlish, Teignmouth, Newton Abbot and Totnes, the railhead for the South Hams once the Kingsbridge branch had closed. From Newton Abbot runs the branch to Torquay and Paignton.

By contrast, with the closure of the 'Withered Arm' lines west of Okehampton, the only sizeable settlement between there and Plymouth is Tavistock. In terms of population density and potential patronage, forgetting the ravages of the elements, the choice for the through route to be kept was clear to the accountants.

I was once told by a railwayman who I met while riding on a DMU to Calstock, on the Gunnislake branch, which includes a surviving part of the Southern Railway route, that back in 1968 it had been intended to keep just one of the two lines just in case, but the demolition contractor misunderstood and lifted both. British Railways was not too bothered and decided to let matters stand. In fairness, I have never read that anecdote elsewhere, so whether or not it is an urban myth I cannot say.

Asked about the South Devon choice, John Edser said: "How much would you be prepared to spend on keeping a diversionary route open?"

Again, when Beeching took over, the railways were losing money hand over fist, because people had chosen to use motor transport instead. The thinking clearly ran along the lines of: if the Dawlish sea wall becomes blocked by storm damage, the cost of replacement bus services for the period it takes to repair the damage is far less than that of maintenance of a second route just in case.

Today there are regular calls for the railheads of the old Southern route, at Bere Alston and Meldon Quarry, the westernmost point of the private Dartmoor Railway, to be reconnected; in view of what we know, and Beeching and his planners did not, about global warming, a decidedly Eighties-and-thereafter model, not a Sixties one.

John, however, believes that there are some lines in Britain which should not have been closed, or if they were, at least should have been mothballed in case the need for them should arise again.

Most people's criticism of Beeching comes from hindsight, which raises the theoretical question as to how far in the future can planners be reasonably and responsibly expected to predict?

At a time when it seemed to many that as far as passenger transport was concerned, the railways were going the way of the stagecoaches that they superseded, the concept of having single inter-city routes which were buoyant and held out hopes of self-sufficiency was paramount. Hard choices based on available evidence had to be made and were.

John Edser's 'wish' list of routes that should have been spared the axe was topped by the East Lincolnshire line from Grimsby to Boston, the original Great Northern Railway main line from Grimsby to London. British Railways instead chose to retain the routes from Grimsby via Lincoln and Newark-on-Trent, and to Scunthorpe via Doncaster, where they picked up the East Coast Main Line to London.

A glance at the map shows that the building of the original main line took full advantage of the flat east Lincolnshire terrain and resulted in a fairly straight route from Grimsby to Louth, from there bending south-eastwards to serve villages and small towns such as Aby, Alford, Willoughby, Burgh-le-Marsh, Firsby (where there would be a later junction for the branch leading to the holiday resort of Skegness), Little Steeping, East Villa, Old Leake and Sibsey before the port of Boston is reached.

Inherent in this list is the reason why Beeching recommended the route for closure.

John explained: "You had Grimsby to Louth, but between there and Boston, there was no real potential for profitable traffic for miles.

"However, with hindsight, closing it was probably a bad thing.

"There has been all this hoo-hah about serving Lincoln. In recent years, there were great plans for a quite big service to Lincoln via Newark, but that seems to have floated away."

The comparatively sparse levels of population in the east of Lincolnshire swung it. Still, British Railways faced a huge fight lasting seven years before the line closed.

THE ORIGINS OF THE EAST
LINCOLNSHIRE RAILWAY

Grimsby expanded rapidly in the early 19th century, after the Great Grimsby Haven Company was formed by Act of Parliament in May 1796. This Act empowered the "widening, deepening, enlarging, altering and improving the Haven of the Town and Port of Great Grimsby".

Once the port facilities had been developed, Grimsby became a boom town, importing iron, timber, wheat, hemp and flax. It grew to the point where new docks became vital to cope with the huge quantity of vessels, and a further Act was obtained in 1845.

In 1845, the dock company effectively evolved into Great Grimsby & Sheffield Junction Railway which set out to build a line between the port, New Holland and Gainsborough. It amalgamated with the Sheffield, Ashton-Under-Lyne and Manchester Railway and the Sheffield and Lincolnshire Junction Railway to form the Manchester, Sheffield and Lincolnshire Railway (later the Great Central) in 1847.

The East Lincolnshire Railway's plans for a line serving Grimsby were published on April 16, 1845. They were backed by local MPs and the Earl of Yarborough. At the same time, the London & York Railway, later the Great Northern, wanted to serve the port. The two companies shared two directors, and a compromise was reached with a common station in Grimsby. This was facilitated by an agreement with the Manchester, Sheffield and Lincolnshire Railway to share Grimsby Town station.

Both the Manchester, Sheffield and Lincolnshire line from Grimsby to New Holland and the East Lincolnshire line from Grimsby to Louth opened to the public on March 1, 1848. Work on building the East Lincolnshire line had started a year before, and such was the rush to build it that navvies worked on Sundays to the disdain of local clergy and newspapers. Some workmen were eventually fined for doing so.

The first train to run along the line was a VIPs and director special on September 17, taking 20 minutes to run from Louth to Grimsby.

There were intermediate stations at Ludborough, North Thoresby, Holton-le-Clay with Tetney, and Waltham for Humberstone.

Building south from Louth continued and Firsby was reached in September 1848. By now the line was operated by the Great Northern.

Construction work at the Boston end of the line began in October 1847, with the driving of piles into the River Witham to lay foundations for a bridge. So many navvies descended on the port that local magistrates warned householders to lock their homes at night. At one stage, eight Baltic ships which had arrived loaded with wooden sleepers were berthed in the port.

The East Lincolnshire line reached Boston on October 2, 1848, when the first train left the initial temporary station at 7.35am bound for Hull via the New Holland ferry. A permanent station opened in 1850.

At Boston, the East Lincolnshire line joined the Great Northern Railway's Lincolnshire Loop.

This 58-mile double-track line was opened in 1848 and briefly formed part of the main route from London to the north of England and Scotland until the section of what is now the East Coast Main Line was built from Peterborough to Doncaster.

There were intermediate stations at Kirton, Algarkirk & Sutterton, Surfleet, Spalding, Littleworth, Deeping St James and Peakirk between Boston and Peterborough. Beyond Boston, the line followed the course of the River Witham to Lincoln via Tattershall and Bardney.

The railway brought huge prosperity to Grimsby, and its opening came a few years after new fishing grounds were discovered on Dogger Bank. The railway in 1848 made it far easier to transport goods to and from the port.

Fast rail links direct to London's Billingsgate Fish Market saw fresh Grimsby fish become renowned across the country.

Because of the port's railway connections, fish and chips became a popular meal, and a British institution known throughout the world.

By the time of its 1950s heydays, Grimsby boasted that it was the largest fishing port in the world.

Coal mined in South Yorkshire was brought by rail and exported through Grimsby.

The East Lincolnshire line received a further boost through the opening of two connections at Firsby Junction.

Firstly, a four-mile branch to the market town of Spilsby opened on May 1, 1868. Infinitely more significant, however, was the opening of a route to Skegness, beginning with the Wainfleet & Firsby Railway, which opened to passengers on October 23, and the extension to Skegness on July 28, 1873.

Skegness had been a fishing village and small port until the arrival of the railway in East Lincolnshire. Accommodation for visitors was being advertised at the Skegness Hotel in 1772, and bathing machines were first used on the beach in 1784. Horse and pony races were staged during the 1820s.

With an excellent sandy beach, Skegness had the ingredients of a holiday resort. The opening of the East Lincolnshire line and Burgh station in 1848 made it easier for visitors to reach Skegness, arriving at the resort via horse omnibus.

However, it was the arrival of a railway in Skegness which really saw it take off, opening it up for cheap day trips and mass tourism. Lord Scarborough set about developing it as a modern resort, laying out new plots for houses, and paving the way for a pier, pleasure gardens, a school and a cricket ground to be built. He was a major shareholder in companies providing the amenities.

Firsby became an important junction and developed to a size far exceeding its position as a country station, even though, as Beeching's planners would later note, the local population could never justify the grandiose facilities. The station had three platforms each 200 metres long and covered with buildings, booking offices, several waiting rooms (male, female and general), restaurants, toilets, baggage and goods halls, crew rooms, staff canteen and several railway offices. The main line tracks were crossed by a substantial footbridge and most of the station was covered by an ornate cast-iron and glass canopy of a type normally only seen at principal city stations. The station also had signalboxes, water towers, extensive goods sidings and engine repair sheds.

In the summer months, thousands of passengers would pass through with their luggage at weekends. In Victorian times, as working conditions improved and holidays became the norm for working class people as well as the better off, Firsby was one of the busiest stations on the east coast. It was the major employer in the area.

In 1908, the Great Northern Railway commissioned a poster to advertise excursions to the resort, the first being from King's Cross at 11.30am on Good Friday 1908. The 'Skegness is so Bracing' poster featuring The

Jolly Fisherman elevated Skegness to national fame as a resort and is now the defining icon for the town. The GNR paid artist John Hassall 12 guineas for it. Hassall had never been to Skegness to find out how bracing it really was, and did not visit the resort until 1936. He is said to have died penniless, but his poster which brought millions of visitors over the East Lincolnshire line into Skegness remains arguably the most famous railway seaside poster of all.

To compete with early road traffic alternatives, in 1905 a series of halts were opened for use by railmotors. Between Grimsby and Louth there were Fotherby Halt, Utterby Halt, Grainsby Halt, Holton Village Halt, Weelsby Road and Hainton Street.

In 1913, the GNR used light railway legislation to obtain powers for a new line from Kirkstead on the Lincoln to Boston line to Little Steeping on the East Lincolnshire line. The purpose was to provide an avoiding route for Boston, relieving summer holiday congestion when trains from Manchester and Sheffield would pour into Skegness. The double track line from Coningsby Junction 1½ miles south of Kirkstead station ran over flat countryside to the East Lincolnshire line at Bellwater Junction. It opened for passengers on July 1, 1913, and became one of the select few extensions of the main line network in Britain in the 20th century/motor age.

A year after the absorption of the GNR into the London & North Eastern Railway at the Grouping of 1923, most of the Grimsby fish trains were rerouted via the East Lincolnshire line when it was realised that it was less congested and the fish could arrive more quickly at its final destination. Sparse population paid dividends here.

BATTLES FOUGHT IN VAIN

The little Spilsby branch struggled to pay its way, and at the start of the Second World War, passenger services were suspended, leaving only a freight service which itself ceased in 1958, when the branch was closed. Yet at the time, few suspected that the East Lincolnshire route could even be considered a candidate for closure, even in 1959 when the whole Midland & Great Northern Joint Railway system which crossed the route at Spalding was axed, sending a pre-Beeching shockwave through the industry.

The last steam-hauled service train to run from Grimsby's own seaside resort, Cleethorpes, to King's Cross was hauled by BR Britannia Pacific No. 70040 *Clive of India* on November 4, 1962. Afterwards the Britannia Pacifics based at Immingham depot hauled fish trains over the East Lancashire Railway.

The last steam engine to haul a passenger train from Cleethorpes to King's Cross in the steam era was the by-then privately owned *Flying Scotsman* on October 21, 1967. With steam on the main line everywhere having died the previous August, No. 4472 returned in July 1969 to work a special over the East Lincolnshire line, but did not stop anywhere to pick up passengers.

By then, the Beeching report had been published, and had horrified Lincolnshire people by listing the whole network north of Boston for closure. That not only included the branch to Skegness and the loop line to Mablethorpe and the 1913 route from Coningsby Junction, but the East Lincolnshire line itself.

The local Transport Users Consultative Committee held an inquiry into the Beeching proposals in September 1964, although locals claimed that already rail workers had begun 'rationalising' infrastructure in readiness for enacting what sceptics saw as a foregone conclusion.

The hearing lasted two days, with protesters ranging from local councils down to ordinary people. A total of 1714 written objections were received, many of them incorporating thousands of individual representations.

One parish council spokesman said that it would take longer to travel from the central Lincolnshire hamlet of New York to London than to fly from London to New York, New York, if the railways were closed.

As stated by AJ Ludlam in his Oakwood Press volume The East Lincolnshire Railway, after the inquiry it was reported: "The lines can be saved only if overwhelming hardship could be caused by their closure. After the meeting there could have been little doubt that such hardship would be caused to thousands of people, that the entire region would be isolated and that economic disaster for the coast would follow."

The transport minister asked British Railways to reconsider, which it did. There was a temporary stay of execution, but only until new closure proposals were drawn up, by which time Beeching had left the railways.

A second TUCC inquiry was held at Skegness in May 1968, again lasting two days. This time, there were 1588 objections. The case for the objectors was opened by Horncastle Conservative MP Peter Tapsell.

It was argued that operating costs could be cut by automating many of the 63 level crossings, and that the British Railways figures for freight usage did not present a fair picture as heavy goods traffic had already been deliberated rerouted away from the line.

The verdict was delivered just before Christmas 1969. It was not the kind of Christmas present that Lincolnshire people wanted to receive. The entire route from Grimsby to Peterborough was to close to passengers, apart from the length between Boston and Firsby, and the line to Skegness, which would now be accessed by trains from Sleaford.

BR said that the lines, including the Mablethorpe loop, were losing £172,000 a year. The minister took into account the TUCC's representation that closure would cause widespread hardship, but decided that many of the rail journeys on the routes were made only occasionally and passengers could be served by alternative rail routes. For instance, around a fifth of users of the East Lincolnshire line travelled from Grimsby to London, and these would be catered for by improved services via Newark.

North of Firsby, additions to existing bus services would provide links to the retained railway route at Market Rasen, the minister decided.

The resulting anger was to no avail. Local residents had pointed out that the alternative transport services that were being offered were not adequate or practical.

BR wanted to close the line the following May, but more time was needed to lay on extra bus services.

Closure took place officially on Monday, October 5, 1970, when a large chunk of the east coast of England suddenly found itself bereft of rail services. The final train was a special to King's Cross run by the Lincolnshire Standard newspaper two days before. On the return leg, the train stopped at as many East Lincolnshire stations as possible so that the train crew could sign autographs. Members of the public packed vantage points at other stations, level crossings and overbridges to wave farewell to the train.

The 14-mile section from Grimsby to Louth was retained for freight to the Associated British Maltsters plant, but the line was singled and much of the infrastructure was removed. The last freight working came on December 28, 1982.

It was a Conservative government which had engaged a man whose staff proposed the closure of the East Lincolnshire line. It was a Labour government that had pledged to reverse the Beeching cuts that oversaw both attempts at closure, and a second Conservative government that allowed it to happen after a decision had earlier been made. None of them came to a decision that there could be a future for the line.

The opening of the Humber Bridge in 1973 led to a resurgence of commercial interest in Humberside, at a time when Grimsby began to sink into decline following the contraction of its famous fishing industry.

Following the pressures placed on the industry during the Cod Wars with Iceland, which ended in 1976, many Grimsby firms decided to cease trawling operations from the town. That ended a way of life and community that had existed for generations. Huge numbers of fishermen became redundant with little hope of finding a job to suit their skills. Some firms switched to industries such as food processing, but the scars of the fishing demise are still very much evident in the town today. I have spoken to many local people who cannot but agree with the verdict of visitors from outside: Grimsby today can be regarded from many angles as grim.

Today, few fishing vessels operate from Grimsby's docks, but the town still has a substantial fish market, of European importance.

What if a new fast link to London via the sizeable towns of Boston and Peterborough had been created? Could the prospect of cheap housing along the Lincolnshire coast have encouraged long-distance commuting? Would more firms have been prepared to relocate there if there were better communications with the capital, combined with cheap land and a ready supply of affordable labour, and perhaps even another means of taking their products out by rail?

Today, the Port of Grimsby and Immingham is the UK's largest port by tonnage. Its prime deep-water location on the Humber Estuary gives companies direct access to mainland Europe and beyond. Immingham has a large Railfreight terminal and a substantial petro-chemical industry.

More than four decades after closure, the coast of Lincolnshire south of the Grimsby/Cleethorpes conurbation lacks direct motorway or dual carriageway access. Many of the A roads are windy affairs which make journeys in or out long-winded affairs, an exception being the A16 running from Boston to Spalding, which largely follows the route of the railway between the towns that was closed in 1970. Otherwise, in providing a quick and efficient means of communication along the seaboard side of the county, linking it to and from London, the East Lincolnshire line is waiting to be bettered.

As it is, the closures of 1970 disenfranchised towns and sizeable rural communities from the rail network in one of England's biggest counties. The question is — how extensive is the true loss in terms of social and economic terms, and how much benefit did the closure bring to the national railway's balance books?

PEOPLE POWER OVERTURNS A CLOSURE

That fact was not lost on local councils to the north of Peterborough when the line closed.

Their representations led to British Rail reopening the line from Peterborough to Spalding from June 7, 1971, with a shuttle service of three trains each way per day. This service was improved in 1982 with the closure of the March to Spalding section of the former Great Northern & Great Eastern Joint Railway when the Lincoln to Cambridge service was transformed into the Lincoln to Peterborough service, which still runs today.

The intermediate stations of Metheringham and Ruskington north of Spalding both reopened in 1975, and there are calls to add Donington to that list. The ideas of reopening stations at Littleworth to serve Deeping St Nicholas or Deeping St James for Market Deeping, taking commuters and shoppers into Peterborough, have been mooted.

However, to travel from Boston to Peterborough you have to take the long-winded route inland to Sleaford, rather than the direct route south to Spalding. Bearing in mind that Boston is still very much a working port, should this comparatively short section not also have been retained, if only as investment for the future?

The A16 could have been built alongside, not on top of it. There would also be a direct route from London to Skegness, a resort which nowadays sees a fraction of the seaside rail traffic that it once did.

A RETURN TO STEAM

Before the Grimsby-Louth section was finally closed, local people had started to campaign for the line to be reopened, to provide a commuter and shopper link to the port, bearing in mind that the villages it once served, in particular New Waltham, had markedly expanded since the days of the Beeching report.

A group, the Grimsby-Louth Group, was formed to fight the final closure of the line following a letter to the Grimsby Evening Telegraph during March 1978.

Members organised a petition and several rail tours in the hope that they could convince the government and British Rail that local people wanted the line.

A five-car DMU railtour organised by the Branch Line Society ran in March 1978.

The group organised the final passenger train, a 'Santa Special' on December 2, 1982, and was made up of two DMUs making a return trip.

The driver of the last passenger train was Tony Jones, one of the future directors of Great Northern & East Lincolnshire Railway plc, a company which evolved out of the campaign group.

After closure British Rail in typical fashion quickly ripped up the track and bulldozed most of the structures, rendering any reopening of the line even more difficult.

The Grimsby-Louth Group became the Grimsby-Louth Railway Preservation Society, a group of volunteers who wanted to restore the whole line, and hopefully run regular public services.

In 1984, the society established an operating base at Ludborough after the trackbed was leased from British Rail.

Following a public enquiry in 1991, a Light Railway Order was granted to the plc, paving the way for rebuilding. Eight and a half miles of trackbed was bought between Louth and New Waltham, but the vital three miles into Grimsby were not offered for sale.

Instead it was used for a dual carriageway running into the heart of Grimsby, North East Lincolnshire Council's A16 Peakes Parkway project. That ended any lingering hopes of commuter trains.

The revivalists had felt powerless to object: they felt that if they had done so, they would have risked the local authority objecting to the Light Railway Order.

So the best hope for what was left of the GNR main line to London lay in creating a tourist attraction. Yes, the railway would return, but would never again form part of the national network, and the route, with so many blockages on the old trackbed, is never again likely to be given the chance to show what could be done with it to tackle the changing needs of the 21st century.

Ludborough station was redeveloped, with the signalbox rebuilt in the original GNR style, a waiting room with a small museum and shop, a platform and a two-lane engine shed and workshop.

In 1998, short passenger rides were offered, and in 2009, the line, now operating under the banner of the Lincolnshire Wolds Railway, had extended a mile to the next station towards Grimsby, North Thoresby.

At the time of writing, it has launched a public appeal for funds to extend its line to the outskirts of Louth where it is planned to build a new station, the original now isolated from the trackbed and converted into a private house.

Tracklaying began around Easter 2000. The first target is to reach the Pear Tree Lane road crossing between Ludborough and Utterby, a distance of three-quarters of a mile. Relaying a line even using volunteer labour costs more than £200,000 a mile of track and materials such as ballast, rails and sleepers need to be bought. Anyone who would like to help the railway is invited to call 01507 363881 for more information.

THE BEECHING PROPERTY BOOM!

It probably never entered Dr Beeching's head, and it was certainly not within his remit, but many of the stations closed as a result of his report have become highly desirable properties, even after lying derelict and vandal-hit for many years.

A classic case is the Louth North signalbox. Bought by the revivalists along with the trackbed, they later sold it off in order to develop funds for other projects, after deciding that any future extension would never go that far into the town.

After closure, the Grade II listed signalbox in Keddington Road became a target for drug users, vandals, flytippers and arsonists.

Tony and Beverley Moss, whose property backed on to the former main line railway, remembered with affection the days when trains used to run along it from Grimsby to Louth. When the revivalists declared the derelict signalbox surplus to requirements, along with adjacent railway land, the couple saw that buying the 'box could end their problems with the ne'er-do-well elements once and for all.

They talked to the local council's planning department and were told that as it was a listed building, they had an obligation to keep it in its present situation.

They then came up with the idea of converting it into a luxury house which they could rent.

With the help of expert advice from conservationists, plans were drawn up for a Tardis-style property, in which the interior would appear much bigger than the outside.

A scheme emerged for an 'upside-down house' with the single bedroom on the ground floor and the open living area and kitchen on the first floor, where generations of signalmen had once pulled levers to send express trains on their way to King's Cross.

Work began in August 2004, and many townsfolk thought it was mission impossible, bearing in mind that arson attacks had left much of the structure a charcoaled hulk.

Local craftsmen were brought in to work on the project, carried out in keeping with the building's railway history. A new traditional level crossing gate, complete with red spot in the middle, was erected alongside the road where the trackbed now forms the property's garden.

Authentic railway signs were affixed to the side of the signalbox in the same position as they had been in the days of steam.

The couple's efforts were rewarded when they received the Louth Civic Trust's Pride of Place award for their work. "It was an eyesore for 30 years, but everyone in the town thinks it's wonderful to drive down Keddington Road now," said Tony.

Their story is replicated all over country, where the railway network's loss has become many a private owner's des res.

CHAPTER SIXTEEN

*Break a newspaper
embargo, save a line!*

THERE ARE many inspirational stories from the Sixties concerning the efforts of local residents to save their railway from closure. For me, one of the finest was the saving of the North Warwickshire Line which, as we saw earlier, was one of the last pieces of the national network to be built in the age of steam.

In the build-up to Easter 1969, an accountant at the Stratford-upon-Avon Herald weekly newspaper noticed that British Rail had reserved space for an advertisement. The paper normally came out on Fridays, but the week in question included Good Friday and so the edition had to appear a day early, on the Thursday.

The accountant, Michael Brockington, telephoned British Railways and asked for the copy to fill the space that had been booked.

Bizarrely, for days British Railways refused what was a perfectly reasonable request. Finally, on the Tuesday, nearing the press deadline, Michael again telephoned British Rail, pointing out that the advertisement could not physically be published if the copy was not supplied there and then.

The advertiser saw sense, and produced the required copy. When Michael read it, he was horrified. It was a statutory notice detailing all the replacement bus services that were to be laid on following the closure of the branch between Tyseley, Shirley and Henley-in-Arden and Bearley Junction. At the time, Michael was secretary of the Stratford-upon-Avon Transport Action Committee, and he immediately saw the implications.

British Rail's post-Beeching closure plans would greatly benefit from publishing the notice just before Easter, when offices would be closed and it would be all but impossible for local people to object to the relevant authorities.

However, British Rail had not taken Michael Brockington into the equation.

In the late Sixties, newspapers were still published using the traditional hot metal process. Michael went into the composing room where the plates for printing were being made up, and did his utmost to get the compositors to run him off a copy of the advertisement, three days ahead of it being released into the public domain, as per the agreement with the advertiser.

He then rushed it to Douglas King, a Birmingham solicitor who was acting on behalf of five local authorities, Warwickshire County, Stratford-upon-Avon Borough, Stratford Rural District, Bromsgrove Rural District and Solihull Borough councils, to prevent the closure of the line, its continuation from Stratford south to Honeybourne, from where DMU services would run on to Worcester, set to be withdrawn from May 5 that year.

Beeching had mentioned the 'modification' to the Stratford-Honeybourne-Worcester services in his 1963 report, but made no mention of any intention to close the North Warwickshire Line. However, one of his core strategies in his bid to streamline the system was to eradicate routes which doubled up, and it was also possible to get from Birmingham to Stratford via Tyseley using the main line via Solihull, Dorridge, Hatton Junction, Claverdon and Bearley station.

The threats to the North Warwickshire Line emerged under the subsequent Labour administration. In June 1968, two months after Barbara Castle was superseded as transport minister by Richard Marsh, support for the line's complete closure came from none other than Knowle

& Dorridge Young Conservatives, whose local station and rail link to Stratford would not be affected.

Birmingham businessman and longtime enthusiast Derek Mayman, the founding director of a successful international company in the construction industry who had become one of the first directors of the Welshpool & Llanfair Light Railway Preservation Company in 1960, and who had been instrumental in obtaining a set of coaches from Austria's Zillertalbahn for use on the mid-Wales line, mounted a vociferous campaign to save the North Warwickshire Line.

However, at the 11th hour, it was Michael Brockington and Douglas King who found themselves holding the trump card. Days before the Easter holiday, Douglas pulled out every stop to obtain a hearing before the High Court went into recess for three weeks. He did so by the skin of his teeth, applying for an injunction to stop the closure.

Michael, who has lived in Welford-on-Avon for the past 40 years, said: "I'm sure that British Rail planned to issue the notice just before Easter when it was too late to do anything about it." Indeed, British Rail had attempted to close the railway before the replacement bus services had been approved by the Transport Commissioners.

As it happened, the High Court threw out Douglas King's application, but he immediately appealed, on the grounds that the Transport Commissioners had not agreed the replacement bus services that were listed. On those grounds, he won.

While the Beeching Axe had disenfranchised major towns like Corby, Mansfield and Leek from the rail network, the halts of Wootton Wawen, Wood End and Danzey for Tanworth would continue to service idyllic rural villages on the North Warwickshire Line.

The injunction remained in place until 1984, when British Rail had it lifted, immediately announcing new plans to truncate the line south of Henley-in-Arden.

By then, the northern section between Shirley, Tyseley and Birmingham Moor Street station had become a thriving commuter line that nobody would then have dared propose for closure, but south of Shirley, passenger numbers tailed off with the passing of every commuter settlement.

Many locals immediately saw this new closure plan for the dog it was. If the line was closed south of Henley, it would lose its passengers to

Stratford, the primary destination. Therefore, it would be easy to come back in two or three years and claim that there was a huge fall-off in passenger numbers, before cutting the line back further to Wythall or even Shirley.

Michael's successor on the transport action committee, Fraser Pithie, swung into action and rode on the trains, collecting around 7000 signatures on a petition.

Eventually, British Rail withdrew the closure notice, after local councils agreed to pay towards the running costs of the four-mile section under threat.

The North Warwickshire Line is a key part of public transport in the West Midlands today. Passenger usage continues to rise, and at Whitlocks End, for long a lonely country halt outside Shirley's urban area, a sizeable park-and-ride car park is often full to capacity, with the modern estate of Dickens Heath a mile away.

Had it not been for a quick-witted, rail-supporting accountant who was prepared to break a newspaper advertiser's embargo, the region would be so much the poorer for it today.

In the High Court hearing covering British Rail's plans to close the line in 1969, Lord Denning, the Master of the Rolls, said that while Midland Red had indeed applied to run the replacement bus services, it had "shown no particular enthusiasm about running them". It was also demonstrated that the replacement bus services would be slower and costlier, and would not match up with the railway route.

While buses have in themselves brought multiple benefits to social mobility and the easing of congestion, it certain respects they might also be considered a public transport disaster of the late 20th century. It has been clearly demonstrated that in many cases, within a few years of bus services taking over from trains on a route, services were withdrawn because of apathy from operators, or the lack of willingness to adapt them to fit the exact needs of the communities that had lost their rail link. The net result was that these communities were left with no public transport in any shape or form, and local residents were left with no alternative but to use the car.

THE NEWEST DAWN FOR THE
NORTH WARWICKSHIRE LINE

The route is now an essential plank of daily commuter and shopper services in and around Birmingham. However, there are those who for decades have argued that it could be much more.

In 2019, plans to develop the branch as a 'main line heritage railway' were announced, under the terms of a ground-breaking new partnership with Tyseley-based steam specialist and Train Operating Company Vintage Trains.

On June 12, the West Midlands Rail Executive, which has responsibility for rail services in its region, and Vintage Trains launched the partnership deal which is designed to see Vintage Trains — and steam — play a greater part in promoting local tourism, with services across the region's network provided for Coventry's City of Culture year in 2021 and in 2022, the Birmingham Commonwealth Games.

However, much emphasis will be placed on promoting the Birmingham to Stratford-upon-Avon route via Shirley and Henley-in-Arden, which is to be marketed as the Shakespeare Line. Vintage Trains has for two decades run the summer Sunday 'Shakespeare Express' along the route, noted for its many surviving original red-brick stations and their buildings dating from the building of the line by the GWR in 1908.

West Midlands mayor Andy Street said: "Vintage Trains do a wonderful job bringing the golden age of steam to many thousands of visitors each year. Riding a steam train through the Warwickshire countryside is certainly a deeply exciting and nostalgic experience and I would urge everyone to give it go.

"But this partnership is also looking to the future. It is about how we make the most of this valuable asset, grow the Vintage Trains network and encourage more community volunteers as well as create more jobs and more apprenticeships."

Vintage Trains Community Benefit Society chairman Michael Whitehouse said: "We will continue to provide exciting tourism experiences on the Shakespeare Line between Birmingham and Stratford-upon-Avon, create more jobs, teach and retain skills at our Tyseley depot and involve the diverse communities along the route in all that we do so that everyone who joins in can be proud of their contribution.

"WMRE wish to ensure express steam trains continue to run in the region for the long term, particularly on the Shakespeare Line to Stratford which they seek to develop as Britain's premier main line heritage railway, so that franchise and heritage trains can run seamlessly together in the timetable for the benefit of the community.

"The plan is to create 'Shakespeare Express' paths from them which can be used daily as market conditions require. This will enable us to augment the service and forward sell to the national and international markets, which plan considerably ahead.

"At present, running only on summer Sundays, we cannot do this and we cannot currently run on weekdays as there isn't sufficient platform capacity in the city. The plan is to create this capacity, most probably at Birmingham Moor Street from 2021.

"Bear in mind that the Shakespeare Line currently has three million passengers per year and Moor Street station currently has an annual footfall of seven million people. By involving all the stations and communities along the Shakespeare Line, we can reach out to all the diverse communities which make up Birmingham: the city centre, the post-war migrants now living in Bordesley, Small Heath and Tyseley, the suburbs of Hall Green and Shirley next to 'Lord of the Rings' Sarehole Mill (Hobbitland, where JRR Tolkien once lived), Henley-in-Arden and, of course, the internationally famous town of Shakespeare's Stratford itself. There will be lots of opportunities to join up tourist centres and tell fascinating stories."

It is estimated that up to 50 jobs including conductors, drivers and maintenance staff needed to operate the trains could be created at Vintage Trains as a result of the partnership.

Vintage Trains aims to identify additional opportunities for heritage services on the main line to provide further value to the West Midlands network, and integrate itself into the work of the wider rail industry in the region.

It will become involved in the future plans for Moor Street station and open up a waiting room/cafe and a small museum at Tyseley's main line station opposite its headquarters, in a bid to embrace the local community.

In short, the twice closure-earmarked branch line might well become a plank of the region's 21st-century tourist economy, as well as an essential commuter artery, and yet, but for an eagle-eyed local weekly newspaper accountant, it would have been lost half a century ago.

CHAPTER SEVENTEEN

Second lives as heritage railways

BACK IN 1962, as we saw in Chapter 3, Dr Beeching opened a new station on the Bluebell Railway, which was the first section of the British Railways main line network to be closed and then reopened as a private venture by volunteers and enthusiasts. Today, such heritage railways account for a major slice of Britain's tourist industry. From such small beginnings, there are well over 100 operating heritage railways and 60 more steam centres in the British Isles. Laid end to end, they would total 510 miles with 399 stations, a greater route mileage than that of the London Underground system and longer than the distance between London and Glasgow. More heritage railways are being planned.

The seeds that grew into the mighty oaks of today's heritage railway sector were sown in 1951, when volunteers took over the near-moribund Talyllyn Railway in central Wales under the leadership of transport historian Tom Rolt, creating Britain's first operational 'preserved' line. It was also the first in the world to be run by volunteers and began a bandwagon that would continue to gather pace, attempting to reverse numerous branch line closures enacted before, during and after the Beeching era.

The idea was not entirely new. In 1929, when Suffolk's legendary 3ft gauge Southwold Railway closed, there were moves by local people to run it themselves, an initiative which sadly came to nothing, probably because there was then no blueprint to follow. Two years after the Talyllyn volunteers ran their first fare-paying trains, Ealing comedy The Titfield Thunderbolt, starring Stanley Holloway, proved a box office hit. The storyline centred around a group of villagers who were battling to keep their branch line operating after British Railways decided to close it.

The film drew considerable inspiration from the book Railway Adventure by Tom Rolt, published the year before, which related his experiences in saving the Talyllyn Railway. Several scenes in the film, such as the emergency resupply of water to the locomotive by buckets from an adjacent stream, or passengers being asked to assist in pushing the carriages, were taken from the book.

The film itself inspired future railway revivalists, conveying the message that ordinary people could 'have a go' and save their local line when the grey men in suits in the Whitehall corridors of power decided it should close. The Titfield Thunderbolt came out in 1953, eight years before Beeching was appointed as British Railways chairman.

During his first two years in the job, before his Report on the Reshaping of British Railways was released in 1963, Beeching rubber-stamped closures which had been recommended by divisional managers and which would have gone ahead had he never been appointed.

In some cases, passenger uptake on many of the winding rural routes that were closed in the Fifties was down to single figures, in others, numbers were moderate, but far from capable of balancing the books. It was not rocket science to come up with the idea that, in theory, buses and cars could do the job better and at a far lower cost to the taxpayer.

There would always be disenfranchised passengers who suffered genuine hardship, even if the majority of those who lost their train services were content to some extent to find alternatives. Those who could not were understandably among the most vocal.

Inevitably, there would be those who would suggest that the closed line should be denationalised and handed over to the people to run, by and for the benefit of the local community, just as in The Titfield Thunderbolt.

Many such protest-cum-revivalist groups would start by aiming high, such as trying to retain an entire route. Such was the case with the Lewes-East Grinstead line, a small part of which was revived in 1960 as the Bluebell Railway, as we saw earlier. It was the first example of a closed section of the standard gauge national network being taken over by revivalists and in the decades that followed, many more would follow.

However, only in a few cases would a revivalist group succeed in taking over and reopening a complete line. The Keighley & Worth Valley Railway (KWVR) was the first such example; the Dart Valley Railway's purchase of the Paignton-Kingswear line straight out of British Rail service was another.

On April 6, 1969, after the Dart Valley Railway bought the GWR Ashburton branch from British Rail, the first preservation era trains ran from Buckfastleigh to a point near the main line north of Totnes, under the new operator's Light Railway Order, with GWR pannier tank No. 6412 behind.

Again, this heritage line was officially opened by none other than axeman Beeching himself — even though it was not one of the many branches that he had infamously closed.

However, in another twist to the battle between road and rail, the revivalists sadly failed to persuade the Ministry of Transport not to take the top portion of the route, the two-mile stretch from Buckfastleigh to Ashburton, for use as part of the new A38 dual carriageway trunk road from Exeter to Plymouth, and therefore the entire branch was not saved, as had been the case with the KWVR.

The year before, British Rail had announced its intention to close the seven-mile Paignton to Kingswear section of the branch from Newton Abbot, in many ways a main line in all but name.

Many eyebrows were raised when the Dart Valley Railway successfully tabled a bid to acquire this section of the line, purchasing it from British Rail in service, without any 'last day' trains and the like that had been a hallmark of the Beeching closures.

The line was bought as a going concern on January 30, 1972, the purchase price being £250,000 with a further £25,000 paid for signalling alterations at Paignton. Most of this was recouped from the sale of the Royal Dart Hotel at Kingswear and other surplus land.

A new independent station was built at Paignton Queen's Park along-side the British Rail station to serve the Kingswear trains, and a winter service was run from January 1, 1973.

However, the operating figures did not stack up for either British Rail or the new owners. It quickly became clear that the Dart Valley Railway could not afford to run a daily service round the year and so from the end of summer 1973 it became a purely seasonal operation.

Dart Valley Railway plc found that the glorious coastal scenery reaped big dividends, while, as the years wore on, the original Buckfastleigh line incurred losses. To cut a very long story short, the Buckfastleigh line was again faced with closure, but was eventually sold to the line's volunteer supporters' association, which had rebranded it as the South Devon Railway. Thanks to freely-given labour, it very much flourishes today. Meanwhile, the Paignton-Kingswear line, now labelled the Dartmouth Steam Railway and River Boat Company, is the only heritage line in Britain to pay annual dividends to its shareholders, relying on paid staff and having built up a transport empire including a boat fleet.

In many cases of lines being acquired by preservationists/revivalists, the intention from the outset was to restore timetabled round-the-year public services, but this rarely happened, and if it did so, did not last. Revivalists found out the hard way that despite the best intentions, there were reasons why lines had been closed. Even with enthusiasts and local people giving their labour free of charge, a 365-days-a-year operation was not possible, let alone viable.

What revivalists could do, however, was to tailor their line to run only the services that people wanted, and were prepared to pay to travel on.

No such option had been open to British Railways. Many of the delightful seaside branch lines, which did a brisk trade in the summer months but carried few passengers once the holidaymakers had gone home, could not, as part of the national network, simply stop running during the winter.

Many such lines were closed because of the extremely high cost of storing vast fleets of coaching stock out of service for summer use during the rest of the year. Had such flexibility been possible, we might still be travelling to Lyme Regis or Ilfracombe in July and August by train. A privately owned heritage railway, however, remained unfettered by such restrictions. It could operate trains for identified markets and when there were sufficient volunteers to man them. However, there would be no service by which local people could travel to work or go shopping whenever they chose.

A very different animal was born. What was on offer was now a tourist attraction in its own right, not simply a means of getting from one place to another by the best form of public transport available.

What could it offer? Not a regular public service, but a living, linear museum, with a totally different business plan and structure.

A popular steam railway might even carry more passengers during its comparatively short operating season than the British Railways passenger services did on the line before they were withdrawn. However, the question remains as to whether the railway is providing a public service as a people carrier, or running trains for their own sake.

Such a question is by no means intended to be disparaging towards revivalists and preservationists. Heritage railways today form a sizeable slice of many a local tourist economy, creating or safeguarding thousands of jobs directly and indirectly. However, only a few can say that they have run 'real' regular public services, as opposed to tourist or enthusiast trains, and it is in this latter category that the would-be emulators of The Titfield Thunderbolt who saved their local branch have ended up. In fairness, some heritage railways have successfully run real freight trains, either as one-offs or as a series to serve an industrial concern next to the line.

Some might give local residents discounted tickets or free travel vouchers, which are much appreciated. Yet none come near to providing a full-blown all-year daily service of the type that British Railways and its predecessors did on the same route.

Again, the message here is that there was often a solid reason, if only by the standards of the day, why such lines closed. On the other hand, if services could have been adapted to suit the specific needs of local people, rather than conforming to a daily timetable that the Act of Parliament which authorised the building of a particular line in the previous century had stipulated, with more room for manoeuvre and greater scope for initiative and imagination, certain closed lines might have been saved, albeit with a local transport subsidy.

This is not to say that heritage railways could never play a part in providing local public transport as opposed to tourist and enthusiast services. The UK landscape has changed much since the years before, during and immediately after the Beeching era, and a station or branch line that might have been used by a handful of passengers a day might now be sitting next to a sizeable commuter housing development.

Provided an operating subsidy is forthcoming, there may well be scope for a heritage railway to introduce peak-hour commuter trains, combined with occasional shoppers' services, alleviating the levels of modern-day traffic congestion on local roads that Beeching never saw in his time.

Heritage railways and museums now carry around seven million passengers a year, according to estimates. They directly employ around 2000 people and are backed up by an army of nearly 18,000 volunteers and many, many more armchair supporters. Many of them run trains over routes that Beeching closed and yet are showing an operating profit, which is almost always ploughed back into infrastructure, or breaking even.

Therefore, does this not show that Beeching got his sums wrong? By no means — in fact, quite the opposite. A revived line that had been earmarked for closure under Beeching and ceased in 1971 was the Minehead branch. Now known as the West Somerset Railway, reopened in stages between Minehead and the first original station on the branch proper, Bishops Lydeard, between 1976-79, it tried to run regular services for local people, using classic diesel multiple units painted in 1950s carmine and cream livery.

Sadly, the hoped-for "real public transport" passenger figures also did not stack up here and the line was severely hampered in its nascent years by not being allowed to run over the main line into Taunton, as did the branch trains under the GWR and British Railways. Fears were raised that it would make a connecting bus service between Taunton and Bishops Lydeard obsolete and a local branch of a trade union successfully objected to the full revival of the line claiming that one bus driver would be made redundant.

It was only in the summer of 2019 that modern-day main line operator Great Western Railway launched a trial DMU service on Saturdays linking Taunton station to heritage services at Bishops Lydeard. Other heritage lines will claim they have provided 'real' public transport as opposed to tourist or heritage trains. The 15in gauge Romney Hythe & Dymchurch

Railway, long billed as a main line in miniature, has run regular school trains for local youngsters. The Swanage Railway, which has managed to rebuild the London & South Western Railway branch line from the resort westwards, was hailed as a huge success after the park-and-ride facility at its eastern passenger terminus of Norden was credited with easing summer congestion on the A351, the spine road of the Isle of Purbeck.

Yet the reality is that none of them have replicated the British Railways services that were axed under Beeching or afterwards, despite the provision of volunteer labour to maintain both rolling stock and infrastructure, therefore reducing or even eliminating labour costs at a stroke.

What has been achieved by preservationists in today's heritage sector is from many angles magnificent beyond belief, giving new generations an insight into the glory days of Britain's railway past and the chance to ride behind steam engines once again polished to perfection, but each of them is a very different animal to the running of a regular public timetable service 365 days a year.

If, of course, a local authority was to step in and subsidise running commuter or shopper services on these lines, it could be a different matter indeed. With fears of a future global fuel crisis and a growing desire to conserve the environment and avoid traffic congestion, fresh new opportunities may well arise here. If it was possible to run seaside branch lines during the summer season only, many more could have been saved by British Railways, but Beeching would be quick to point out the enormous cost of storing and maintaining the rolling stock for the rest of the time when it would not be used, as well as that of maintaining the route infrastructure throughout the year. In any age where the car is king, such figures would never stack up.

THE NORTH YORKSHIRE MOORS RAILWAY: A PINNACLE OF HERITAGE REVIVAL

In terms of passenger numbers, the biggest of all heritage lines in Britain, and possibly the world, is the North Yorkshire Moors Railway (NYMR), which runs from Grosmont to Pickering and also extends its services over Network Rail's Esk Valley line to reach Whitby. The North Yorkshire Moors Railway began life in 1836 as the Whitby & Pickering Railway, designed in 1831 by *Rocket* designer George Stephenson as a late horse-drawn line.

In 1845, the railway was acquired by the York & North Midland Railway that re-engineered the line to allow the use of steam locomotives and re-equipped the Beck Hole Incline with a stationary engine. The permanent stations and other structures that were constructed along the line remain today.

The company also added the line south from Pickering to Rillington Junction at Malton so there was a connection to York and London.

In 1854, the York & North Midland Railway became part of the North Eastern Railway, which in the early 1860s bypassed Beck Hole Incline so that locomotives could use the entire route. The end result was the line we have today. The bypassed section of the original route is now the 3.5-mile Historic Rail Trail.

Beeching listed the route for closure in his 1963 report and accordingly the final passenger service ran on March 6, 1965, although the line was used in June that year to stable the Royal Train for the Duke of Edinburgh's visit to the RAF Fylingdales early warning station. Freight ended in July 1966.

Local councils had fought hard but in vain to save both the Whitby-Pickering-Malton and Whitby-Scarborough lines, but were thrown breadcrumbs in the form of the Esk Valley Line to Battersby Junction and Middlesbrough. A winding route indeed, but better than no railway at all.

The demise of the Whitby to Pickering line was at first met with silence. However, local man Tom Salmon, who had wondered how to fight the closure plans as soon as Beeching announced them, set up a meeting at his home in Ruswarp in June 1967 to see if anything could be done to save it, as despite the haste elsewhere in ripping up tracks soon after the last trains had passed by, this line was still intact.

Several local railwaymen familiar with the line attended the meeting. They included retired BR driver Fred Stuart, a Whitby councillor who had fought the closure and even suggested using the rates to subsidise it.

In true Titfield fashion, he said: "If BR or the local authorities will not operate it, can we try?"

At a packed public meeting at Goathland on November 18, 1967, the North Yorkshire Moors Railway Preservation Society was established, with Fred as its first chairman and Tom as secretary.

While the wonderfully scenic coastal route from Whitby to Scarborough was by then being dismantled, British Rail agreed to hold off on the Malton route for six months while the society became established.

At first, it was agreed with British Rail to begin by reopening the Grosmont to Eller Beck section, with a new halt being provided near Fylingdales to provide access to the National Park.

The first item of rolling stock arrived on August 9, 1968, in the form of AC Cars diesel railbus No. 79978. Then came a first-class sleeping car to be used as volunteer accommodation. In November 1968, British Rail agreed to give the society complete access to the 18 miles of track and use maintenance trolleys for carrying out essential repairs. Around the same time, a new company, the North Yorkshire Moors Railway Ltd, was formed.

The initial aim was to reopen the railway from Grosmont southwards through the spectacular glacial gorge in Newtondale, maybe rebuilding it to Pickering at a later date.

Early the following year, the British Railways Board approved the sale of the whole line to the summit at Eller Beck and the trackbed only to Pickering. May 19, 1969, saw a 10% deposit of £4250 paid.

On January 25, 1969, Hudswell Clarke 0-4-0ST *Mirvale* arrived on the line and steamed from Pickering to Grosmont, with British Rail permission, attracting huge crowds in the process.

It was followed eight weeks later by Andrew Barclay 0-6-0ST *Salmon* and an 1898-built E Burrows and Sons 0-4-0 well tank owned by the Newcastle University Railway Society.

In the second half of 1969, British Rail singled the double track section of the line between Grosmont and Levisham. The move sparked a race against time to buy the remaining single track line through Newtondale.

North Riding County Council and the North York Moors National Park planning committee persuaded British Rail to hold off lifting the remaining track to Pickering.

However, by early 1970, it was apparent there was insufficient money to buy the remaining track to Pickering. British Rail gave the society a deadline of August to come up with some money, or lifting would begin.

Mirvale and *Salmon* became the stars of an Easter 1970 steam gala that British Rail allowed to be held at Goathland, and it raised vital funds for the society.

Many heritage railways, including some of today's biggest, started out by running industrial locomotive types, wholly unauthentic to a main line setting, but which satisfied the general public's craving to see steam in the years following its demise on the main line in August 1968.

However, more appropriate locomotives for a former North Eastern Railway route were on the horizon. The North Eastern Locomotive Preservation Group had been busy elsewhere preserving NER P3 J27 0-6-0 No. 2392 and T2 (Q6) 0-8-0 No. 63395, and the NYMR was a ready home. Also arriving in 1970 was Lambton, Hetton & Joicey Collieries 0-6-2T No. 29.

During a steam gala on June 27-29 that year, the Q6 and No. 29 hauled three-coach trains from Grosmont to Goathland, using volunteer BR steam drivers.

On March 27, 1971, the NYMR Preservation Society transformed itself into the North Yorkshire Moors Historical Railway Trust.

In early 1971, the British Railways Board agreed a price of £42,500 for the whole 18 miles of trackbed from Grosmont to High Mill, Pickering. The English Tourist Board offered a £30,000 grant towards the line purchase.

By now, membership had risen to around the 6000 mark and a multitude of fundraising events were staged, from raffles and sponsored walks to collecting Green Shield stamps.

On July 23, 1971, a special train hauled by No. 29's sister engine No. 5 ran from Grosmont to Pickering carrying Alderman J Fletcher, chairman of North Riding of Yorkshire County Council, and his guests. It bore fruit big time, for on November 3, 1971, the council voted to negotiate with British Rail to buy the 12-mile line between Eller Beck and Pickering.

The idea was that the county council would buy the track and sell it to the NYMR over 20 years. The move would save the revivalists from having to re-lay the line in the future.

A fresh obstacle arose when Pickering Urban District Council considered allowing a supermarket to build on Pickering station. The Department of the Environment then saved the day by giving the station listed building status protection.

Finally, the big day arrived, when the whole line would be reopened to the public — but as a heritage railway, not in its pre-closure format.

The first timetabled heritage services were run on Easter Sunday, April 22, 1973, with the official opening on May 1 that year. The first public train was a DMU hired from British Rail. The first public steam-hauled train was hauled by No. 2392.

The Duchess of Kent arrived at Whitby by air to perform the official opening. She unveiled a plaque at the Angel Hotel where plans for Stephenson's original line were made in the 1830s, and then travelled by car to Grosmont to be greeted by a large crowd. There, she unveiled a commemorative plaque and was presented with a painting.

The duchess activated a signal to give the 'all clear' for the seven-coach royal reopening special train, double headed by No. 29 and No. 2392, to proceed.

At Pickering, a brass band led the duchess as she walked from the station to the Black Swan Hotel where she unveiled another plaque.

Since then, the NYMR has gone from strength to strength, building up a sizeable fleet of main line steam locomotives and hiring others in from time to time.

Steam apart, one of the big draws for tourists is the upland scenery, which they can experience from the elevated heights of a train in remote areas not accessible by car. In this respect it is also a brilliant facility to national park walkers, who use the train to get straight into deepest moorland.

It is also a line for all seasons, not just the summer. 'Santa Special' services are run in the Christmas period and winter moorland scenery adds greatly to their appeal.

An enormous publicity boost to the line's fortunes lasted several years when it was used for location filming of the TV drama Heartbeat, set in the Sixties. Goathland station became Aidensfield, and it also doubled up as Hogsmeade in the Harry Potter films.

Other TV appearances have included the programmes Casualty, Brideshead Revisited, All Creatures Great and Small, The Royal, Poirot and Sherlock Holmes.

Such nationwide exposure has helped push the line's annual passenger numbers to around the 350,000 mark — a major heritage success story.

The NYMR has also extended regular services over Network Rail metals, with some of its locomotives passed for running over the Esk

Valley line, between Whitby and Grosmont and westwards to Battersby Junction and even Middlesbrough.

Many supporters were concerned about the extension of regular services into Whitby, fearing that the extra cost of running the trains and Network Rail track access charges would not be covered by a rise in passenger numbers.

They were proved wrong. In 2005/6, the Carnforth-based West Coast Railway Company ran a pilot service from the heritage line to Whitby, and in 2007, the NYMR became a Train Operating Company in its own right, able to do the job under its own licence. So once again, a through journey over George Stephenson's route from Whitby to Pickering was possible.

From time to time, the missing 6.5 miles from Pickering, where the original station roof has been replaced with the aid of Heritage Lottery Fund grant aid, to Rillington Junction, has been the subject of calls for reinstatement, finally reversing the last part of the Beeching closure.

Such a move would create a second through route to Whitby for public trains from the main York to Scarborough line, while having the potential to bring in more visitors by rail to the NYMR.

However, the problems of extending the NYMR south of Pickering are compounded by the presence of a large road junction and supermarket immediately beyond the station and houses built on the formation just north of Kirby.

Also, extending NYMR services to Malton is seen as being of little gain, as the section between Pickering and Rillington Junction comprises flat and featureless landscape, largely unappealing to tourists.

PRE-BEECHING PASSENGER CLOSURES, NOW HERITAGE LINES

These lists refer to complete routes which were formerly run as part of the national network and which individual heritage lines mostly run over particular lengths.

> » **Battlefield Line:** Nuneaton-Ashby closed to passengers 1931, closed to goods 1970.
> » **Lynton & Barnstaple Railway:** closed 1935.
> » **Pontypool & Blaenavon Railway:** closed to passengers 1941.

» **Caledonian Railway:** Brechin-Bridge of Dun closed to passengers 1952.
» **Bure Valley Railway:** Aylsham-Wroxham section of County School-Wroxham closed to passengers 1952.
» **Weardale Railway:** Bishop Auckland-Eastgate section of Bishop Auckland-Wearhead closed to passengers 1953.
» **Kent & East Sussex Railway:** Headcorn to Robertsbridge closed to regular passenger trains 1954.
» **Wensleydale Railway:** Northallerton-Hawes closed to passengers 1954.
» **Bo'ness & Kinneil Railway:** closed to passengers 1956.
» **Welshpool & Llanfair Light Railway:** closed 1956.
» **Chinnor & Princes Risborough Railway:** closed to passengers 1957.
» **Bluebell Railway:** East Grinstead-Lewes closed to passengers 1958.
» **South Devon Railway:** Totnes-Ashburton closed to passengers 1958.
» **Cholsey & Wallingford Railway:** closed to passengers 1959.
» **Rudyard Lake Steam Railway:** Leek-Macclesfield closed to passengers 1960.
» **Northampton & Lamport Railway:** Northampton-Market Harborough closed to passengers 1960.
» **Midland Railway-Butterley:** Butterley-Ambergate-Mansfield closed to passengers 1961.
» **Swindon & Cricklade Railway:** Andover-Andoversford closed to passengers 1961.

HERITAGE RAILWAYS ON ROUTES CLOSED BY BEECHING

This list includes both routes contained in the 1963 Beeching Report and those previously endorsed for closure during his first two years as British Railways chairman.

» **Avon Valley Railway:** Mangotsfield- Bath Green Park closed to passengers 1966.
» **Bala Lake Railway:** Ruabon-Morfa Mawddach closed to passengers 1965.
» **Berkeley Vale Railway:** Berkeley Road-Sharpness closed to passengers 1964.

» **Bluebell Railway:** Haywards Heath-Ardingly-Horsted Keynes closed to passengers 1963.

» **Buckinghamshire Railway Centre:** Marylebone-Nottingham Victoria closed 1966.

» **Bodmin & Wenford Railway:** Bodmin Road-Padstow closed to passengers 1967.

» **Brecon Mountain Railway:** Newport-Dowlais-Brecon closed to passengers 1962.

» **Cambrian Railways:** Gobowen-Oswestry closed to passengers 1966.

» **Churnet Valley Railway:** Leek-Uttoxeter closed to passengers 1965.

» **Colne Valley Railway:** Haverhill-Chappell & Wakes Colne closed to passengers 1961, freight 1965.

» **Devon Railway Centre, Cadeleigh:** Exeter-Dulverton line closed 1963.

» **East Anglian Railway Museum:** Shelford- Marks Tey (but Sudbury to Marks Tey never closed).

» **East Lancashire Railway:** Manchester Victoria-Bury-Bacup closed to passengers 1966.

» **East Somerset Railway:** Witham-Yatton closed to passengers 1963.

» **Embsay & Bolton Abbey Steam Railway:** Leeds City-Ilkley-Skipton closed to passengers 1965.

» **Gartell Light Railway:** Bath Green Park-Bournemouth West closed 1966.

» **Great Central Railway:** Marylebone-Nottingham Victoria closed as through route 1966, to local passenger services 1969.

» **Gwili Railway:** Carmarthen-Aberystwyth closed to passengers 1965.

» **Helston Railway:** Gwinear Road-Helston closed 1962.

» **Isle of Wight Steam Railway:** Ryde Pier Head-Ventnor/Cowes closed 1966.

» **Keith & Dufftown Railway:** Keith-Dufftown-Elgin closed to passengers 1965.

» **Keighley & Worth Valley Railway:** Keighley-Oxenhope closed 1962.

» **Lappa Valley Railway:** Newquay-Chacewater closed 1963.

» **Lakeside & Haverthwaite Railway:** Ulverston-Lakeside (Windermere) closed to passengers 1965.

» **Launceston Steam Railway:** Okehampton-Padstow closed to passengers 1966.

» **Mid-Hants Railway:** Winchester City-Alton closed 1973.

» **Lavender Line:** Tunbridge Wells-Brighton-Uckfield-Lewes closed 1969.

» **Lincolnshire Wolds Railway:** Peterborough-Grimsby Town closed to passengers 1970.

» **Llangollen Railway:** Ruabon-Morfa Mawddach closed to passengers 1965.

» **Nene Valley Railway:** Rugby-Peterborough East closed to passengers 1966.

» **North Norfolk Railway:** Sheringham-Melton Constable closed 1964.

» **North Yorkshire Moors Railway:** Malton-Whitby closed 1965.

» **Plym Valley Railway:** Plymouth-Launceston closed to passengers 1962.

» **Severn Valley Railway:** Bewdley-Shrewsbury closed to passengers 1963.

» **South Tynedale Railway:** Haltwhistle-Alston closed 1976.

» **Spa Valley Railway:** Three Bridges-Tunbridge Wells West closed 1985.

» **Strathspey Railway:** Aviemore-Craigellachie/Forres closed to passengers 1965.

» **Wells & Walsingham Railway:** Dereham-Wells-next-the-Sea closed 1964.

» **West Somerset Railway:** Taunton-Minehead closed 1971.

» **Welsh Highland Railway:** Caernarfon to Dinas section, part of Caernarfon-Afon Wen standard gauge line, closed in December 1964.

HERITAGE LINES ON ROUTES NOT PROPOSED FOR CLOSURE BY BEECHING BUT SUBSEQUENTLY CLOSED

» **Dartmoor Railway:** Okehampton-Bere Alston: closed to passengers 1968, Exeter to Okehampton closed to passengers 1972.

» **Dartmouth Steam Railway & River Boat Company:** Paignton-Kingswear privatised in 1972.

» **Gloucestershire Warwickshire Railway:** Stratford-upon-Avon-Gloucester closed to passengers 1968.

» **Mid-Norfolk Railway:** Wymondham-Dereham: closed to passengers 1969.

» **Peak Rail:** Peak Forest Junction-Matlock closed 1968.

» **Swanage Railway:** Wareham-Swanage closed 1972.

» **Vale of Rheidol Railway:** Aberystwyth-Devil's Bridge sold by British Rail 1989.

» **Wisbech & March Bramley line (not yet operational in 2011):** closed in September 1968.

CHAPTER EIGTHEEN

Cuts unravelled

SINCE THE upsurge in rail traffic that began in the 1980s, and greater appreciation of the environmental damage caused by huge volumes of road traffic, both in terms of pollution and congestion, there has been a sea change on the railway network.

The traditional tearing up of railway lines, often within days of them having closed, has ceased. At many locations around the country lie branch lines that are 'mothballed', the tracks intact, albeit heavily covered in vegetation.

One such example is the Anglesey Central Railway that runs from Gaerwen Junction on the Bangor-Holyhead line to Amlwch. It lost its passenger services to the Beeching Axe on December 5, 1964, with all stations closed and goods yards, passing loops and sidings removed. However, the entire branch was saved to serve the Associated Octel bromine extraction plant at Amlwch.

In 1993, Octel's daily freight traffic was transferred to road haulage and all traffic on the Amlwch branch ended. The Octel plant closed in 2003 and has since been demolished, but the track remains in place. While local revivalists have sought to reopen it as a tourist line under the banner of Lein Amlwch, in 2011 the Welsh Assembly asked Network

Rail to carry out a study into its possible reopening to serve the local community.

Similarly, the Trawsfynydd branch — in effect an extension of the Conwy Valley Line from Blaenau Ffestiniog — which served the former Trawsfynydd nuclear power station in Snowdonia, is still in place, 20 years after the complex closed down. There are periodic calls for it to be revived to carry tourists, but the key point is — it too has not been ripped up, as would have speedily been the case in the Sixties and Seventies. Scrapping a potential provider of 'green' transport is very much seen as politically incorrect in today's climate.

Who knows how many lines would have reopened by now if British Railways had adopted a similar approach back then?

Since Beeching produced his report in 1963, road traffic levels have grown significantly, bringing gridlock to some areas. Housing developments of the Seventies and Eighties have turned small villages, which in the days of steam barely justified a station or halt, into thriving commuter settlements more than capable of justifying a rail connection.

At the same time, recent years have seen record levels of passengers on the railways. For instance, around 1.2 billion passenger journeys were made in 2007/08, a rise of 45% on the figure from a decade earlier.

At the time of writing, 2019, there is also ever-increasing demand for more capacity on the network, and some of the Beeching cuts have been reversed.

Several closed stations have reopened and passenger services restored on lines where they had been withdrawn under the Sixties cuts. Many of them are in urban areas where the Passenger Transport Executives established by Barbara Castle's 1968 Transport Act have been tackling congestion by promoting rail use.

THE BIGGEST REVERSAL OF THEM ALL

As we saw in Chapter 6, the writing was on the wall for the Carlisle to Edinburgh Waverley Line as soon as the doctor referred to it as "the biggest money loser in the British railway system". Its closure has long been regarded as the biggest and most severe cut of the Beeching era.

However, the rebuilding of the northernmost section in recent times as the Borders Railway has proved to be one of, if not the, most successful of all the Beeching closure reversals. Beeching had seen a clear choice between the two principal routes from the West Coast Main Line to Edinburgh, one from Carlisle running through sparsely populated or uninhabited hill country for much of the way, with several significant gradients, or the shorter route from Carstairs Junction, which passes through a far more densely populated area. It was obvious which one would stay.

The closure left the Scottish Borders as the only region of Britain without a rail link, and Hawick, today's population 14,801, 56 miles from Edinburgh and 42 miles from Carlisle, as the largest town farthest from a railway station. Despite the passage of time, there were people who remained determined that one day they would get their railway back.

It had taken campaigners more than 46 years to roll the clock back, but at last they saw their endeavours bear fruit when the first passenger trains ran on the rebuilt railway on September 5, 2015. The opening of the 'new' £294 million, 30½-mile line between Newcraighall — south-east of Edinburgh — to Tweedbank, covering about a third of the 98-mile Waverley Route, proved to be a landmark achievement for several reasons.

Indeed, it was the longest domestic line to open in Britain since the West Highland Extension between Fort William and Mallaig in 1901.

On the day of the official opening by the Queen, three days after the first public services, steam appeared on the line in the form of John Cameron's A4 No. 60009 *Union of South Africa*.

It had been 48 years since the last steam locomotive had run over the Waverley Route.

The last steam railtour to work over the line came on December 3, 1966, when LNER B1 4-6-0 No. 61278 headed the Scottish Region's 'Last B1 Excursion' from Edinburgh via the Glasgow & South Western Railway route to Kingmoor, returning to Waverley via Galashiels.

With the demise of steam on the national network less than a year away, Carlisle Kingmoor shed retained a substantial allocation of BR Standard Britannia Pacifics throughout 1967 and although these were only normally rostered to work south from the city they did very occasionally venture north.

As late as November 1967, one of the class, No. 70011 *Hotspur*, found itself on a northbound freight over the Waverley Route, but this was topped by what is regarded as the very last steam train over the line later in the month when sister No. 70022 *Tornado* deputised for a failed Sulzer Type 2 diesel on a 2S52 Carlisle-Edinburgh semi-fast, just a month before the closure of Kingmoor shed, and withdrawal.

Steam, however, would never been forgotten by the public at large, and neither would the Waverley Route.

In the late Nineties, there was talk about reopening the southern section of the Waverley Route from Carlisle as far as Riccarton Junction to extract timber from Kielder Forest, but again it came to nothing.

In January 1999, the Campaign for Borders Rail (CBR) was formally launched at a Burns Supper in Melrose station and collected thousands of signatures on a petition pressing for a rail route to the region to be relaid.

An independent study published in February 2000 concluded that the reopening of the Borders rail link could be financially viable, and on June 1, 2000, the Scottish Parliament debated whether to rebuild the entire Waverley Route.

CBR's UK parliamentary officer Nick Bethune said: "The original Scottish Borders Railway feasibility study carried out by consultants Scott Wilson for the Scottish Executive in 2000 was very downbeat about the line's tourist potential despite the Borders being renowned for Sir Walter Scott's home at Abbotsford, several historic abbeys and delightful scenery.

"It said that 'existing tourist attractions are not likely to benefit from the proposed rail service' and that 'south of Gorebridge the line runs through moderately attractive scenery and that some tourists will travel on the line 'for the ride' but there is no reason to believe they will spend significant amounts of money in the Borders'."

In 2002, the Waverley Trust Group was launched to promote a community railway to and through the Scottish Borders and argued the case for a more innovative and tourist-friendly railway than that proposed by the promoter.

The WRT's research in conjunction with CBR ultimately led to the Tweedbank terminus being redesigned (lengthened) to accommodate tourist charter trains.

On January 6, 2005, marking the 36th anniversary of the last passenger train, a rally was held calling for the Waverley Route to be rebuilt. Six months later, a Scottish Parliament committee supported reinstatement of the northern 35 miles from Edinburgh to Galashiels.

In June 2006, the Scottish Parliament gave the green light to the Waverley Railway Bill to restore the rail link between Edinburgh and Tweedbank. On March 27, 2007, work began to examine the formation of the old line prior to its rebuilding. On March 4, 2010, Scottish Transport Minister Stewart Stevenson visited Galashiels to cut the first sod of the new railway, thereby activating the act of parliament under which the railway has been rebuilt.

In December 2012, Network Rail appointed BAM Nuttall as the main contractor for what was to be named the Borders Railway.

The project, which involved both ScotRail and Network Rail, included seven new stations — at Shawfair, Eskbank, Newtongrange, Gorebridge, Stow, Galashiels and Tweedbank.

In August 2013, it was reported that developers and property buyers alike were driving a housing boom along the Borders Railway corridor, with the number of new homes built in Midlothian more than doubling in the space of a year. New houses completed in 2012 rose to 916 from 451 the year before. Summarising its successes, CBR said that in addition to its core achievement — the return of a railway from Edinburgh through Midlothian to Tweedbank — local rail campaigners, notably CBR, Waverley Route Trust and Stow Station Supporters Group, could take credit for some important successes, a number achieved in the face of official resistance.

These included creating the Borders Railway name in 2003 and in 2011 persuading Parliament to include a station stop at the original North British Railway's Edinburgh-Hawick branch station at Stow.

In 2013, CBR successfully campaigned for the requirement for new ScotRail operator Abellio to allow steam-hauled tourist trains to fit in with scheduled public passenger services, and cut maximum waiting time at the A7 pedestrian crossing from bus to Gala railway station from 90 to 30 seconds, thereby improving convenience and safety for rail passengers.

The following year CBR successfully lobbied for the first train of the day to Edinburgh being retimed to make a connection with the 6.25am departure from the capital to London.

CBR also persuaded Transport Scotland to upgrade the Borders Railway's Class 158 DMUs by improving window-seat positioning and increasing luggage-cycle carrying space. A series of steam trips run by operator Abellio ScotRail over the revived railway sold out well before it opened for the start of the regular public half-hourly DMU services.

Scottish Borders Council leader David Parker opened the new Tweedbank terminus to the public on Saturday, September 5, 2015 — and immediately vowed to continue to campaign for the line to be extended the full length of the Waverley Route to Hawick and Carlisle. That day saw a select group of lucky local residents who had been awarded 'golden tickets' travel over the line for a sneak preview.

They travelled on three trains leaving Tweedbank, Galashiels and Stow, each carrying 160 passengers. Many had special links to the line, having campaigned for its return or been involved in the old Waverley Route. Others making the trip were nominated by the public or won competitions.

However, they were not the first passengers on the reborn line. Among those was veteran campaigner and Waverley Route legend Madge Elliot, 87, who was given a special ride over the line from Tweedbank to Newcraighall during driver training trips on Sunday, July 26, with her family.

Madge fought hard to save the route before it closed. She spearheaded a petition to keep the line open and in 1968 — along with son Kim and Liberal MP David Steel — hand delivered it to Prime Minister Harold Wilson.

When final closure was scheduled for Monday, January 6, 1969, Madge and her campaign group continued their protest by having a simulated coffin placed aboard the last train to leave Hawick station travelling to St Pancras.

She was later awarded an MBE, for 28 years of tennis coaching in Hawick, and on June 4 saw Freightliner Class 66 No. 66528 *Madge Elliot MBE* named after her at a ceremony at Waverley station.

After her trip, Madge told BBC Scotland: "I never had any doubt it would come back again. It was such a daft thing to do, to close our railway.

"The scenery is absolutely beautiful. We can attract visitors from all over the world to this part of the country."

Scotland's Infrastructure Secretary Keith Brown, who also travelled that day, said: "Madge Elliot is a legend of the Borders and the railways, and it is absolutely fitting that she be the first member of the public to travel on this line as she was so instrumental in having it reinstated."

The iconic route takes customers between Tweedbank and Edinburgh in 55 minutes, with a half-hourly service for most of the day.

The first fare-paying passengers for the journey were carried on Sunday, September 6, on the 8.45am service from Tweedbank to Edinburgh, some queueing for hours for a place on the historic journey. Crowds gathered to watch Class 158 vehicles Nos. 158701/716/727 pull up and depart.

First in the queue for tickets were Andrew Whitworth, from Harrogate, and Miles Glendinning, from Edinburgh. Andrew said: "It's righting a wrong, because the line should never have been closed back in 1969."

The first public southbound train was the 9.11am Edinburgh to Tweedbank and long queues formed well before departure time. It was formed of three Class 170 DMUs.

Coun Parker, who also rode on the first train out of Tweedbank, said: "We always said that this was the beginning, Tweedbank was only ever going to be the first stop on this railway. All of us now need to come together again, redouble our efforts and get this line down to Hawick and Carlisle.

"The fact that we've already sold out all the steam trains before the line has even opened just shows how much appetite there is for a railway.

"We'll only ever realise the proper economic benefits when we get to Hawick and Carlisle and I'm convinced we can make that happen."

Edinburgh City Council leader Coun Andrew Burns said: "It will play an important role in increasing connectivity to and from the capital, providing a convenient route for visitors and commuters.

"Not only will it ease the journey for those working in and outwith the city, but, with the last train leaving Edinburgh just before midnight, it will allow those from Midlothian and the Borders to enjoy everything the city has to offer."

An Abellio ScotRail spokesman said that more than 2500 journeys were made on the Sunday. "The level of interest in the Borders Railway has been remarkable, with thousands of people turning up to travel in recent days, particularly at weekends with families making a day of it," he said. "On Monday (September 7), the first day of commuter services, numbers varied but it proved popular; for example 220 people travelled to Edinburgh on the 7.28am from Tweedbank." CBR's next objective is to see the Borders Railway extended to Galashiels and Hawick through to Carlisle, completing a reborn Waverley Route.

South of Scotland MSP Claudia Beamish who, with support from the CBR, successfully campaigned for the platforms to be redesigned to accommodate 12-coach tourist charter trains, said: "In the face of opposition from policy makers, the CBR stood firm in their belief that reopening this line would be good for the Borders, but good for Scotland too.

"I am determined to continue to try to convince those in my own party and the Scottish Government of the importance of getting the line extended through Hawick to Carlisle and will be glad to work on this with CBR."

Nick Bethune added: "The Borders Railway should be recognised as one of the greatest achievements of grassroots rail campaigning in British history."

CBR chairman Simon Walton added: "The physical obstacles to extending the line to Hawick initially are far fewer than had to be overcome in construction between Edinburgh and Tweedbank, such as the massive multi-million-pound structure needed to burrow under the Edinburgh city bypass.

"A reinstated railway through to Carlisle would provide a strategic diversionary route, relieving pressure on the busy West Coast Main Line."

Passenger numbers in the first three years of the Borders Railway indeed validated the vision of the long-time campaigners. By the third anniversary of its opening, September 6, 2018, more than four million journeys had been made.

Alex Hynes, the ScotRail Alliance managing director, said: "The Borders Railway continues to provide a strong and reliable transport connection, benefiting employment, leisure, tourism and business.

"Reaching the milestone figure of more than four million passenger journeys demonstrates the success of what was an ambitious project and I look forward to its continued growth."

Michael Matheson, Scotland's Cabinet Secretary for Transport, Infrastructure and Connectivity, said: "The Borders Railway has been a phenomenal success as it continues to grow in both popularity and bringing benefits to the local economy. The increase in passenger numbers since it opened three years ago demonstrates it is acting as a catalyst for investment while opening up employment, leisure and education opportunities for communities along its length.

"We continue to look at ways to develop the potential of the line and the recommendations from the Borders Transport Corridors Study will, in turn, feed into the ongoing Strategic Transport Projects Review."

If a route so damningly written off by Beeching can be demonstrated as playing a key role in transport needs half a century on, could other routes lost in or just after his day be likewise revived to perform a local transport revolution too, the pro-rail lobby asks.

Before the Borders Railway opened, rail revival in Scotland had already proved its worth.

Laurencekirk station on the main line between Aberdeen and Arbroath was closed in 1967 but reopened in May 2009, making it the 77th new or reopened station in Scotland since 1970.

Services on the Edinburgh-Bathgate line that reopened in 1986 now carry four times as many passengers as originally estimated. This enormous success led to the rebuilding and reopening of the 14-mile closed section between Airdrie and Bathgate in 2011.

Services on the Larkhall-Hamilton/Anniesland-Maryhill lines that reopened in 2005 have been carrying around 40% more passengers than previously predicted.

The Stirling-Alloa line was reopened on May 19, 2008 after a 40-year gap and carried three times more passengers than estimated.

AND THERE'S MORE TO COME!

Following the success of the Borders Railway, in early August 2019, the Scottish Government announced that it was to spend £70 million on a five-year project to reverse another Beeching cut, in order to return passenger trains to Levenmouth in Fife.

The announcement came half a century after passenger services were halted on the five-mile route, part of a line that had extended to St Andrews, until freight east of Leven ceased in 1966 and that section of the route closed.

Passenger services to Leven ceased in 1969, but the route remained open as a freight-only line to serve the Cameronbridge whisky distillery, Kirkland yard and Methil power station, the terminus of the line. Carbon dioxide produced by the distillery at Cameronbridge was carried by rail, while coal slurry from collieries around Fife was delivered to Methil power station using the line.

The last services ran on the line in 2001, at the time Methil power station was mothballed.

Still in situ, the line was completely disused until 2011, when one mile of the route was reopened to serve a loading point for the opencast coal mine at Earlseat. Freight services ran on this section of track 2012-15.

Campaigns for the reinstatement of passenger services on the route have occurred since passenger services were withdrawn.

Nowadays, the Levenmouth area is by far the largest urban area in Scotland unserved by any direct rail link, with a population of around 33,000. The catchment area of the line, which would include parts of the East Neuk, would rise to around 43,000. The Levenmouth Sustainable Transport Study suggested there would be 750,000 passengers getting on or off trains in the area each year by 2037.

Scotland's Transport Secretary Michael Matheson confirmed the project would now go forward to the detailed design phase. It is planned that the reopened rail link will see trains stop at Leven and Cameron Bridge, running on via Thornton to link east Fife with Edinburgh and Dundee for the first time since 1969. The new passenger trains will join the Fife Circle Line at Thornton North Junction, and the overall journey time from Leven to Edinburgh is expected to take around 70 to 75 minutes.

Mr Matheson said: "I am extremely pleased that the case has been made for the Levenmouth rail link and I look forward to seeing this project being taken forward to the next stages of design.

"The detailed appraisal work that has been carried out suggests that improved transport links, which give Leven a direct rail link to the capital, will lead to an enhanced local economy, bringing better access to employment and education and the potential for new investment."

Fife's Green MSP Mark Ruskell said: "There's also the possibility to use the line for freight and take hundreds of lorries off local roads and I expect this to be explored more in the next feasibility stage. "This announcement needs to just be the start of a more ambitious plan for expanding the rail network in Scotland."

Scottish Liberal Democrat leader and North East Fife MSP Willie Rennie said: "Grit, charm and bloody-mindedness has won the campaign to bring back the railway to Levenmouth.

"The Levenmouth Rail Campaign, with the staunch support of local people, has persuaded the authorities that there would be a powerful economic, social and environmental benefit with the reopening of the line."

GREEN SHOOTS SOUTH OF THE BORDER

The prime example of the reversal of a Beeching closure in England is the Robin Hood Line between Nottingham and Worksop via Mansfield. Formed from two separate closed railways, it opened in stages between 1993 and 1998.

Before then, Mansfield had been the largest town in Britain left without a rail link. It is one of the great idiosyncrasies of Victorian route planning combined with Beeching closures that towns like Mansfield and Leek can end up being disenfranchised from the national network, while you can still buy a ticket to those aforementioned village stations on the North Warwickshire Line.

Some reopenings took place fairly soon after closure. The section of the Lincoln to Peterborough line between Peterborough and Spalding closed to passengers on October 5, 1970, but reopened on June 7, 1971; Ruskington & Metheringham station on the Sleaford to Lincoln line reopened in October 1975. The Great Western Railway's Birmingham terminus of Snow Hill had been largely demolished, but a new replacement opened in 1987, along with the tunnel that ran south beneath the city centre to Moor Street and the old line to Kidderminster and Worcester. A new service between Birmingham and London, terminating at Marylebone rather than Paddington, was introduced.

The former line from Snow Hill running north to Wolverhampton has been reopened as part of the Midland Metro tram system. Several cities such as Manchester, Nottingham and Sheffield have built new modern light rail tram systems, some using old railway trackbeds in part.

Also in the West Midlands, the line from Coventry to Leamington was reopened on May 2, 1977, followed by the Coventry to Nuneaton line in 1988. A new station is to be provided at Kenilworth in 2013. The Walsall-Hednesford line was reopened to passenger traffic in 1989 and extended to Rugeley in 1997. However, despite such successes, reopening has not been all plain sailing: the adjoining Walsall to Wolverhampton line saw its passenger trains withdrawn in 2008 on economic grounds.

In London, Snow Hill tunnel (not a Beeching closure) was reopened for passenger use in 1988, providing a link between the Midland Main Line from St Pancras and the network south of the River Thames via London Bridge station. Named Thameslink, it now offers a north-south cross-city rail link that also connects Bedford to Brighton.

Part of the Varsity Line closed in 1967 by the Wilson government, the Oxford to Bicester Line was reopened in 1987 by the Network SouthEast sector of British Rail, and many believe that one day it will again be possible to catch a train from Oxford to Cambridge.

The London to Aylesbury line was extended north along the surviving freight-only part of the former Great Central main line to a new park-and-ride station called Aylesbury Vale Parkway, which opened in December 2008. Beeching had viewed South Wales as a declining industrial region, arguably with great clarity of vision in view of the pit closures that took place two decades later. His report led to the loss of most of the valleys' network.

However, since 1983 the trend has been very much reversed, with four lines reopened within 20 miles — Abercynon-Aberdare, Barry-Bridgend via Llantwit Major, Bridgend-Maesteg and the Ebbw Valley branch via Newbridge, with 32 new stations opening.

While Scotland has repeatedly found itself at the forefront of closure threats, rail reopenings south of the border have been something of a revelation. Across Britain, more than 200 stations were reopened in the 1980s and early '90s, and in spite of the overall reduction in track and station capacity during the past 45 years since Beeching's cuts began to bite hard, the network today carries around 30% more passengers than it did then.

COULD MORE LINES REOPEN?

In 2009, Britain's Train Operating Companies issued a blueprint for reconnecting 40 stations on 14 routes to the national network at a cost of around £500 million, many having closed during the Beeching era, in order to improve access to rail for up to a million potential users.

Michael Roberts, chief executive of the Association of Train Operating Companies, said: "We have established that there is a strong business case for investment to bring a number of towns back on to the rail network.

"Now we need to safeguard these routes and develop the detailed case for investment."

A report by ATOC also called for seven new park-and-ride stations, at Rushden (Northamptonshire), Peterlee (County Durham), Kenilworth (Warwickshire), Ilkeston and Clay Cross (Derbyshire), Ossett (West Yorkshire) and Wantage (Oxfordshire), to be built on existing lines, and identified 20 more lines that could be reopened on employment grounds.

The report compiled by Chris Austin, ATOC former director of public policy, said the case for reopening more local stations and building 'parkways' had been boosted by lack of parking at main stations and congestion on roads leading to them.

The areas that would be served by the 14 lines identified in the report were:
  » Aldridge and Brownhills in the West Midlands
  » Ashington and Blyth in Northumberland
  » Bordon, Hythe and Ringwood in Hampshire
  » Brixham in Devon (served by a park-and-ride at nearby Churston on the Dartmouth Steam Railway rather than the original branch to the town)
  » Cranleigh in Surrey
  » Fleetwood, Rawtenstall and Skelmersdale in Lancashire
  » Leicester to Burton in the East Midlands
  » Wisbech in Cambridgeshire
  » Washington in Tyne and Wear

Not all of the railways would need to be relaid: most of them are still served by freight-only lines.

Chris Austin said: "They are all large towns which have changed radically since the railways went 40 years ago. Many were old coal mining or manufacturing centres, which now generate large numbers of commuters who need to use the train.

"All the schemes, with support from national and local government, could be completed over the next two decades. At the very least the land needs to be left as a possible rail corridor, rather than being built on."

One of the major criticisms made of Beeching was that he failed to take into account future trends like population growth and greater demand for travel. The ATOC report suggested ways of redressing the balance, although it had to accept that because vacant trackbeds had not been safeguarded, many of those running through urban areas had been built over and would therefore be difficult or impossible to reopen.

The report flew in the face of a White Paper published by the Labour government in 2007, which said there were no plans to reopen branch lines and even hinted that it might no longer be appropriate to protect their trackbeds from building development.

ATOC suggested that other lines which could be prioritised for reopening included the Uckfield to Lewes line in East Sussex, part of which is now occupied by the Lavender Line, the Bristol to Portishead branch and Yorkshire's Harrogate-Ripon-Northallerton route.

The restoration of the Manton Curve in Rutland would facilitate direct services between Kettering and Peterborough, while reopening the electrified Woodhead line from Manchester to Sheffield would increase capacity between the two cities.

In 2011, ATOC pointed out that passenger use of existing rural branch lines was very much increasing, by as much as 55% in 12 months alone.

It produced figures that showed passenger levels on the Par to Newquay line rose by 54.8% from 2008/09 to 2009/10, and 56.1% from 2007/08 to 2009/10, while Derby to Matlock rose by 42% and 72.1% and Truro to Falmouth by 37.8% and 56.1%.

It reported that many of the fastest-growing branch lines connect to seaside resorts and towns and, as in the pre-Beeching eras, showed high points during the summer months. Nevertheless, there was an underlying trend of rising passenger numbers on the rural railways, due to the increasing popularity of home-grown attractions and concerted efforts to attract local people and visitors back to the railways.

Some of the lines saw growth after operators put on more services to meet demand from commuters and holidaymakers alike.

CHAPTER NINETEEN

The final verdict

S o what should we really make of Dr Beeching today, 50 years after he became British Railways chairman and "the most hated civil servant in Britain". Was he a bogeyman — or a benefactor?

Of course, if we long for the steam era through rose-tinted spectacles and long for the days when country towns and villages were served by a dense network of cross-country routes and branch lines, which meant that you could travel almost anywhere by train, then he will be damned without redemption by our sentimentality, and we should read no further.

Likewise, if we view the relationship between Transport Minister Ernest Marples, who had vested interests in road building and, as we saw earlier, ended up fleeing Britain with vast unpaid tax bills, and the man he chose to pay a near-pop star salary to bring hard-hitting business principles to British Railways at a time when it was plunging ever deeper into a mire of unprecedented debt, we might be forgiven for thinking that dark forces of self-interest conspired to bring about the demise of the national network that was, in favour of alternative transport.

Understandably, there was no love lost between Beeching and the tens of thousands of lowly paid rail workers who were left on the scrap heap with meagre pensions by the cutbacks, which they considered to be vindictive and impersonal to their dying day, accusing him of mercilessly wielding his axe with vitriol, glee and even spite.

In 1962, there were 474,536 people employed by British Railways, the figure fell to around 307,000 by 1968.

Yet Beeching could not be blamed for their historic low wages and the inherited hopeless level of overstaffing on lines for which public demand was disappearing fast — and maybe their venom might instead have been better directed at former rail passengers who had bought a car.

However, if we place everything in its true context, we must look outside the bubble that is Britain. The hard fact is that countries through-out the western hemisphere had been closing unremunerative lines since the 1930s. What was happening in Britain in the Fifties and Sixties was also taking place in North America, the continent, where swathes of rural metre gauge lines were being closed, and closer to home, Ireland. Countries like the USA were years ahead of Britain in terms of diesel-isation, electrification and route rationalisation.

Everywhere, those in power were having to come to grips with the unparalled phenomenon of the soaring levels of private motor transport, from motorbikes to luxury cars. It was certainly not a problem limited to Britain, and likewise Beeching and Marples cannot in any way be blamed for the railway closure trends in other countries. Indeed, global evidence indicates that closures at this time were unavoidable.

Dr Richard Beeching was awarded a controversial salary more typical of the higher-paid private sector than a civil servant. He was also given a remit, which broadly said that the deficit must be cut at all costs, and he was given scant leeway to recommend that loss-making lines should be retained on social grounds. Such judgment was ultimately left to Marples, who did redeem some routes recommended for the axe by Beeching and who has also been accused of delaying other closures as the 1964 General Election loomed.

The hard fact is that some railway lines still running in the Fifties and Sixties should never have been built at all, because they had been designed and built more than a century ago in starkly different socio-eco-nomic conditions, with hope of riches that never materialised.

Other lines had become so poorly patronised that it would have been cheaper to pay for the daily users to share a taxi.

Take the GWR's Cheltenham to Kingham and Banbury route, for instance. How many people would travel daily to Cheltenham or Banbury from, say, Bourton-on-the Water or Chipping Norton? Take away the line's coal and agricultural traffic, and what business case do you have left?

One often-expounded argument against Beeching was the failure to recognise the full importance of loss-leaders.

Closing any branch line wiped away its contribution to main line traffic at a stroke. In fact, this aspect was addressed in The Reshaping of British Railways, although the doctor's response was not as flexible as it might have been.

Beeching and others assumed that disenfranchised villagers would merely use motor transport to reach the nearest main line station and so often they were proved wrong.

On the other hand, by the early Sixties many remote branch lines had so few regular passengers that their revenue contribution to the main line was negligible and in such cases it is difficult to argue with Beeching's logic.

The savings that Beeching promised to make never materialised. By closing almost a third of the network, he managed to achieve a saving of just £30 million, while overall losses were still above £100 million.

His Trunk Route Report in 1965 which called for even more drastic closures, disenfranchising large regions as well as towns and villages from the network, was such an embarrassment that he parted company with British Railways soon after, ahead of schedule.

Yet if the rationale behind the original 1963 report was so wrong, why did Harold Wilson's Labour Government which had publicly pledged to stop the Beeching cuts before winning the General Election in 1964 not only immediately renege on its promises, but in some cases speeded up the closures.

Labour Transport Minister Barbara Castle introduced a key social element that led to the potential retention of unviable lines and set in place the Passenger Transport Executive model by which integrated urban transport could be developed — as happened successfully — but let us not forget she too still closed thousands of miles of routes as recommended by Beeching and then added several more routes into the bargain: a strong recognition of the fact that widespread closures in an increasingly car-dominated country were inevitable.

In a great decade of change, when the steam era that had served the country so well during two world wars was visibly disappearing, with new futuristic forms of transport jumping off the drawing board, and where the car provided a liberating force to even modest-income families, there were those who believed that modernised or not, the days of the railways were numbered.

THE BIGGEST FAILING OF ALL

For me, the biggest mistake of the Beeching era and the years that followed was the speed and ruthlessness by which closures were implemented, leaving little possibility of going back should circumstances change — as they have done all over the country.

New towns subsequently appeared on the landscape, and with inner-city redevelopment, sizeable communities were springing up on the outskirts of cities. Meanwhile, country towns and villages that previously could not support their local branch line would eventually add housing estates and become much-sought-after commuter belt settlements.

With soaring levels of car ownership, surely it was obvious that rush-hour gridlock in cities would occur within the foreseeable future, and buses without dedicated lanes would fare no better than cars in jams. Where there are bus lanes, they so often serve the purpose of slowing cars to a snail's pace in the remaining 'public' lane — often people need their car for their job, and using public transport is not an option.

Countries like France got it right. Yes, withdraw the worst loss-making services, but keep the trackbed, if not the track itself, intact for potential future use should circumstances change.

In Britain, such options were discarded too quickly or never even considered; tracks being lifted sometimes within days of closure leaving no going back, and the land sold off. The problem is that any land that is sold off in urban areas will be sooner rather than later redeveloped. The cost of repurchasing former railway land in cities and demolishing buildings in the way of any reinstatement schemes immediately makes most of them non-viable. Building new termini on urban fringes rather than in the city centres defeats the object.

What has long rankled with me is the case of the closure of the GWR Stratford-upon-Avon to Cheltenham line, which in post-Beeching years had been retained for freight. In 1976, more than a decade after Beeching, a derailment at Chicken Curve near Winchcombe damaged the track and led to a British Rail decision not to bother repairing the line. Most of the 28-mile route was lifted three years later, and the trackbed through Stratford used for a town bypass, although a grass strip capable of accommodating a single track was left.

Fast forward a third of a century and the houses now built around the site in Stratford have changed hands many times. While in the late Nineties, Network Rail's predecessor Railtrack was seriously looking at reopening the route for freight as a bypass for the Lickey Incline. I have no doubt there would now be an overwhelming — 'not in my back yard' — protest, as well as problems with crossing the new roadway on the level. Had the trackbed been preserved intact, while letting everyone know that the railway might come back one day, this situation and many others like it would have been avoided.

I looked at badly gridlocked Bath, and attempts being made to regenerate the former coalmining towns of Radstock and Midsomer Norton. Why not, I wondered, reinstate the Somerset & Dorset main line linking all three, as a commuter route, so people could buy cheap housing and commute to Bath and Bristol? I was informed as a rough estimate that it would cost at least as much in actual pounds (forgetting inflation) to rebuild that section of line as Beeching managed to save by closing an entire third of Britain's rail network.

WHAT IF?

What if Dr Richard Beeching had never been appointed in 1961? The regions of British Railways would certainly have closed more and more branch lines as they had been doing for several years, probably without any reference to a central guiding criteria.

Allowing them to carry on doing their own thing may have ended up with the network's finances in an even greater mess and maybe led to more closures than were recommended by the Beeching report.

It is worth pausing for a minute, looking back on the maps in this volume, and then seriously asking — how many of the Beeching closures would have happened in the Sixties anyway, with or without him?

Similarly, another British Railways chairman in Beeching's place might well have closed more lines sooner, before the subsequent and enlightened social need policies of later years could save them.

Furthermore, if the recommended cutbacks had not been made at the time and the British Railways deficit left to spiral further out of control, with only vain hopes being thrown at it, would the delay have ultimately led to far more drastic rationalisation being imposed, such as that outlined in the horror story that was the Serpell Report in 1982, and with the full blessing of the over-burdened taxpayer? We will never know.

Nothing anyone could have done would have prevented the rise of the car and the mass exodus of passengers from rail to road, which offers greater personal flexibility. It was a global phenomenon, not unique to Britain.

What was being attempted by Beeching, however, was the identification of instances where passengers would still prefer to travel by train, as well as cases where the carriage of freight by rail offered clear advantages over road haulage. While there may have been elements of tunnel vision in both the remit he was given by Ernest Marples and his own approach, he made an honest attempt to achieve these goals and thereby save the railway network from a far more dire predicament.

He applied a simple business principle.

A factory employs 20 men on the production line. Suddenly someone invents machinery that can do the job of 19 of them, leaving just one to oversee it. That one position is what may then be termed a "real job" — it is essential for production to be maintained and cannot be replaced by technology, and the other 19 should therefore be made redundant, according to the accountant's recommendation.

The accountant's remit by nature is purely mathematical. Therefore ruthless by nature, it cannot involve consideration as to whether sacking the 19 would cause hardship, or the loss of their incomes would have a negative effect on the local economy outside and so on. That final decision is up to the factory owners.

In the case of British Railways, Beeching was the accountant and the owners were firstly the Conservative and then the Labour governments. The buck stopped with them.

However, if the powers that be outside the firm look at the redundancies in a wider context, such as the cost of unemployment benefit, retraining, supporting local business deprived of income from the workers who have lost their wage, and so on, they might well decide that a subsidy to the factory to retain some of the jobs, maybe in the event of increased production at a later date, would serve the local economy well.

No country has been able to support a large railway network of its original size and a modern road network side by side.

Economies were inevitable, but who knows what lines might have been saved if the social aspect of closures had been more fully addressed by transport ministers some years before Barbara Castle's 1968 Act, maybe even as soon as the pledge-breaking Harold Wilson came to power in 1964?

For a man accused of trying to destroy Britain's railways, Beeching's innovations regarding bulk freight such as the merry-go-round coal hoppers and the Freightliner container system, proved highly successful and are still in use nearly half a century on.

So much changed in the Sixties, including the nationalised railway network, which emerged from the decade streamlined and slimmed down, even if it was never as sleek and shiny as those who told us that the Seventies were "The Age of the Train" in TV advertising would have had us believe.

Yes, rationalisation could and almost certainly should have been done better, and while the Sixties promised so much hope and optimism, the decade came packaged with liberal lashings of naivety and lack of real foresight in so many cases.

Nonetheless, the reduced railway network has managed to ride the storm of threats to its existence like the Serpell Report. With the opening of the High Speed 1 Channel Tunnel rail link to the award-winning St Pancras International station, and the promise of a new high-speed rail link from London to Birmingham, Manchester and the north, and an east-to-west cross-link line beneath London, and passenger figures at their highest in many decades, the future for rail is now looking more promising than at any time since the 1955 Modernisation Plan.

We all miss the rural branch lines, look at them wistfully in magazines like *Heritage Railway* and on archive cine footage, and we know that the closure of trunk routes like the Great Central was short-sighted. Too many large towns became cut off from the network and not enough emphasis was placed on the fear that motor transport would at the rate of expansion bring cities to gridlock sooner than later.

Yet evidence, backed by a mountain of hindsight, shows that while Beeching made mistakes, he appeared to honestly and efficiently follow a given remit, albeit one that was too brutal in parts.

The cutbacks, while largely inevitable, may also be viewed as having reshaped Britain's railways into a slimmer, fitter beast that at last, after disappointing decades in the doldrums, is now gearing up to the fresh challenges of the 21st century, able to hold its head high in an age where the car will forever remain king.

Yes, it is so easy to make Dr Beeching a scapegoat, especially when you take into account the speed and clinical efficiency in which he went about his deficit-cutting task. He merely took the Queen's shilling and carried out the duties he was given by not one but two democratically elected governments, on both sides of the political fence.

In trying to make sense of global transport trends at the beginning of the greatest decade of change, the like of which had never been seen before, he steadfastly and determinedly tackled a job which under no circumstances was ever likely to bring him universal popularity, and led to him taking the public rap for the final decisions of those in higher authority on both sides of the political fence, both during and after his term in office.

Maybe this particular hatchet man erred more on the side of the heroic than any of us want to believe.

Baron Beeching lived in Lewes Road, East Grinstead, from the 1960s until he died at Queen Victoria Hospital in 1985.

Beeching Way in East Grinstead was named after him as it lies on the route of one of the lines made obsolete by his report.

He first developed signs of heart trouble in 1969. The following year, he became chairman of building materials group Redland plc, and later became chairman of ship owners Furness Withy.

When once asked about his career with the railways and if he regretted his cuts, he famously and somewhat pompously said that he regretted not having closed more lines. He maintained this stance to the end.

The Bluebell Railway, where, as we saw in Chapter 3, Beeching opened a new halt in 1962, months before the publication of The Reshaping of British Railways, completed its northern extension to rejoin the main line at his latter-day residence of East Grinstead in March 2013. There, a new station was developed and the reconnection produced a mini-boom for local tourism. Irony abounds from many angles here. In spring 2011, veteran TV reporter John Sergeant used Scotland's Bo'ness & Kinneil Railway as a backdrop to an item on the Beeching cuts he recorded for BBC's The One Show.

A special train hauled by Class 26 diesel No. 26024 made two trips over the heritage line from Bo'ness to Birkhill to allow the film crew to get the train in motion effect while John did an interview.

Travelling with John was rail expert David Spaven who provided detailed examples of how the cuts savaged the UK network by about a third.

John said: "We think of Beeching as being a bad guy. We think, looking back, if we hadn't had this guy, lots of lovely railways could have been preserved.

"But it was very much a problem of the time and people thought that railways then were old-fashioned and they were uneconomic. So something had to be done — and that was a savage reappraisal of the entire railway network.

"My conclusion is that Beeching is neither a hero nor a villain but very much a man of his time."

INDEX